ßLACK WOMEN IN THE ACADEMY

*The Secrets to Success
and Achievement*

Revised and Updated Edition

Sheila T. Gregory, Ph.D.

University Press of America, ® Inc.
Lanham • New York • Oxford

Copyright © 1999 by
Sheila T. Gregory

University Press of America,® Inc.
4720 Boston Way
Lanham, Maryland 20706

12 Hid's Copse Rd.
Cumnor Hill, Oxford OX2 9JJ

Library of Congress Cataloging-in-Publication Data

Gregory, Sheila T.
Black women in the academy : the secrets to success and
achievement / Sheila T. Gregory. —Rev. and updated ed.
p.   cm.
Includes bibliographical references and index.
1. Afro-American women—Education (Higher) 2. Afro-American
college students. 3. Afro-American college graduates. 4. Afro-
American women college teachers. 5. Academic achievement—
United States. 6. Educational surveys—United States. I. Title.
LC2781.G74   1999   378'.0089'96073—dc21   99—15084 CIP

ISBN 0-7618-1412-4 (pbk: alk. ppr.)

⊖™The paper used in this publication meets the minimum
requirements of American National Standard for Information
Sciences—Permanence of Paper for Printed Library Materials,
ANSI Z39.48—1984

UCD WOMEN'S CENTER
*D*edication

With love, respect, and appreciation

to my mother Tenicia Banks Gregory

and my father Dr. Karl Dwight Gregory,

who like many Black educators

have devoted their lives

to furthering the knowledge

of all persons--young and old,

Black and White--through

teaching, mentoring, and community service.

§

And for all women of color

and their families.

In Memory of Bernice Marie Barnes

My dearest teacher, treasured friend, and guardian angel

(1917-1995)

*C*ontents

IX.   *WHERE DO WE GO FROM HERE?*

APPENDIX

*L*ist of Tables

*F*oreword

African American women, while the most numerous of women of color in the faculty of institutions of higher education, are still only 2.2 percent of full-time faculty. Half of those are in the historically black colleges and only one percent are represented in predominantly white institutions, and of those, most are in the community colleges. That is to say, black women are not equally or well represented throughout the full spectrum of institutions of higher education. Moreover, in the decade from 1981 to 1991, black women lost ground in gaining tenure, dropping from 58 percent of those awarded tenure to 56 percent. Their numbers are, in addition, concentrated in fields such as education, social work, and nursing, and are practically invisible in fields such as engineering and science. Furthermore, many of these women leave academic life for a variety of reasons, diminishing their already slim presence in the academy. These are the facts, but these facts must be placed in a larger historical context to fully understand them.

Ever since Emancipation, Black women have had a special calling to teach. In the male dominated society of the nineteenth century, and barred from most other occupations, women flocked to teaching as an honorable alternative to domestic work. As black colleges were being established throughout the South, Black women, at first, found themselves employed more as faculty members because the Black colleges emphasized the humbler trades--home economics, nursing, and teaching--while the white women's colleges stressed the liberal arts. The early advantage of Black women compared to other women of color lasted well into the current period of higher education desegregation. But the advantage did not last due to Black women being concentrated in a narrow range of professions and suffering discrimination in trying to enter other fields. But try they did, and gradually, under tremendous odds, Black women began to fight their way into the range of teaching positions in higher education institutions, both black and white. They learned, as Paula Giddings has said, "the harsher lessons of being Black and a woman in America."

From Mary McLeod Bethune to Johnetta Cole, and many thousands of women lesser-known, Black women have struggled in the academy against the twin forces of sexism and racism. Some have prevailed, others have not.

Sheila Gregory has told their story. But she has told it in a unique way. Many historians have written eloquent stories of the struggles of Black women academics; many sociologists have documented their struggle with facts. Dr. Gregory has done both. She has recaptured the history of the Black woman's odyssey in academe and the forces that have acted upon her, from the family to the church and the community. Then she has conducted an in-depth study of Black women who are currently in the academy, have returned to the academy, or have left the academy, and in each instance she gives reasons for their choices. She concludes with recommendations for retaining Black women in the academy.

This is a powerful study and very timely. As we attempt to increase the number of people of color in the academy, the area of least progress has been in the faculty. Finding reasons for the barriers and recommendations to overcome them is especially useful. It is even more useful to have a study of African American women at this time, because their struggle is unique and the barriers they have to overcome are formidable. Sheila Gregory has produced an excellent study and we are indebted to her for it.

Reginald Wilson, Ph.D.
Senior Scholar
American Council on Education

*P*reface

This project grew out of my interest and research in the area of recruitment and retention of Black scholars. Being raised by two Detroit educators taught me to appreciate and love reading and learning. My parents reinforced in me at an early age the value of hard work and dedication to one's family, friends, community, and career.

Naturally as a young Black woman, I wanted to know exactly what I needed to do to be successful. I wanted to formulate a strategy--a road map to success. I decided to conduct a series of pilot studies to see what was in store for me two years later when I finished my doctorate. As I interviewed numerous faculty of color nationwide, I learned that although Black faculty had achieved some success, much more work was yet to be done. I knew I was responsible for creating my own success, but first I had to define success for myself.

I believe that although there may be multiple barriers in our paths to success, we have the power to choose what we do with our lives. The attitudes we espouse and perceptions we have of ourselves directly influence our success and challenges in life. I began to learn how to position myself for empowerment and when to let go of aspects I could not control. According to Susan L. Taylor in her inspiring 1993 book, *In the Spirit,* we create our own possibilities through our power to choose.

The purpose of this book was to identify the secrets to success and achievement for Black women scholars. In so doing, the book begins by examining the history of Black women and their families, and identifying the common barriers to success and achievement. A healthy portion of this book is devoted to explaining the research study upon which it was based, and identifying the primary factors that influenced the decisions of Black women faculty to remain in, return to, or voluntarily leave the academy. Since the largest percentage of women in the study (53%) were successful achievers and maintained a relatively high job satisfaction rate, the book attempts to further explore the career and life choices of these women. How can Black women faculty and higher education institutions help to create opportunities for success and achievement? How can colleges and universities better attract and retain talented Black women scholars? Why is this necessary?

In this revised edition, I have updated the statistics on the status of women both inside and outside of the academy and have incorporated recent research in the field, along with findings from my ongoing research on 20 groups of international faculty and women of color in the United States. I also would like to make special note of the fact that the word "minority" is not my choice of terms. I try not to use the term because of the negative connotation it implies and the knowledge that we are rapidly becoming a majority. However, since the term is the language used in most of our federal documents, it will sometimes be necessary to use the term for accuracy and consistency.

Black women have participated in higher education for well over a century. Although the journey has been difficult, significant achievements have been made, and many have reaped the benefits of their contributions. Today, fewer Black women doctoral recipients are choosing academic employment, and many of those who do enter the academy later leave for employment in business, industry, and the professions. Many speculate that the present decline of Black faculty is expected to become even more severe as the growth of the academic labor market levels off.

Jack Schuster contends that by the year 2004, nearly 340,000 faculty members will be needed to replace those who are expected to retire. Projections suggest that there will not be adequate numbers of qualified faculty and few faculty of color available to replace the retiring faculty. As we enter the new millenium, we can now see this coming to fruition. It is not uncommon to pick up the Chronicle of Higher Education and see numerous full-page advertisements for dozens of faculty positions at one institution for any given academic year.

Between the years 1975 and 1984, the percentage of Black women faculty declined from 4.6 percent to 3.6 percent. Not only has the national pool of Black Ph.D.'s shrunk in many disciplines, but Black women Ph.D.'s are still most likely to be: concentrated among the lowest academic ranks, receive the lowest salaries, be employed primarily by two-year colleges, teach part-time, and earn doctorates primarily in education, the social sciences, and the professions. Although these factors clearly threaten the current and future status of Black women professors, the implications of their absence are even more disturbing.

The declining presence of Black women in the academy has numerous implications for women faculty as individuals and colleagues, and for students, family, community, the academy, and the nation. As individuals, Black women faculty often experience isolation because of the lack of a critical mass. In 1987, for example, Snyder reported that approximately 2 percent of all faculty in American colleges and universities were Black women. In predominately white institutions, according to Blum, 1.9 percent were Black men and women. Many Black women faculty have reported that they need other Black and minority faculty, within or outside the department, to share common ideas and concerns and to affirm each others presence when the institution fails to do so. Isolation according to Menges and Exum (1983), has been frequently cited as a major factor influencing the decisions of Black and other minority faculty to seek alternative employment.

Much research has pointed to the need for Black scholars to write about their experiences and substantiate evidence to help challenge the numerous stereotypes that negatively depict Black women and other minority faculty. Further research on Blacks could help to identify and possibly address concerns associated with the Black family and help improve the conditions of the community.

In academia, Black women have contributed a wealth of research in various disciplines that have significantly impacted the curriculum. In the last decade alone, the writings, art, and poetry of Black women have graced American classrooms. The intellectual work generated and the networks developed as a result of the data Black women have contributed and constructed have been significant and sorely need to continue.

Black women have had a rich tradition of employment in education at all levels. Many have sought careers in the teaching profession because of the desire to make a difference in the lives of others. Education in the Black community has historically served as a vehicle for many Black families to escape poverty. One important purpose of education in the Black community has been to prepare the next generation for leadership roles in the community and society. As in the home, Black women were the teachers and role models for all young students, but they played a special role in the lives of Blacks, women, and other minority students. This leadership cannot continue if Black women faculty role models do not exist in the classroom.

There is compelling evidence that Black women faculty can have a profound impact on the lives and perceptions of students. Recent studies from Black scholars such as Blackwell, Brown, Mommsen, and Wilson have continuously cited the lack of mentoring as one of the major reasons colleges and universities have had difficulty recruiting and retaining Black and other non Asian American minority students. Smith and Zorn (1981) have indicated that many Black students perceive the absence of Black faculty members as paralleling their current low status and future outlook on campus. Furthermore, Blackwell (1983) has found that the number of Black faculty at a college or university is the most important predictor of the first year Black student enrollment, retention rate, and total number of Black student graduates. DeFour & Hirsch (1990) have argued that the mere presence of Black faculty on campus provides evidence to minority students, perceiving that they too can complete their education and become competent and successful professionals. If Black students cannot find any Black faculty with whom they can affirm their presence or serve as academic role models and mentors, fewer Black students are likely to graduate. Therefore, fewer still will be adequately equipped to improve the socioeconomic conditions of their family, compete in the work force, or make significant contributions to the community and society at large.

The lack of Black women in higher education can also have a detrimental impact on non-minority students, faculty, and staff. Sometimes the absence or small participation of Black women academics can send the erroneous message that Black women are not qualified to be scholars, professors, administrators, or even doctoral students. Many Black women faculty in various studies reported that their qualifications were continuously challenged.

From a national perspective, it is in the best interest of the nation to ensure that each and every person has access to quality higher education. Furthermore, we must be willing and able to nurture all available talent and provide support systems to help ensure their success. Research suggests that unless alternative strategies are employed, there will not be adequate Black women faculty to meet the mentoring needs of the anticipated increasing numbers of Black and other college students of color.

The personal and professional factors that influence career mobility among Black women faculty represent a serious and important gap in academic research. If we are to successfully expand and retain the pool of Black women faculty, primarily among the upper academic ranks, it is important to discover the reasons why an increasing number of Black women academics at two and four-year American colleges and universities leave academe. It is also important to learn what influence salary, tenure status, institutional type, intention to leave, marital status, number of dependents, support systems, and external barriers play on the career mobility of this severely underrepresented population. By examining the characteristics of those that remain, return, or voluntarily leave the academy, we can create a model of academic success and achievement to better understand these dynamics.

Shirley Vining-Brown recognizes the necessity for such research and states, "there is a need for more precise answers of why minorities are losing interest in graduate training and academic careers. A more precise model and additional data would identify the reasons given by [Black] respondents as to why they chose academic or non academic careers and why they left academe" (1988, p. 29).

Acknowledgments

I am grateful to my family, friends, and colleagues who helped to make this book possible, including:

God almighty, who continues to give me the inner strength and tenacity to keep going;

My precious daughter, Courtney Gregory Jones, who continuously provides incredible joy, hope, excitement, meaning, and challenge to my life;

my parents, Karl and Tenicia Gregory who have given me more love, faith, and encouragement than I could possibly express in this book;

my husband, Tony Jones, for being in my corner and keeping me laughing;

special thanks to my guardian angel, Bernice Barnes whose presence I constantly feel even though she has gone on to a higher place;

my siblings, Karin and Kurt Gregory who have always provided their love and support;

my Uncles Alti, Victor, and Ralph, my Aunts Wendy and Lois, and my many cousins, especially Mario Morrow who keeps me inspired;

my godparents, Pat and Elizabeth French, who have always supported my personal and professional endeavors;

the members of the Association of Black Women in Higher Education, the Black Caucus of the American Association for Higher Education, and the National Congress of Black Faculty who offered their support and encouragement;

the women upon which this study is based who generously shared their time and life experiences with me;

Reginald Wilson who graciously offered to write the foreword to this book;

Delores Smalls, Felicienne Ramey, Yolanda Moses, Mary Brown, E.J. Josey, Wornie Reed, and William Harvey who provided quotes to endorse this book;

Michael Tierney, who served as my dissertation chair and helped to guide me along the arduous path to completion;

Howard Stevenson, Antonio McDaniels, and Vivian Gadsden who served on my dissertation committee and offered continuous advice, encouragement, and motivation to keep me focused on the task at hand;

George Keller, previous Senior Fellow and Chair of the Higher Education Division at the University of Pennsylvania, who hired me as his assistant, edited my first publication, inspired me in the classroom, extended his friendship, and continues to support my professional endeavors;

Beecroft Osirike and Saburah Abdul-Kabir who helped to input the data and preserve my sanity;

Susan L. Taylor, Editor-in-Chief of *Essence* Magazine, for her book *In the Spirit* that helped to encourage and inspire me when the work seemed insurmountable;

my warmest thanks to several mentors not yet mentioned, including Bobby and LaJuan Jones, Otis Hill, Thelma Malle, and Nate Essex for the continued support and guidance;

and to a handful of my friends Ramona Thomas, Erica O'Neal, Marisol Sosa, M.J. Warrender, Mary Carter, Karen Ferguson, Elena Robinson, Clifton Camp, and Traci and Joann Wilkerson who unfailingly lent support and encouragement through phone conversations, faxes, E-mail messages, handwritten notes, hugs, jokes, chocolates, flowers, and trips to Baskin Robbins. I love you.

Thank you all.

I. *Introduction*

OVERVIEW

Black Women in the Academy: The Secrets to Success and Achievement is divided into nine chapters. Chapter One is an introduction that sets the context for the book and offers useful caveats for the reader. Chapter Two contains selected historical data focusing on three important aspects in the lives of Black women: resilience of Black women and their families; strengths of the Black church and community; and an overview of the formidable gains made by Black women in the workforce. Chapter Three features a bird's-eye view of the status and achievements of Black women professors and scholars in the academy. It contains five primary sections: a summary of important studies examining the academic labor market over the past four decades; a review of the literature on academic mobility; the rise of intellectualism among Black women; rites of passage; and a discussion of the choice patterns made regarding career and family.

Chapter Four presents the conceptual framework of the study from an economic, psychosocial, and job satisfaction theoretical approach. Then each of the following eight factors --salary, tenure status, institutional type, intention to leave, marital status, number of dependents, support systems, and external barriers--are examined by a review of the literature. Chapter Five contains the results of the study and is divided into four sections. The first section provides a descriptive comparison of a similar 1981 study of Black women Ph.D.'s and is followed by an examination of the decision patterns of this study as compared to a 1988 study employing similar characteristics. The third section offers a description and rationale for the inferential analysis employed for this study, and the final section in this chapter presents the decision model of career mobility representing the three distinct groups in which the sample fell.

Chapter Six presents the major findings, an examination of the common barriers to success and achievement, and a section exploring the personal lifestyle choices of Black women faculty. Chapter Seven provides recommendations in three primary areas: tenure and promotion; career advancement; and suggestions for creating opportunities for success and achievement. Chapter Eight has been added in this revised addition and provides insights into the plight of faculty women in twenty-one different countries (Central and South America, Puerto Rico and Cuba; Hawaii; Canada; West Indies [Jamaica, Barbados and Trinidad-Tobago]; Japan; China; Korea; Norway; West Germany; Netherlands; Britain; Australia; New Zealand; India; Israel; Turkey; Jordan and; Egypt) around the world and concludes with selected comparisons of international faculty. The final Chapter offers a summary of recommendations for policymakers and addresses some of the areas for future research and exploration.

CAVEATS

Although *Black Women in the Academy: The Secrets to Success and Achievement* is the first book since 1981 to examine the career and family life of Black women Ph.D.'s, it will not satisfy the needs of every reader. The findings of this study represent the experiences of 384 Black women faculty, past and present, from two-year and four-year American colleges and universities and cannot be generalizable to the 8,771 Black women doctorates. Furthermore, numerous environmental, family, and personal factors that are well beyond the scope of most measures were difficult to capture in this survey instrument. However, every attempt was made to discount the possible indirect effects of these complex variables. To aid the reader and provide additional information, the research methodology for this study, which includes the research design, description of the variables, study design, and limitations of the study are provided in the Appendix. In addition, a lengthy 44-page bibliography is included for additional reference.

II. *In the Beginning*

'HERSTORICAL' BACKGROUND

The history of Black women in the United States can best be described as a struggle for survival and identity, and the desire to protect and support her family. Black women have emerged from what Hudson-Weems (1989) terms a 'tripartite' form of oppression of racism, classism, and sexism. However, in spite of limited resources and low socioeconomic status, Black women have managed to survive and achieve great strides.

When studying Black women, it is important to contextualize the framework of their perspectives by comprehensively analyzing the historical components which help identify their thoughts, feelings, and experiences. Perhaps the most useful tool is the original model developed in 1908 by W.E.B. DuBois. In his book, *The Negro American Family*, DuBois stresses the importance of recognizing the historical relationships of African heritage and tradition of the Black family. This study will maintain the structure provided by DuBois, in an attempt to provide a clearer, more comprehensive understanding of the experiences of Black women.

In Elizabeth Peterson's book, *African American Women: A Study of Will and Success* (1992), she passionately describes the power of Black women. The power, she says, has to do with the relationship with ourselves, and those with God, family, friends, and community. All of these relationships bring power to Black women, because it is there where Black women are most comfortable in expressing themselves, and most likely to be affirmed for who and what they are. She says:

> The Black female's ability to define herself comes from a belief that no human has the right to define another. Each person is a unique creation of God; and with God, the individual elicits her

own becoming....The Black female who understands this knows that only she has the responsibility to determine her path. The Black woman knows that she is constantly in a state of becoming as she reconnects with God, family, and community, and as she is moved in different directions (pp. 86-87).

Traditionally, most Black women have shown great resilience when faced with life's challenges. This strength has sometimes been misconstrued and stereotyped in such terms as "superwoman" or "matriarch." Unfortunately, many unfavorable studies by social scientists who are rarely women and almost never people of color, have been based on these misconceptions. In the past 25 years alone, Black scholars such as Billingsley, Hill, Nobles, Staples, Walker, and Willie have sought to challenge these stereotypes which have served to negatively characterize Black women and ignore the strength of her passion for survival and achievement.

Resilience of Black Women and Their Families

Rodgers-Rose stresses in her 1980 book, *The Black Woman*, that "the history and lives of Black women cannot be separated from the history and lives of Black men and their children" (p. 12). Therefore, the Black family--primary and extended--will be the focus of this section.

Historically, Black families have had different family structures than most other cultures. While research on the complexities of the primary and extended Black family is widely available, there are presently no existing social research studies on how these complex relationships can influence career mobility.

The Black family can best be described as a social system (Billingsley, 1968) which emphasizes the interdependence of familial and community relationships. In a 1973 study of successful Black professionals, Epstein found that the choice of marriage and motherhood were important features in the lives of Black women which appeared to form a pattern that limited their occupational status. But what about the stable numbers of Black educated women who chose not to marry? Some remained single, according to Epstein, because they were unable to find a mate of similar social rank and education. Most of the Black women in Epstein's study had three common characteristics: they typically married late (if at all), they were not coerced into marriage by their parents, and they rarely felt anxious about becoming married. For some professional Black women, marriage did not appear to be as important as it was in the past (Bell, 1970). As Epstein pointed out, Black women who married college educated men rarely considered leaving the workforce because, in many cases, the husband's education was not a guarantee of financial success or occupational security. Black women often reported that "the quality of their lives are determined by their own endeavors and was less a response of their husbands' occupational situation" (Epstein, 1973, p. 925).

In a similar study, Fichter (1964) found that roughly half of all respondents indicated a preference for combining the familial roles with occupational roles. It is important to recognize, however, that the career decisions of Black and other women are often influenced by forces outside their control that can often affect the timing and outcome of the choices they made regarding family and career. Examples of such forces are discussed in Chapters Three and Four.

Bell (1970) states that to Black women, the role of the mother is more important than the role of the wife. According to the Asante proverb, "It's a woman who gave birth to a man; It's a woman who gave birth to a chief" (Young, 1986). As illustrated by this proverb, Black women have historically maintained a high status in the Black community and a unique and special relationship with their children. While marriage was important, Nobles (1975) points out that "the special bond between a mother and child is so deeply rooted in African heritage and philosophical orientation, that it has traditionally placed a great and unique value on children because they represent the continuity of life." The needs of the child are almost always of primary importance.

Historically, Black women have maintained strong bonds with their children. In a recent survey by Peterson (1994), the mother-daughter bond was stressed as the most important theme among women in the relationship of the family. However, this "connectedness" did not necessarily represent a matriarchal order or favoritism towards daughters. In fact, in some cases, women in this study reported that sons were more coddled by their mothers, while daughters were given greater responsibility. In most cultures, women continue to have the primary responsibility for raising the children. According to Peterson, what is unique in most Black families is that the mother-daughter bond often lasts long past childhood and is reinforced over time with each new generation. In most Black families, the values of family togetherness and interdependence are stressed, and young women are taught "to take responsibility for themselves and the family" (Peterson 1992, 67). Traditionally, the eldest daughter has the primary responsibility for caring for the family and heading the household in the absence of the mother.

In most Black communities, a great value is placed on the role of education because many believe it is the only means for successful employment in American society. The key to a child's future, as well as the future of the community, was also recognized. Although many Black families lacked the financial resources to enable each child to attend school, many Black mothers sacrificed everything to ensure that at least one child attended school. Often, once that child completed school and obtained a job, he or she took responsibility for providing for the younger children and the family.

The education of Black women has always been considered an important investment in the future. In 1964, Silberman found that a greater value was placed on the higher education of daughters than sons in the Black community. Education originally became a primary concern to Blacks as they sought to erase the myth of intellectual inferiority. Black teachers often became the only means to establish schools and educational associations in the community, and teach Black youth and adults. Noble (1956) found in an earlier study of Black women college graduates that 90 percent cited "preparing for a vocation" as the most important reason for going to college. In most Black families, there was a strong belief and commitment to advancing to ensure that each generation could go further and achieve more than the one preceding them.

Strength of the Black Church and Community

One of the greatest sources of strength and what was often at the center of the Black community was the Black church. Its role was to provide spiritual, moral, emotional, social, political, and economic support. Little data is available from scholars on the effectiveness of the Black church based on the attitudes of the Black community. However, the National Survey of Black Americans has found that most Blacks have very positive views regarding the Black church (Taylor, Thornton, and Chatters, 1987). For example, 80 percent of all respondents indicated that they felt black churches had served to improve the conditions of Blacks.

Black women traditionally have been very active in the Black church. The participation of Black women have predominately been in church activities such as singing, ushering, teaching, counseling, caring for the needy membership, and coordinating. The function of Black women previously had been primarily one of subordination, rather than one of leadership. However, in the past 20 years, Black women have begun to redefine their roles and status in the Black church, as well as in the job market.

Black women have consistently had relatively high participation rates in higher education. A college education often provided a vehicle for professional jobs in education, health care, social work, and other helping fields. Today, an increasing number of Black women are seeking graduate and professional degrees in a variety of non-traditional fields, such as theology.

In a 1978 study, Taylor compared the number of Black Canadian theology students in 1972 and found that only 2.7 percent of them were women. Just five years later in 1977, the number of Black women theological students increased more than five-fold to 13.5 percent. The Black religious community, particularly evangelists, had also witnessed the emergence of deaconesses, ministers, preachers, bishops, and other spiritual directors.

Much speculation has been focused on the role of the Black church in terms of its religious and social value. For example, Murray and Harrison (1981) argue that young college-educated Black women are returning to the Black church not only for its religious value, but for the social interaction they are increasingly unable to receive in the workplace due to their relatively small numbers. The works of Taylor (1978) and Murray and Harrison (1981) suggest that Black women will continue to assume greater power and opportunities for leadership in the Black church as growing numbers of Black women acquire higher statuses and take on more powerful roles. According to Murray and Harrison, "The movement toward altered roles for women within the church is paralleled in Black women's search for redefinition within the framework of her African heritage" (p. 119).

Hill (1972) has identified five major strengths, and maintains they are the means for survival, advancement, and stability in the Black community. These characteristics are strong kinship bonds, adaptability of family roles, strong religious orientation, strong work orientation, and strong achievement orientation. These values and ethics, Hill contends, have helped to keep Black women and their families together, and have strengthened their roles as wife and mother.

An essential aspect in the Black community which has richly benefited Black women and their families are what McAdoo (1980) referred to as extended family support networks. These extended networks "provided emotional support, economic supplements, and most important, protected the families integrity from assault by external forces" (p. 125). This system of mutual aid was based on the African heritage of communalism and was most likely a consequence of socialization that had traditionally encouraged respect and assistance to elderly family members (Chatters, 1986; Taylor and Chatters, 1986). However, these patterns were also typically influenced by socioeconomic conditions (Mutran, 1985). Extended families were important features in the Black community because they helped provide a source of strength and protection (Hill, 1972). This enabled Black families to cope with problems by "banding together to form a network of intimate mutual aid and social interaction with neighbors and kin" (Billingsley, 1968, p. 25). The network enabled women to work while friends, family, or neighbors stayed home and cared for the children. This mutual interdependence was also a means for many Black women to cope with poverty and racism (Stack, 1974). The unspoken words were often "you take care of mine and I'll take care of yours" (Jeffers, 1967, p. 21).

Extended networks in the Black community have provided enormous emotional and economic support for the elderly. According to a 1986 U.S. Census Bureau projection (U.S. Department of Commerce, 1986), the Black elderly population will reach 4 million by the year 2000, exceeding the White elderly population by 26 percent. This demographic trend alone will have significant implications for Black women who are typically the primary caregivers (Barresi and Menon, 1990) of aging parents. Caregiving is often characterized by a mutual exchange of assistance between adult children and their elderly parents (Taylor and Chatters, 1986) but can be provided by non-immediate family members such as friends, neighbors, and church members (Billingsley, 1968; Chatters et. al., 1986; Taylor, 1985; Taylor and Chatters, 1986).

Research on Black families suggests that cultural values encourage responsibility towards aging family members (Barresi and Menon,

1990). "Elderly Blacks tended to prefer to receive assistance, care, and support from a daughter, followed by a son, spouse, sister, brother, friend, neighbor, and finally parents" (Barresi and Menon, 1990, p. 223). When assistance from immediate family members was not available, non-immediate family members were preferred. In the absence or unavailability of immediate family and non-immediate family members, formal support was sought (Chatters et. al., 1986; Taylor, 1985; Taylor and Chatters, 1986). Often in Black families, the aging parents resided either in the home of an immediate family member, or close by to enable care to be more readily accessible (Taylor, 1985). Since some elderly Black women have, at one point or another, acted as surrogate mothers, a greater number of members are often available to provide care.

Formidable Gains in the Workforce

The participation of Black women in the labor force has remained consistently strong. For married women, participation has been relatively unrelated to their husbands' education, occupation, or income (Douglass, 1979). The participation of Black women in the workforce has helped to shape their views about themselves and others. During the 1980's, for example, the labor force participation of Black women rose by 29 percent, and in 1987 women accounted for 50 percent of the total employment of Blacks in the workplace. In 1987, the number of Black women in the workforce outnumbered Black men by 21,000. Furthermore, between 1980 and 1990 the labor force participation rate of Black women increased from 53.1 to 57.8 percent. Also between 1980 and 1990, the number of Black families headed by women rose to 54.9 percent (Department of Labor, 1991). Black women have traditionally supported and sustained themselves and their families (Evans, 1989). By and large, Black women have been primarily dependent upon themselves, whether by choice or necessity. This was evidenced by the increasing number of single Black women, and the dramatic rise in the percentage of Black single parent households headed primarily by women (Jones, 1983).

Black women have historically faced numerous barriers to reach parity in the labor force. Although an increasing number of Black women have made formidable gains in the workforce, many still remain at the bottom of the socioeconomic scale, and continue to be concentrated in service and lower level occupations (U.S. Department of Commerce, 1980).

III. *Women as Professors and Scholars*

A BIRDS-EYE VIEW OF THE ACADEMY

In academe, African American women have not fared any better. In 1991, African American women represented 5.8 percent of the enrollment in American colleges and universities as compared to 4.5 percent for African American men (U.S. Department of Education, 1992). African American women also maintained greater proportional representation within their race than white American women (Guy-Sheftall, 1989). In spite of the high college participation rates, African American women faculty continued to be concentrated among the lower ranks, primarily non-tenured positions, promoted at a slower rate, paid less than their male and white female counterparts, located in traditional disciplines, and primarily employed by two-year colleges (Brown, 1988; Redskin and Phipps, 1988; Zumeta, 1984). Currently, the academic labor market for African American women appears to be precarious, despite improvements in recent years with regard to doctoral degree attainment, and affirmative action and diversity efforts. This section will briefly discuss the history and status of the academic labor market and provide evidence to help explain the major correlates of academic mobility among the faculty ranks.

Academic Labor Market

During the past 4 decades, economists, and social scientists such as Bowen and Schuster, Bowen and Sosa, Cartter, Exum, Finnegan, and Wilson have contributed several important studies that have sought to explain the academic labor market.

Over fifty years ago, Logan Wilson introduced the concept of self-study of academic careers from entry into the profession, through retirement. Wilson contended that once the first academic position was secured, productivity in the form of publications and citations was the primary factor that led to rewards such as promotion and tenure, and often mobility.

In 1966, Cartter was the first to predict an excess supply of Ph.D.'s in the 1970s, based on a study of over 4,000 ratings from graduate departments around the country. In subsequent studies, he incorporated adjustments to the academic labor market, new needs of faculty, enrollment projections, economics and financing of higher education, and market imbalances. He argued three points at which market forces influence the system: (1) the number of job openings and the salary rates offered which influenced turnover for inter-institutional movements; (2) the hiring of new first-time faculty directly from graduate school; and (3) the flows of senior faculty between academic and nonacademic positions.

In a 1984 study of women and minority faculty, Exum, Menges, Watkins, and Berglund contended that the small numbers of women and minority faculty in tenured and non-tenured positions in elite universities, were mostly due to the nature of the internal academic labor market itself, rather than solely due to racism, sexism, or the small pool of qualified women and minority candidates. The five internal factors of the academic marketplace identified in the study which provided the greatest barriers for women and minorities were: (1) the way faculty positions were filled; (2) the customs relied upon; (3) the nature of competition for faculty; (4) non acceptance of important problems in the market; and (5) the absence of clear job descriptions and formal evaluations.

In 1986, Bowen and Schuster predicted a significant shortfall of high quality faculty between the year 2000 and 2010 based on an analysis of cohort size and the academic labor market. They argued that college enrollments would decline in the late 1980s and early 1990s, and increase rapidly as we approach the year 2000 and as the offspring of the baby boomers reach college age (Stapleton, 1988). Furthermore, they predicted that the rate of faculty attrition would increase at the same time as the large numbers of new faculty of the 1950s and 1960s reach retirement age. Bowen and Schuster stated that "some of the best talent has been, and is being, attracted to medicine, law, business, engineering, science, and other fields, and away from academic careers" (p. 168).

Bowen and Sosa in 1989 studied faculty in the arts and sciences, and presented a model that calculated 96 separate projections for supply and demand, including the rates of resignation, retirement, and death. They projected a continuation of the relatively constant annual numbers of new Ph.D.'s who accept academic positions in the arts and sciences. They concluded that the most important variable of supply and demand is the institutions' student-faculty ratios.

More recently in 1993, Finnegan explored the career patterns of faculty employed by two year comprehensive universities. Finnegan found: (1) the labor market was segmented by organizational type which supported the findings of Brown (1967); (2) careers typically evolve as individuals interact with various external forces of the labor market; and (3) comprehensive universities differ from research universities because employment histories tend to be closely tied to different aspirations, fluctuations on the labor market, and changing institutional natures.

Major Correlates of Academic Mobility

In the past 25 years, a handful of studies by such scholars as Brown, Burke, Caplow and McGee, Crane, Curry-Williams, Mommsen, Moore and Wagstaff, and Rosenfeld and Jones, have helped to identify the major correlates of academic mobility. Some of these studies have found that academic faculty move outside academia as well as within, because it often leads to higher salaries. However, according to Kornhauser, movement outside of the academy can often mean lower prestige among peers, and problems adjusting to less autonomous work. As the academic labor market tightens, it is expected that more Ph.D.'s will begin their careers outside the academy.

The earliest study on faculty mobility was conducted in 1958 by Caplow and McGee that provided a sociological study of academic organizations and faculty mobility at nine major universities. They argued that personal contacts could greatly influence which candidate was interviewed and recruited, and gave graduates from more prestigious institutions an advantage into higher status job positions. They concluded that the prestige of a candidate rather than scholarly performance had the greatest influence on mobility to more prestigious institutions. This study design involved the faculty personnel decisions of 304 vacancies, terminations, and appointments at nine major research universities. However, it is important to consider that in the 1950's when the study was conducted, the Brown vs. Board of Education decision had recently been decided in 1954. Up until the late 1950's, 96 percent of all full-time African American faculty were employed by HBCU's (Thomas, 1981). Today, the total number of full-time African American faculty employed at HBCU's are fewer than 45 percent (Smith, 1992). Furthermore, Caplow and McGee noted that both women and minority faculty were placed "outside the prestige system and therefore of little interest to hiring departments" (Burke, 1988, p. 32). They further stated that "discrimination on the basis of race appears to be nearly absolute. No major university in the United States has more than a token representation of Negroes on its faculty..." Therefore, in 1958 when this study was conducted, only a very small and statistically insignificant number of African American or women faculty could possibly have participated in this study. The few African American or women faculty who may have participated, if at all, were employed during one of the most challenging periods where resistance to hiring women and minorities were at one of the highest points in the history of higher education. Consequently, the findings of this study are grossly inadequate in explaining the decision patterns of African American women professors.

In 1967, Brown conducted an elaborate study analyzing the academic labor market in terms of supply and demand, mobility and turnover, and job choice of nearly 10,000 college faculty. Brown characterized professors as "mobile," arguing that the ability to change institutions could be crucial to advancement, and that the appearance that one was willing to move was often important even for upward mobility within an institution. Brown identified seven major factors influencing the decision of faculty to leave their positions: (1) competency of administrators; (2) research facilities and opportunities; (3) teaching loads; (4) salary; (5) courses taught; (6) competency of colleagues; and (7) congeniality of colleagues. Brown's study was conducted in the late 1960's and early to mid 1970's. This period was a relatively prosperous one for many African American women faculty. African American women faculty were seeking and securing faculty positions in greater numbers at four-year institutions other than HBCU's. A limited number of African American and women faculty also successfully joined the faculty ranks at some predominantly white institutions. In contrast, the academic labor market today is not nearly as advantageous for African American women faculty. While the numbers of African American women doctorates are steadily increasing, fewer are choosing academic employment and fewer still remain in the academy because of more attractive career options in other industries. In addition, the progression rates for African American faculty are lower today than for any other group (Brown, 1988). The characterization Brown ascertained that professors were mobile in 1967, cannot be completely supported today. While some African American women faculty appear to be mobile and have enjoyed opportunities within the academy, a growing number are securing positions outside the academy where benefits are often greater. Pragmatically, this study fails to provide ample evidence about the decision patterns of African American women professors in a historically comparable period.

In 1970, Crane examined the academic marketplace using the Cartter (1966) ratings to study mobility among 780 faculty in six disciplines between 1963 and 1966. Crane found that for younger faculty, prestige of the doctorate rather than past performance was a useful predictor of future performance. In support of this contention, Robert Merton (1968) argued that rewards often had a "cumulative effect" which increased the scientists' ability to secure resources for scholarly research, thus increasing the likelihood of successful future performance. The Crane study focused on characteristics of new faculty to predict future performance, yet it failed to examine the factors influencing the decisions of faculty to remain in, return to, or voluntarily leave the academy.

In 1974, Mommsen studied 1,383 African American faculty and found three major factors which contributed to job choice: (91%) the presence of colleagues with similar interests; (87%) existence of adequate research facilities; and (82%) opportunities for specialization. Mommsen concluded that intrinsic factors were more influential in determining job choice than extrinsic factors. While the Mommsen study provided a wealth of solid literature in an area of research sorely lacking, the study also suffered from the threats of history. The study examined three cohorts that received doctorate degrees through 1944, between 1945 and 1959, and between 1960 and 1969. During this historical period, cohorts experienced the depression, World War II, Korea, the Civil Rights Movement, and the initiatives of John F. Kennedy and Lyndon B. Johnson to name a few. Although the later historical events may well have been experience by most African American faculty in this sample due to a mean age of 50.9, relatively fewer had experienced the depression or World War II which may provide alternative reasons for mobility. Also, Mommsen focused on job and career choice, rather than on the factors influencing faculty to remain in, return to, or voluntarily leave the academy

Also in 1974, Moore and Wagstaff surveyed over 6,000 African American faculty in predominantly white institutions. They found the following five factors as most influential in the decision to leave their position at predominantly white institutions: (1) perceived racial discrimination; (2) desire to work at a traditionally black institution; (3) difficulty in obtaining tenure and promotion; (4) low priority placed on teaching at the school; and (5) the expectation to participate in African American activities and groups. Although the Moore and Wagstaff study was most closely associated with the design of this study, Moore and Wagstaff focused exclusively on African American faculty at predominantly white institutions.   The study was also conducted over twenty years ago and may have suffered from the threats of history. In addition, the study design failed to account for psychosocial factors related to marital status, household responsibilities, and number of dependents.

In 1981, Rosenfeld analyzed the career mobility of 207 men and women faculty to determine what differences could be influenced by gender. Rosenfeld found that women were in lower tenure track ranks or in non-tenured positions.   Geographic mobility was the most significant predictor of mobility, and was typically associated with the size of the labor market. Rosenfeld concluded that women were less likely to follow typical career paths, but warned that the types of moves could differ and influence the rates of mobility.   Rosenfeld speculated that women considered the process of obtaining the Ph.D. as a major career goal, and were less cognizant than men about what the future career would bring. The sample in this study was taken from the American Psychological Association for doctorates who received their Ph.D. degrees between 1955 and 1962, and who held teaching positions in 1970. Because psychologists have been found to be more mobile than most other professionals (Harmon, 1965) and less than 3 percent of all psychology teaching faculty are African American women, this study severely limits generalizability. Rosenfeld does, however, discuss the constraints of marital status on mobility and suggests why some faculty women have greater or less mobility.

In 1985, Curry-Williams examined the factors that influenced the decisions of "other-race" faculty to accept, remain in, and consider leaving faculty positions at four public southeastern universities. Curry-Williams found that half of all African American faculty cited "limited affirmative action efforts for African Americans" as the primary factor influencing them to leave the predominantly white institutions. This study only examined faculty from four public southeastern universities and focused primarily on court-ordered desegregation to compare faculty from HBCU's to faculty from PWI's. The study, for the most part, compared white faculty with African American faculty and were confined to the policies and practices prevalent in the South. These policies may likely have been very different than other institutional policies across the country. Although the study included family factors, it failed to include a sufficiently adequate percentage of African American women faculty in the study and could not separate the findings to determine the specific nature of this population.

In a 1987 study of the career patterns of mobility among academic psychologists, Rosenfeld and Jones found that the differences between men and women in the variable affects of geographic mobility were influenced by the life-cycles and chosen careers of the respondents. For example, women were most often found in larger cities, which seemed to inhibit their mobility. The higher the productivity, the quicker the movement to the first job for women. Women's mobility appeared to be less affected than men by their life-cycle stages, but more than men by their career position. Rosenfeld contended that actual or perceived geographic mobility or immobility, affected career advancement for women. This study was based in part on the research collected from Rosenfeld's 1981 study discussed earlier in this section. Comparisons were made regarding the mobility and perceived mobility of faculty women and men, however, few were African American faculty women. Furthermore, the study exclusively examined the mobility of faculty in the discipline of psychology and failed to generalize its application to the larger population.

In 1988, Burke replicated the 1958 Caplow and McGee study using the original framework to examine the mobility of 305 faculty in the academic marketplace. Burke contended: (1) selection decisions were based primarily on research interests and capabilities of the candidate; (2) resigning assistant professors and senior professors cited intellectual isolation and incompatibility as mobility factors; (3) a third of assistant and associate professors left higher education altogether; and (4) spouses employment (18 percent for women and 19 percent for men) was a major factor in the appointment and resignation of staff. As in the Caplow and McGee study, Burke examined faculty personnel decisions in the arts and sciences departments of six major research universities. While the numbers of African American women faculty at these six institutions were most likely to be relatively greater than the Caplow and McGee study in 1958, the findings did not offer comparison by ethnicity or race. In addition, the study did not include psychosocial factors or explain why some faculty chose to remain in, return to, or voluntarily leave the academy.

Also in a 1988 study of field mobility, Brown examined the career patterns of minority faculty, analyzing a 10 percent sample of over 79,000 from the National Research Council's Survey of Doctorate Recipients between 1975-1986, which included science, engineering, and humanities doctorates. Brown concluded that: (1) the pool of African American doctorates had decreased to its lowest point since 1975; (2) a smaller percentage of African American doctorates were choosing academic careers and instead opting for careers in business and industry; and (3) the progression and retention rates for African American faculty were lower than any other group. Brown found the most common reasons African American Ph.D.'s had given for obtaining employment in a non-Ph.D. field were: (1) more attractive career options; (2) position in Ph.D. field not available; (3) better pay; (4) undefined other; (5) promoted to new field and; (6) geographic location, (7) personal preference, and (8) family constraints, respectively. This study provided numerous comparative data for this study, but lacked evidence on why African American faculty are remaining in the academy, why some return, and why others voluntarily leave. The study was also limited to science, engineering, and humanities doctorates and displayed the absence of standard errors that rendered it impossible to determine the statistical significance of survey data.

STATUS AND ACHIEVEMENTS IN THE ACADEMY

The present condition of intellectual African American women has been shaped by historical and societal forces which have influenced the ways in which African American women view the world, themselves, and their relationships with family, community, and career. Traditionally, over half of all African American women doctorate recipients choose academic employment, but the numbers are declining as more opt for careers in business, industry, and the professions. What gave rise to the emergence of intellectual African American women and how does it influence the choices of African American women professors? What are the primary characteristics of African American women professors and which factors appear to influence mobility? What career decisions are African American women professors likely to make and what implications do those choices have on African American families, the community, the academy, and society at large? The following three sections will attempt to answer these questions.

Emergence as Intellectuals

In the African American community, the traditional purpose of a formal education for women was social and cultural refinement to assist her in becoming a good wife and mother (Coleman-Burns, 1989). Literacy was also a primary concern because it was important for reading the Bible and teaching the children (Perkins, 1983). Most African American women, like white women, were encouraged to study in "helping" fields, such as education, nursing, and social work (Moses, 1989) and many often prepared themselves to become primary and secondary school teachers (Coleman-Burns, 1989). In 1833, Oberlin became the first college to admit both women and African Americans, and the first to graduate African Americans (DuBois, 1900). DuBois' 1900 study indicated that 50 percent of African American women college graduates from 1860-1899 were married, and the census report referred to by DuBois indicated that ten times as many African American women than white women were employed, which was probably due to economic necessity. In 1890, for example, only 30 African American women held baccalaureate degrees, compared to over 300 black men and 2,500 white women (Graham, 1992).

The education of African American women has traditionally served multiple purposes. Coleman-Burns wrote in 1989, that the primary purpose of education for Black women was to "prepare members of the next generation to take their rightful place as tomorrow's leadership" (p. 152). This was important for African American women, because historically it was the mother who determined the status of their children and had the primary responsibility for child rearing.

In the early 20th century, the African American community began to recognize the need to train African American women for potential leadership roles in the community (Bell-Scott, 1984). African American women used education as a means to further the struggle of equality. This struggle produced a "new breed" of intellectual African American women, according to Coleman-Burns. "The black community's priority on education for black women has been unprecedented from any similarly oppressed class. As a result of this commitment to the education of females and the opening up (real or perceived) of white institutions of higher education to larger numbers of blacks in the 1960s, the intellectual imagination of scholarly African American women has been unleashed" (p. 146).

Baran (1965) describes two types of intellectual roles. The first was the "intellect workers" who only served to distribute and apply the current culture of the status quo, but were not intellectuals because their role according to Baran, was "to obstruct any change of the existing order" (p. 7). The role of the intellectual, however, was to "change the existing order of things in favor of the better one" (p. 7). Traditionally, African American women have been the persons to dispute the dominant patterns during historical periods of protest and other movements. Coleman-Burns (1989) argued that to be an intellectual, one must be able to articulate, create, and apply culture. Many Black teachers, writers, artists, performers, and others have been doing this for years. It appears that only now were Black women getting the credit for achievements they were denied in the past.

Most early African American women leaders focused primarily on women and youth organizations to meet the needs of the African American community (Gilkes, 1983; Perkins, 1983). One of the first African American women's educational societies was the Female Literary Association of Philadelphia. In the preamble (Perkins, 1983), the group indicated that it was their "duty...as daughters of a despised race, to use our uproot endeavors to enlighten the understanding, to cultivate the talents entrusted to our keeping, that by so doing, we may in a great measure, break down the strong barrier of prejudice, and raise ourselves to an equality with those of our fellow beings, who differ from us in complexion" (p. 19). In 1896, a group of educated African American women formed the National Association of Colored Women whose motto was "lifting as we climb." The accomplishments of the group focused on community development and included the establishment of orphanages, elderly homes, educational institutions, and religious programs (Perkins, 1983).

According to Cornel West (1994), some African American intellectuals are often unable to obtain respect and support from the African American community, particularly the middle-class population, because of a growing distrust and suspicion of the intentions of black intellectuals. Sometimes members of the African American community perceive that upwardly mobile persons, who physically remove themselves and their families from the African American community, are intentionally abandoning their culture and people for material gain. West describes two types of African American intellectuals, "the successful ones, distant from (and usually condescending toward) the black community, and unsuccessful ones, disdainful of the white intellectual world. But both camps remain marginal to the black community--dangling between two worlds with little or no black infra-structural bases" (p. 61).

West describes the overall climate for African American intellectuals in society as typically hostile and often requiring reliance on their own resources, such as African American institutions, organizations, and journals. Unfortunately, according to West, institutional support for African American intellectuals are not readily available. "In short, the black infrastructure for intellectual discourse and dialogue is nearly nonexistent" (p. 60). West also argues that African American intellectuals have failed to create and maintain their own organizations to constructively criticize and promote the intellectual works of people of color, which has resulted in a decline of intellectual activity in both quality and quantity among African Americans. According to Howard-Vital (1989), without intellectual activity, "African American women will become invisible, isolated, and powerless...Unless we African American women take an aggressive, unrelenting, lead in identifying who we are, we will continue to react to distortions and perceptions created by others" (p. 189-190).

Rites of Passage

The current status of African American women in academe has been varied based on the type of position one holds. While the characteristics of African American women faculty at two-year and four-year American colleges and universities differ, as do faculty of liberal arts and research institutions, the major issues of salary, teaching versus research, and tenure and promotion practices are common concerns for all faculty. Research suggests that some of these factors may influence African American women to seek employment in sectors outside academe. Often, these characteristics can affect career mobility when they are combined with lifestyle choices, such as motherhood or a desire to hold a position which can further the needs of the community.

Many faculty believe that the value of one's work and contribution in an American college or university are reflected in the salary (McCombs, 1989). If one gives credence to this argument, the academy has far to go to affirm the contributions of African American women.

In a 1988 AAUP report on the status of full-time women faculty with doctorates in the academy, salary differentials between men and women faculty were shown to be 11.8 percent for professors, 7.4 percent for associate professors, and 9.5 percent for assistant professors in all institutions. National data indicates that overall, women and minority faculty were consistently paid less than white males at every faculty rank (Exum, 1983). Finkelstein had found that women were still paid less than men, even after controlling for rank, institutional type, and discipline (1987).

Many studies indicated that women tended to be disproportionately over-represented in certain fields and disciplines which most often led to lower ranks with lower pay (Halaby, 1979). Other studies suggest that since African American doctorate recipients tended to be women, older when they receive their doctorates, married, had more dependents, incurred greater debt by the time they complete their doctorates, and earned their degrees primarily in education, the social sciences and the professions, greater salaries may have been one of the most significant factors in their decisions to voluntarily leave academic employment for a position outside the academy (Brown, 1988; Zumeta, 1984).

Teaching, research, and administration were typically the job responsibilities for most faculty at two and four-year American colleges and universities. Usually, the type of institution where one was employed, determined which responsibilities were given priority and considered more highly in promotion and tenure decisions. The primary work activity of most African American faculty at four-year American colleges and universities was teaching, followed by administration and research, as compared to Asian American faculty who engage more heavily in research, than teaching or administration. In two-year institutions, teaching was the primary work activity and research is rarely emphasized. (Table 3.1).

TABLE 3.1

Primary Work Activity of Minority Science, Engineering, and Humanities Ph.D.'s Employed as Full-Time Faculty in 2 and 4-Year Institutions: U.S. Educated, 1985 (in percent*)

Type of Institution/ Primary Work	African American	Hispanic	Asian American	U.S. Total
4-Year Institution:	(3,355)	(2,589)	(1,490)	(180,077)
Teaching	60.9	54.3	39.9	58.6
Research	11.7	22.4	41.6	21.6
Administration	17.4	15.9	8.7	17.3
2-Year Institution:				
Teaching	70.2	70.4	86.2	83.1
Research	-0-	-0-	-0-	1.4
Administration	21.2	29.6	5.8	11.4

** Within group percentages do not add up to 100
because no-report and other cases were excluded.*

Source: National Research Council, Survey of Doctorate Recipients, 1985.

Although many African American women faculty found teaching personally rewarding, as opposed to the politics of administration, unclear expectations of scholarly research, and ambiguous requirements of promotion and tenure, teaching as a primary work activity had its consequences. For example, African American women faculty typically engaged in more teaching, advised greater numbers of students, and participated in more committee work than white men. As a result, they may have conducted less research and published fewer articles than their white men or women counterparts (Moses, 1989). African American women also tended not to be included in collaborative research projects with their peers. Furthermore, they often lacked sponsorship and rarely had access to resources for research (Moore, 1981) which could lead to greater prestige, higher future economic gains, and enhanced job mobility. Women typically were found to teach more hours on average then men (Austin and Gamson, 1983). They also taught mostly undergraduates and had less contact with graduate students and were therefore less likely to be awarded teaching assistants (Freeman, 1977).

In a 1996 study of faculty research productivity and motivation, Tien and Blackburn found that intrinsic motivation (for example, research interests) rather than extrinsic motivation (for example, a promotion) played a more important role in the research productivity of faculty. They admitted that intrinsic motivation of faculty was difficult to measure because of the imprecise nature of the instruments, and the lack of theory base for generating a hypothesis, but had support of their findings from other studies (Behymer, 1974; Finkelstein, 1984). One possible reason for those conflicting findings was that motivation tended to change over time. Therefore, measuring a faculty members motivation after their publication had been accepted (Creswell, 1985), would not yield the same result had that professor completed the same instrument while they were still trying to find a home for their work.

Tien and Blackburn also found that full professors published the most, but assistant professors published more than associate professors. The fact that most associate professors were tenured may help to explain why productivity decreases after they are promoted to associate professor and tenured. For many women, Black and minority faculty, getting tenure was a dream come true because it provided job security, which was often more important than a promotion with a higher salary.

Some research has indicated that faculty research interests and academic rank were both major correlates of the faculty research productivity (Bentley, 1990; Creswell, 1985; Finkelstein, 1984; Fox, 1985). While many studies suggested that faculty research interests correlated highly with research performance (Blackburn, Behymer, and Hall, 1978; Fulton and Trow, 1974), another recent faculty study showed that research interest did not predict publications (Blackburn, Bieber, Lawrence, and Trautvetter, 1993) and negatively correlated with research involvement (Steitz, 1982).

Sometimes, when African American faculty engaged in scholarly research, they encountered several roadblocks. Blum argued that "because of the small representation [of blacks in full-time faculty positions], scholarship on issues germane to Blacks were often judged by their white colleagues. Too often, say many minority faculty members, those colleagues were conservative and unappreciative of nontraditional subjects or nontraditional views" (1988, p. A5). Numerous studies mentioned that African American faculty often indicated having research trivialized and devalued if it focused on black issues or issues of a social concern (Exum, 1983; Mitchell, 1983).

In a 1988 AAUP Report of the Status of Women in the Academic Profession, the percentage of men of all institutions who were tenured in 1988 were 69 percent, as compared to 46 percent for women. Furthermore, women were disproportionately in non-tenure track positions. In 1988, 18 percent of full-time faculty were currently in non-tenure track positions, compared to 7 percent of men (July/Aug., 1988).

Research suggests that although academe still claims the greatest share of African American doctorate recipients (ACE, 1993), many appear to be beginning to avoid careers in the academy (Brown, 1988). In 1975, for example, 67.6 percent of all reporting doctorate recipients planned to work in the academy. In the following eight years, the numbers choosing academe continued to decline. In 1984, academe claimed a small, but greater number of doctorate recipients, although the numbers continue to fall, reaching only 48.5 percent of the all African American doctorate recipients. In comparison, a growing number of Hispanic, Asian American, and white doctorate recipients were also showing a declining interest in academic employment. This data appeared to suggest that while fewer numbers of doctorate recipients as a whole were joining the academy, the number of African

American doctorate recipients choosing academic employment were declining at a more rapid pace than any other group.

Some African American faculty had opted for careers in academic administration. African American women have a long tradition of leadership in education, but their status as administrators was not impressive either. For example, in 1985, only 3.4 percent of administrators were African American women as compared to 30.4 percent of white females. The majority of African American administrators were employed at historically black institutions and were primarily concentrated in student affairs and specialized positions. Like faculty, African American women tended to be older, married, concentrated in two-year institutions, and paid approximately 15 percent less than their male counterparts (Moses, 1989).

Another area where there has been a gain of African American women is in the professions, particularly health care. For example, the number of African American women in the health care professions grew from 9.4 percent in 1960, to 17.4 percent in 1980. In the mid-1980s, health care became the dominant employer of African American professional women (Woody, 1989).

Making Choices About Career and Family

Studies suggest that there are numerous individual, family, and societal factors that can affect the choices of African American women and may influence career mobility. Several studies have examined the individual constraints women often experience such as marital status, number of dependents, and spouses' income on job mobility (Felmlee, 1980). Some studies suggest that women often compromise advancement of their careers (Marwell et al., 1979; Sagaria, 1988) to eliminate the risks to marriage and family. While some women may choose to either marry early or marry late after they had established their careers, others may have completely forgone marriage and children (Aisenberg and Harrington, 1988; Marshall and Jones, 1990). African American women, however, had traditionally combined family and work.

Black women have historically maintained a rich tradition of managing family, work, and community, but they often did it at a cost (Moses, 1989). In many cases due to work history and economic necessity, Black women were socialized early to combining their roles as wife, mother, and worker (Willie, 1974). Support was typically provided from social networks in the community (Hill, 1972), however adolescents in the home served as the primarily means of household support for employed mothers by providing childcare and household help. Malson (1983) suggests that African American children viewed their mothers as role models. Since most mothers worked and served multiple roles, African American children typically did not view employment and homemaking as mutually exclusive. Furthermore, those views and attitudes often carried over into practice as adults.

In a study of the career mobility of Black women community workers (1983), Gilkes found that "women's career orientations and patterns of occupational mobility were organized around the goals of community work--empowerment of the black community and change in the quality of individual and group life and in the larger social structure" (p. 115). The careers of these women were shaped and determined primarily by "unpredictable crises and conflicts imposed and arising within the black community...Job tenure was determined more by changes in their own nation-class consciousness and black community politics than by 'better opportunities' and promotions offered within mainstream professional and sub-professional networks" (p. 124). Black women in this study appeared to accept positions which enabled them to further the interest of the black community and when the work was done, they moved on to secure a new position where they could be more effective in the community.

While research institutions graduate 61 percent of African American doctorates and 76 percent of Latino doctorates, African American make up only 2.9 percent of tenured faculty and Latinos constitute only 1.9 percent of tenured faculty (Fields, 1998). Howard University, which is a Black Research 1 institution, Wayne State University, Temple University, and Emory University show the highest percentage of African American faculty members with tenure.

In 1995, Howard had 516 Black faculty, representing 68 percent of the university's faculty. Of these professors, 61 percent or 356 were either tenured or on tenure track. Columbia had the second largest number (216) of overall Black faculty, but only 3 percent or 41 faculty were tenured or on tenure track. Following Howard, the top four institutions with the greatest numbers of African American faculty that were tenured or on tenure track include the University of Michigan, Ann Arbor with 98 faculty, the University of Maryland-College Park and Temple University both at 85, and Ohio State University-main campus with 83 faculty.

The current 5,278 African American scholars in research institutions throughout the United States constituted roughly 3 percent of the faculty at these institutions.   Among faculty with tenure (119,838), only 2.9 percent or 3,479 were African American.

Although more than half of all African American doctorate holders and the majority of African American women doctorate recipients were employed in academe, they typically had the lowest faculty progression, retention, and tenure rates in the academy. Furthermore, most were concentrated among the lowest ranks, and in two-year and four-year colleges and universities as opposed to large research institutions.

After a decline in 1977, African American women substantially increased their share of doctorate degrees. In 1986, they received 60.9 percent of all doctorates awarded to African American candidates, compared to 34.9 percent in 1975 and 38.7 in 1977.   African American women who obtained doctorates tended to be older than the average student, take longer to attain the degree, be married, and were most likely to earn their doctorate degree in education, the social sciences, or the professions (Moses, 1989).

According to the National Research Council, a significantly growing number of African American Ph.D.'s were opting for careers, while 12.5 percent chose government, and only 1.6 percent chose business and industry. However, the number of African American education doctorate recipients choosing academic employment dropped from 60 percent in 1975, to 38.3 percent in 1986, while their corresponding representation in business and industry more than doubled from 1.6 percent in 1975, to 3.3 percent in 1986. In six of the seven disciplines represented, the numbers of African American and Hispanic Ph.D.'s recipients choosing academic employment declined. Those in engineering, however, rose slightly from 33.3 percent in 1975 to 37.6 percent in 1986. In all reported disciplines, with the exception of the physical sciences, the total number of African American doctorates choosing business and industry careers doubled, and in engineering, more than tripled from 11.1 percent in 1975 to 37.2 in 1986 (Table 3.2).

TABLE 3.2:

Percentage of U.S.* African American and Hispanic Ph.D.'s in Selected Fields with Interests in Academe vs. Non-Academe Sectors: 1975-1986.

Field/ Ethnicity	Academe		Sector Government		Business/ Industry		Other	
	1975	1986	1975	1986	1975	1986	1975	1986
Physical Science								
Black	46.2	26.7	11.5	13.3	34.6	53.3	7.7	6.7
Hispanic	43.8	40.0	18.8	16.0	31.2	44.0	5.6	-0-
Engineering								
Black**	33.3	37.6	55.6	25.2	11.1	37.2	-0-	-0-
Hispanic	25.0	38.9	8.3	16.7	66.7	44.4	-0-	-0-
Life Science								
Black	75.0	52.2	25.0	8.7	-0-	21.7	-0-	17.4
Hispanic	76.5	77.8	5.9	16.7	11.2	5.5	5.4	-0-
Social Science								
Black	79.4	56.4	11.2	11.9	-0-	6.9	9.3	24.8
Hispanic	82.1	49.3	5.1	20.0	12.8	10.7	-0-	20.0
Humanities								
Black	93.5	85.0	1.6	2.5	-0-	-0-	4.7	12.5
Hispanic	94.7	91.3	2.6	4.3	-0-	-0-	2.5	4.2
Education								
Black	60.0	38.3	12.5	18.2	1.6	3.3	25.9	40.0
Hispanic	62.9	45.7	11.4	14.7	1.4	6.0	24.3	33.6
Professions/Other								
Black	88.5	66.0	3.8	16.0	-0-	6.0	7.7	12.0
Hispanic	88.3	68.4	-0-	-0-	-0-	15.8	11.7	15.8

* Includes native born and naturalized citizens.

** Percentages for Black Ph.D.'s are based on N of 9 individuals in 1975 and 8 individuals in 1986.

Source: National Research Council, Office of Scientific & Engineering Personnel, Survey of Earned Doctorates, 1975-1986.

African American women have traditionally remained in education because of the potential for challenging current paradigms and providing leadership for young developing scholars. But each African American woman had a different history and unique experience that helped to shape her identity (McCombs, 1989). "For black women, the challenge is to enter and remain within the university and perform all responsibilities without losing integrity. The central problems of isolation, alienation, promotion, and tenure play an important role in determining who will remain" (McCombs, 1989, p. 141). Menges and Exum (1983) argued that sustaining a career in academe requires more than securing a position; it required surviving promotion and tenure, which most often determined who would remain and who would leave the academy.

McCombs (1989) contended that the "participation [of black women] and the struggle that ensued between academia and themselves is one of necessity, not choice...African American women who decided to enter the university do so with the understanding that it would be a new experience, but it would also be a challenge to their traditions" (p. 137).

Scholars have offered much speculation for the reasons why African American faculty leave academe. Brown suggested the following reasons: (1) fewer African Americans took postdoctoral appointments prior to taking faculty positions, (2) most engaged in teaching over research, and (3) promotion and tenure requirements were not always clear or decisions fair. Others contended the lack of job security (Bowen and Schuster, 1986), a tight academic labor market (Shapiro, 1983), and overburdening service roles (Staples, 1986) had contributed to the severe loss of African American faculty among the ranks.

Research suggests, in general, that the primary factors which could influence African American women to leave academic employment included: family factors affecting spouse and children; geographic location, such as climate, size, proximity to friends and family, and areas of interest; job characteristics of the work itself; people in and environment of the department; the people, environment, and facilities of the university; salary, fringe benefits, and opportunities for other income; and the opportunities for advancement, professional development, promotion, and tenure.

IV. *The Decision to Remain in, Return To, or Voluntarily Leave the Academy*

Currently no scholarly research exists on the success and achievements of Black women professors. The focus of most research has typically been on "minority" or "women" faculty and the dominant emphasis of these studies has centered primarily on desegregation, affirmative action, and recruitment and retention efforts. To date, no studies have specifically examined the influences of marital status, number of dependents, tenure status, job satisfaction, and support systems (or lack thereof) on the career mobility of Black women professors.

Given that there are no existing conceptual or theoretical models currently available to address the concerns of this study, the two main purposes of this chapter was to attempt to isolate the findings from previous research which may contain elements relevant to this study, and propose a conceptual framework from which a more precise economic and psychosocial model of the career mobility of Black women professors can be developed. A "more precise model" will more fairly examine the experiences of Black women professors and discover what factors influence career mobility, as well as what role these factors play in the success and achievement factors of Black faculty women.

The first section provides a conceptual framework based on economic, psychosocial, and job satisfaction theory. In order to gain a better insight and appreciation of the experiences of Black faculty women, the second section offers an economic and psychosocial model, focusing on the eight major independent variables which have been suggested to influence career mobility of Black faculty women, supported by empirical research.

CONCEPTUAL FRAMEWORK

The factors that influence career mobility often differ based on the circumstances, needs, interests, desires, and experiences of each individual faculty member. Even in the case of an individual, for example, the value given to any one factor can change as the circumstances change and as rational value judgments are placed on the perceived costs or benefits of alternative employment opportunities. The categorical dependent variable in this study was the decision of Black faculty women to remain in, return to, or voluntarily leave their present institution for alternative academic or nonacademic employment. The following eight variables were examined to determine what influences, if any, these choices have on the decision: (1) salary; (2) tenure status; (3) institutional type; (4) intention to leave; (5) marital status; (6) number of dependents; (7) support systems; and (8) external barriers.

The conceptual framework draws upon economic, psychosocial, and job satisfaction theorys to help explain the decisions of 384 Black faculty women. These theories, which often overlap, provide a useful foundation for examining career mobility, as well as for explaining the impact of job satisfaction on economic and psychosocial factors, and the factors which influence patterns of choice.

Economic and Psychosocial Theory

Theoretical studies on academic faculty suggests that extrinsic factors, such as salary, compensation, benefits, and tenure (which typically commands greater economic returns) are the primary factors which influence career decision patterns. Faculty often weigh the perceived costs and benefits of perceived alternatives. Economic theorists stress the importance of rational decision-making and view salary, compensation, and other expected gross returns as the primary reasons workers seek alternative employment (Weiler, 1985).

Research on Black faculty have consistently cited factors such as isolation, the absence of support groups and a critical mass, greater likelihood of more dependents, marital status, and a myriad of external barriers to help explain the decisions of Black faculty to leave academic employment. Psychosocial theories tend to lend credence to these extrinsic factors which focus primarily on the individual, family, personal characteristics (i.e. age, marital status, number of dependents), and external forces (i.e. environment, community, support systems, and external barriers) to help explain why Black faculty might leave for alternative employment (Gregory, 1994b). The following section will explore the impact of job satisfaction on the behaviors of Black faculty women. Job satisfaction theory is useful because it can help to explain the relationship between job dissatisfaction and turnover, and what influences job satisfaction may have on economic and psychosocial theory.

Job Satisfaction Theory

Job satisfaction is defined as a measure of the quality of work life and has been shown to influence behavior and performance of workers to leave an organization (Price and Mueller, 1986). In the past 25 years, over 250 articles have been written related to faculty job satisfaction in higher education according to the Educational Resources Information Center. Although researchers cite a number of leading scholars from which to base their framework (Brayfield and Crockett; Eckert and Stecklein; Herzberg; Herzberg, Mausner, Peterson, and Capwell; Herzberg, Mausner, and Snyderman; Hulin and Smith; Likert; Locke; Morse; Smith, Kendall, and Hulin; and Vroom), Herzberg's theory is the most widely accepted and employed framework used to explain job satisfaction. Herzberg contends that intrinsic factors, which most often pertain to the work itself, contribute primarily to job satisfaction. The five major variables of job satisfaction or intrinsic factors Herzberg (1972) identified were: (1) achievement; (2) recognition; (3) the work itself; (4) responsibility; and (5) advancement. Extrinsic factors, Herzberg explains, such as the environment and conditions surrounding the work, were typically the leading cause of dissatisfaction. The five major dissatisfiers or extrinsic factors identified were: (1) company policy and administration; (2) supervision; (3) salary; (4) interpersonal relations; and (6) working conditions.

Landy (1989) has identified six techniques often employed to measure job satisfaction: (1) job descriptive indexes; (2) overt behavior scales; (3) action tendency scales; (4) interviews; (5) attitude scales; and (6) critical incidents. Although Herzberg used critical incidents to measure job satisfaction, the most common job satisfaction measure was the job descriptive indexes. However, Landy stresses that "there is no best way. But no matter how job satisfaction is measured, the technique must be capable of producing reliable and valid data, or those data are worthless" (p. 475).

According to the literature on job satisfaction, economic factors such as salary has been cited as a determinant of job satisfaction as well as one of the common sources of job dissatisfaction. Although most would agree that salary is often one of the contributing factors influencing Black faculty mobility, there is much debate about the degree to which salary impacts one's decision to leave. For example, some faculty may perceive they are being paid less because of the amount of work performed or their contribution to the institution, and this can lead more to job dissatisfaction than the specific amount paid (Ivancevich and Donnelly, 1968). Others may compare their salaries to a greater salary they could command for similar work outside of academe (Morse, 1953).

Other studies suggest that job turnover is the result of numerous psychosocial factors influencing job dissatisfaction (Herzberg, Mausner, Peterson, and Capwell, 1957; Vroom, 1964). For example, a primary factor found to influence overall faculty dissatisfaction is the extent to which work interferes with and limits one's personal life (Carnegie Foundation, 1986). Furthermore, certain aspects of work and non-work experience have been found to be related to job satisfaction (Near and Sorcinelli, 1986). Also, studies indicate that the thought of quitting, the intention to search for alternative employment, and the actual act of quitting are significantly related to job satisfaction (Mobley, Horner, and Hollingsworth, 1978). Studies suggest that job satisfaction appears to play an important role early in the process, and becomes less important as the individual matriculates through the stages of one's career (Mobley, Horner, and Hollingsworth, 1978). However, other scholars warn that regardless of the level of job satisfaction, the more difficult it is to obtain a position, the less likely it is to quit the one you have (Hulin and Smith, 1964).

Research on academic faculty indicates significant differences in levels of satisfaction among faculty at different ages and career stages (Baldwin and Blackburn, 1981; Ladd and Lipset, 1976). Numerous studies also suggest gender differences in job satisfaction. For example, faculty women tend to report more stress (Brown, Bond,

Gerne, Krager, Krantz, Lukin, and Prentice, 1986), less satisfaction (Project in the Status and Education of Women, 1986), fewer promotions (Astin and Snyder, 1982; Aisenberg and Harrington, 1988), lower salaries (Astin and Snyder, 1982; Sandler, 1986; Schoen and Winocur, 1988), and greater attrition from the ranks (Project in the Status and Education of Women, 1986). Other studies suggest that faculty women may possess greater awareness of their feelings (Heppner and Gonzales, 1987) and be more vocal about expressing them (Balswick and Avertt, 1977). However, the relationship between gender and job satisfaction has been found to be inconsistent (Moch, 1980). A more recent study of academic careers among faculty members at a mid-western state university reported low rates of job satisfaction and yet a high importance to factors dealing with career, marriage, and personal factors (Thoreson, Kardash, Leuthold, and Morrow, 1990).

Several studies have emerged which examine job satisfaction among ethnic groups. For example, Blacks have been found to report more dissatisfaction than whites in predominantly white organizations (O'Reilly and Roberts, 1973; Smith, et al., 1974; Weaver, 1974). In contrast, other studies have argued that Blacks are more satisfied than whites (Gavin and Ewen, 1974) and often expect more favorable job related rewards than whites (Greenhaus and Gavin, 1972). In an attempt to explain these conflicting findings, Moch (1980) produced a similar study which controlled for race and found that social (extrinsic) and psychosocial (intrinsic) factors were statistically significant for Black workers and extrinsic factors were most influential in job dissatisfaction.

According to Davis (1985):

...it appears that as a group, black faculty are less satisfied with their college/university positions than are white faculty..... Black faculty, relative to whites, perceive themselves to be less respected, to receive less satisfaction from their positions, and to have less certain employment futures (p. 90).

In 1986, Ball examined the factors of life satisfaction among Blacks. Ball contended that married, divorced, and widowed Black women were more satisfied with their lives than were separated or single Black women. Ball further argued that Black men who were married were significantly less satisfied than were separated, divorced, and widowed Black men. This finding demands further research.

Understanding these factors can help academics learn what factors influence satisfaction or dissatisfaction among Black faculty women, what impact these factors have on career mobility, and what might be done to intervene and help prevent the loss of Black faculty women from the academic ranks.

FACTORS WHICH MAY INFLUENCE CAREER MOBILITY

Salary

Economic theorists have traditionally claimed that salary or the opportunity to gain greater economic returns, are the primary reasons most workers voluntarily seek employment elsewhere. Theoretical studies on the behaviors of academic faculty would appear to lend some credence to this claim. However, many studies suggest that salary is very often only one of the contributing factors, and not always the primary factor which influences mobility among academic faculty. For example, some studies suggest that the decision to leave is often a combination of tangible benefits of the position, such as greater salary, more research support, or better facilities (Matier, 1990), and intangible benefits of the current work environment, such as autonomy, influence, sense of belonging, and institutional reputation (Blackburn and Aurand, 1972). A limited number of academic studies exist which focus on the influence of salary on faculty turnover intentions (Ehrenberg, et al., 1990; Marshall, 1964; Matier, 1990; McKenna and Sikula, 1981; and Weiler, 1985).

In a 1990 study, Ehrenberg, Kasper, and Rees examined faculty turnover using AAUP data and found that greater levels of compensation tended to increase retention rates for assistant and associate professors, but not for full professors. In addition, they contended that this growth increased as faculty moved from graduate schools, to four-year undergraduate institutions, then to two-year institutions, respectively.

Also in 1990, Matier studied two four-year universities--one urban and one rural--and examined the decisions of tenure-track faculty to leave their current place of employment after receiving firm offers for attractive career options. The faculty respondents had not been denied tenure at the time of the study and adequately represented a broad range of disciplines. Matier found that approximately 60 percent reported that they would leave their current position if given a greater increase of tangible benefits such as salary, better facilities, and research support.

In 1985, Weiler examined tenured faculty members who resigned from the University of Minnesota between 1980 and 1984. Weiler found that the five primary factors that influenced the decision to leave in order of importance were: (1) personal factors; (2) salary or salary potential; (3) availability of research funds; (4) locational factors; and (5) reputation of the new employer.

In a similar 1981 study of career mobility among business professors, McKenna and Sikula examined the causes of turnover and the frequency of career moves among 187 business schools. McKenna and Sikula concluded that, although there were numerous variations in the reasons for turnover among faculty in different academic ranks, the 5 major reasons for leaving were: 1) promotion opportunities elsewhere; 2) greater pay; 3) greater career opportunity for a spouse; 4) dissatisfaction with present administration; and 5) alternative employment at a more prestigious institution.

In a 1964 study of economic professors, Marshall found five major factors which had the greatest influence on the decision of faculty to leave their positions. Salary ranked first, followed by the lack of promotional opportunities, geographic location, unsatisfactory working conditions, and fringe benefits.

In contrast to the previous studies that have suggested that salary was the primary factor influencing academic faculty to leave for alternative employment, Schuster (1986) contends otherwise. Although salary is a often a factor in faculty mobility, Schuster argues, it is not always the primary factor. For faculty members, Schuster states that, "the intrinsic rewards of academic life--not salaries--have always been the most important issue. But faculty members, however, do not view compensation as unimportant" (p. 278). According to a recent study by the National Center on Education Statistics, "sizable portions of faculty members indicated that they would consider leaving their institutions, and higher education altogether, if the right opportunity appeared..." (Schuster, 1990, p. 37).

In support of Schuster's contention, numerous scholars (Aurand and Blackburn; Brown, 1967; Ladd and Lipset, 1976; McGee, 1971; Stecklein and Lathrop, 1960) have found that salary was not the primary factor in the decision of faculty--even at the highest levels and most prestigious institution--to leave their present position. The most important factors in the decision to leave were: (1) nature of the job duties; (2) competency and congeniality of colleagues; and (3) the opportunity for research and professional development (Finkelstein, 1984; Ladd and Lipset, 1976).

Previous studies have debated the impact of salary on career mobility of faculty. Brown (1967) found that the value of salary and the actual salary received was inversely related, which suggest that salary was increasingly less important as faculty moved into higher academic ranks and therefore, were less likely to be a primary motivator in the decision to leave. In support, McGee (1971) found that faculty earning the greatest salaries among liberal arts institutions had the lowest rates of mobility, while the lower salaried faculty tended to be more mobile. Yet Ladd and Lipset (1976) found that a greater salary was the most significant factor of faculty--of all ages and rank--to leave their present institution.

Limited research is available on the career mobility of women. However, the majority of data confirms discrepencies in salary between academic and nonacademic industries (Brown, 1988; Hansen, 1985; and Maxfield, 1981) along ethnic lines (Felmlee, 1982; Mincer and Polachek, 1974; Sorensen, 1983; Spilerman, 1977; and Tuma, 1976) and among faculty women (Astin and Snyder, 1982; Bernard, 1987; Johnson and Stafford, 1979, Thoreson, et al., 1990).

According to the National Science Foundation (1990), women academics, as compared to men, typically have careers that are more frequently interrupted. In addition, they usually do not hold a doctorate, accumulate less professional experience and training, and have different work histories (Eckert, 1971; Mincer and Polachek, 1974; Zuckerman, 1987). Furthermore, women are traditionally concentrated in academic disciplines and institutions that offer the lowest pay and less prestige (Bayer, 1973; Finkelstein, 1984). Women also spend more time teaching and publishing, and are rarely involved in governance (Bayer and Astin, 1975; Cameron, 1978). Salary differentials can, in part, be explained by lower tenure rates for women (46 percent for women and 69 percent for men), a paucity of women in the highest paying disciplines and institutions, and heavy concentration in the lower ranks (Hexter, 1990). In 1989, salary differentials between faculty men and women ranged from 7 percent for instructors to as high as 13.1 percent for full professors.

Many academic studies suggest that in general, 12-month faculty salaries remain far below salaries found in business and private industry (Brown, 1988; Hansen, 1986; and Maxfield, 1981). For example, according to the National Research Council's Survey of Doctorate Recipients (1986), the average 12-month salary for Black faculty in the sciences, engineering, and humanities was $35,968, as compared to $42,950 outside academe, and this gap appears to be widening (Table 4.1).

According to the United States Department of *Education Digest of Educational Statistics* (1992), in 1985 there were a total of 114,259 full-time faculty men among the professor ranks in institutions of higher education. In contrast, there were only 15,011 (or 8 percent) full-time faculty women in similar positions during the same period. Also in 1985, the average salary for full-time faculty men among the professor ranks was $43,833, as compared to $38,252 for faculty women.

Gender often has a significant impact on faculty salaries. Comparable worth is often an issue because women professors are typically paid less than their male counterparts in virtually all employment sectors (AAUP, 1989; Mayfield and Nash, 1976). In a study of women professors at historically Black colleges in the South, Mayfield and Nash contended that 32 percent of women professors reported experiencing salary discrimination, although 92 percent of those respondents indicated they would still choose the same position regardless of salary discrimination. According to the AAUP (1989) Annual Report on the Economic Status of the Profession, (1988-89), the 1988-89 average academic year salaries of faculty women by category, affiliation, and rank, were substantially less than the average salary for men in all cases. In 1991, Smart examined gender equity in the academy, and found that the gender of faculty was the most significant factor of academic rank and salary, whereas the type of institution, academic discipline, and the nature of the work itself were all secondary determinants of the same.

In the 1985 article entitled *Salary Differences Across Disciplines*, Hansen examined the reasons for the widening gap among disciplines of academic faculty. Hansen argued that because of the decline in real faculty earnings since the 1970s, the private sector has lured away many academics by offering higher salaries. The same market forces that drove up salaries in the private market, argues Hansen, also

TABLE 4.1 :

Median Annual Salaries of Minority Science, Engineering,
& Humanities Ph.D.'s employed Full-Time, By Years Since
Ph.D. & Type of Post-Graduate Sector: U.S. Educated, 1985.

Salary and Years Since Ph.D.	African American	Hispanic	Asian American	U.S. Total
All Years:				
Academe*	$35,968	$34,911	$35,765	$37,376
Non-academe	42,950	45,738	43,318	47,401
Total	37,844	38,250	40,773	41,028
% difference**	16	24	17	21
5 Years or Less:				
Academe*	$29,757	$26,450	$28,317	$28,313
Non-academe	36,863	39,256	39,279	37,479
% difference**	19	33	28	25
6-10 Years:				
Academe*	$34,203	$33,843	$33,692	$32,977
Non-academe	42,861	49,650	47,783	43,682
% difference**	20	33	29	25
11-15 Years:				
Academe*	$40,226	$39,648	$32,762	$38,101
Non-academe	54,586	49,200	42,659	50,723
% difference**	26	19	23	25
16-20 Years:				
Academe*	$45,231	$45,011	$52,450	$42,973
Non-academe	-0-***	-0-***	72,024	55,832
% difference**	-0-***	-0-***	27	23

*   Excludes medical schools.
**   Difference between non-academic and academic median salaries,
        expressed as a percentage of non-academic median salary.
*** Median salaries are not reported for cells with fewer than 10
        sample individuals.

Source: National Resource Council, Survey of Doctorate Recipients,
        1985.

increased salaries in selected academic disciplines, such as engineering and computer science. The demand for professionals in these areas not only appears to influence the exiting of many faculty for private sector positions, but also claims a rapidly increasing number of graduate students.

Research on Blacks in the academy offers a contrasting picture. Some studies suggest, for example, that since Black doctorate recipients tend to be women who are older when they receive their degrees, are most often married, have more dependents, incur greater debt by the time they complete their education, and earn their doctorates primarily in education, the social sciences and professions, greater salaries may be one of the more significant factors in the decision to leave academic employment (Brown, 1988; Zumeta, 1984).

According to Curry-Williams (1985), most national studies indicate that extrinsic factors, such as salary, benefits, and geographical location, have the greatest influence on the decisions of Black faculty to leave their institutions. However, several studies conducted on Black faculty do not support this contention, and in fact, suggest that salary is not a primary factor in the decision of most Black faculty to leave (Hoskin, 1978; Moore and Wagstaff, 1974). Moore and Wagstaff (1974), for example, found that the factors influencing Black faculty to leave predominantly white institutions were perceived racial discrimination, desire to work at a historically Black colleges, difficulty in obtaining tenure and promotion, low priority of teaching at the school, and the expectation to participate in Black activities. Hoskin's work on Black administrators are consistent with Moore and Wagstaff's work. Hoskin (1978) found that the primary reasons Black administrators left predominantly white institutions were: limited opportunities for promotion; perceived racial discrimination; extra efforts required for promotion due to ascribed status; low seniority; and poor relationships with colleagues. Despite research on the contrary, Suinn and Witt (1982) have found that Black faculty are willing to be the first minority in a department, provided that the community offers a presence of ethnicity.

In summary, most non-minority scholars agree that salary differentials are often a contributing factor to varying degrees, which may influence a faculty member to leave their current position for alternative employment. However, most minority scholars do not support this contention. The decision to remain in, return to, or voluntarily leave is most often a combination of variables relating to both the current and alternative position. These influential variables may include both work and non work-related factors, such as the extrinsic and intrinsic benefits to the individual and the family.

Tenure

According to the American Association of University Professor's (AAUP) 1940 Statement of Principles, tenure offers: (1) the freedom to teach and conduct research; and (2) economic security. Tenure is described as an arrangement by which faculty appointments continue until retirement age, although they are subject to dismissal for adequate cause or termination due to financial exigency or change of institutional programs in higher education institutions (AAUP, 1973). Tenure also allows a faculty member to participate in the personnel decisions of other colleagues (Bowen and Schuster, 1986).

Tenure track faculty positions in American higher education are typically measured by the ranks of assistant, associate, and full professor. Rank has been shown to be the most important determinant of tenure and the most important predictor of salary (Bayer and Astin, 1975). It has been well documented that women are more likely to be at less prestigious institutions--those which are public and do not grant doctorate degrees (Cole 1979) or in non tenure-track positions (Bernard, 1964). Because women are typically clustered in lower academic ranks, they are less likely to be granted tenure, and therefore less likely to experience job security and academic freedom (Freeman, 1977).

According to the United States Department of Education *Digest of Education Statistics* (1992), less women are tenured in 1990 than a decade ago. In 1980-81, 49.7 percent of full-time faculty women in all institutions were tenured, compared to 70 percent for faculty men. In 1990, the percentage of tenured women dropped to 45.2 percent for women, while the percentage for men remained relatively the same at 67.7 percent. More women in public two-year colleges continue to be more successful in gaining tenure in 1980 and 1990 than are women in four-year colleges and universities. The rate of tenure among women in private two-year and four-year colleges and universities, however, do not indicate a significant difference. In 1980, 37.2 percent of women at private four-year colleges and universities held tenure, as compared to 39.5 percent of women in two-year private institutions. And in 1990, 39.7 percent of women held tenure in four-year colleges and universities as compared with 39.1 percent in two-year institutions, respectively.

Numerous studies based on different fields and samples have found that women are underrepresented in the higher academic ranks. Typically, women are less likely to be granted tenure and are often promoted more slowly than are men (Astin & Snyder, 1982; Bayer and Astin, 1975; Bernard, 1964; Cole and Cole, 1973; Hurlbert and Rosenfeld, 1992; Long, Allison and McGinnis, 1993; Rosenfeld and Jones, 1986; Szafran, 1984). According to Graham (1973) "the most important single observation about women in the academic world is that their numbers decrease dramatically as the importance of the post increases" (p. 163). In a study of career mobility among faculty men and women, Rosenfeld supported this contention by stating:

> Women as compared with men were found in lower tenure ranks or in non tenure-track positions.... These differences seem due not only to the slower rate at which women move between career ladder ranks, but also to the differences by sex in types of career mobility men and women have (1981, p. 358).

Research on Black faculty and their status among tenure ranks are not encouraging. Studies indicate Black scholars are almost absent among the tenure ranks in most predominately white institutions (Benokraitis and Feagin, 1978). In 1985, Black faculty women were concentrated most heavily in assistant professor and instructor ranks that are most often non-tenured positions (Table 4.2).

Several studies indicate that minority faculty often find promotion and tenure to be ambiguous, inappropriate, unrealistic, or unfairly weighed (Banks, 1984; Gregory, 1995a; Ladd, 1979; Lincoln and Guba, 1980; and Outcalt, 1980). Some minority and women faculty never reach tenure because they were often caught in the "revolving door" syndrome. This often occurs when faculty members are appointed on tenure track, kept for four to six years, evaluated unfavorably for tenure, and required to leave. This "up and out" process may be repeated at numerous institutions until the individual eventually chooses to leave the academy altogether (Aquirre, 1981; Banks, 1984; Gregory, 1995a; Valverde, 1981).

TABLE 4.2:

Full-time instructional faculty women in institutions
of higher education: Fall 1985

	Total	African American	Other Minority	White
Professors.........................	15,011	801	677	13,533
Associate professors.........	25,936	1,606	1,183	23,147
Assistant professors..........	39,845	2,972	1,959	34,914
Instructors........................	32,160	2,465	1,488	28,207
Lecturers...........................	4,668	327	300	4,041
Other faculty.....................	10,443	600	602	9,241

Source: United States Equal Employment Opportunity Commission,
          Higher Education Staff Information Report File, 1985.

Some African American faculty have found through their
experiences that obtaining tenure is increasingly difficult. Many are
subjected to emotional and psychological abuses during the tenure
review process. Some argue that focusing only on research puts many
faculty of color at a disadvantage because they often focus more on
teaching, mentoring, and community service. These activities often
deterred Black and other minority faculty from their research, thereby
decreasing their chances of receiving tenure.

"For faculty of color, tenure is torture," says Dr. Alice Brown-
Collins, an African American social psychologist who is a tenured
professor at the University of Vermont. "Whether they receive tenure
or not, a very large percentage of Black and female academics find the
tenure process bitter and traumatic because even if you get tenure,
unless every vote was unanimous, it means that now you get to spend
the rest of your life with some people who thought you weren't good
enough to be there." She adds, "The people of color we've spoken to
almost always report that coming up for tenure for strips them
psychologically.   The   department   because   a   personal   and
psychological minefield. You don't know what people are going to do,
or whom you can trust. Departments are intimate institutions and
people have long memories. If you ever had a disagreement with
someone, it will come up during tenure."

Most four-year colleges and universities around the country state in their policies and procedures that "Teaching, research and service" are given equal weight when a scholar is considered for tenure, although in reality, only tenure is given serious consideration. In other words, if you have a strong publication record in mainstream, referred journals, you will probably receive tenure even if your teaching and service record are less than exemplary. Ironically, in graduate schools of education where our goal is to teach others to teach, counsel and lead other teachers, we still adhere to research as the major and sometimes the only criteria for tenure.

The truth is that somebody has to teach undergraduates, advise students, serve on committees, mentor students, and be responsible for a host of other responsibilities that are not rewarded by tenure and rarely recognized during promotion. That 'somebody' is usually a caring and creative woman or person of color who is committed to quality teaching, mentoring students, and sincere service to one's campus and community. Unfortunately, the more successful they are in these activities, the less likely they will have published and the harder it will be to make a case for tenure. In support of this contention, Chamberlain (1998) argues that women often choose to participate in time-consuming activities, such as family or teaching, that reduce their scholarly productivity and consequently hinder their career progress.

To add insult to injury, the requirements for tenure seem to become more rigorous each year. As a previous member of the promotion and tenure committee, we were only able to vote on faculty of equal or lesser rank than ourselves. Although I did not vote on tenure cases because I was not a tenured faculty member at that institution, I was present during discussion. I can honestly say that there is nothing more upsetting than to realize that most, if not all of the senior faculty on the tenure committee who are judging your academic worth, achieved their tenure with far fewer accomplishments than you, at a time when the standards were not so rigorous.

> Individuals have the right to know about issues that affect their lives, and how and by whom decisions are made is essential information. Treating people with dignity requires that we ensure they understand the process; to do otherwise makes a mockery of an organization that presents itself as a community (Tierney and Bensimon, p. 138).

Harriette Richard, a psychologist at Northern Kentucky University stated that, "it is particularly destructive to African American faculty because a personal commitment to mentoring was a clearly acknowledged, necessary part of what they did for themselves and their community." In addition, research clearly indicates that mentoring is important because it directly influences the number of Black and other minority students attending and graduating from colleges and universities (Blackwell, 1989). In fact, the mentoring of minority students was one of the primary reasons cited by colleges and universities for diversifying their faculty.

One possible barrier to tenure for many Black faculty women are the extraordinary time demands placed on them due to their relatively small numbers (Banks, 1984; Gregory, 1994b). For example, Merton (1957) argues that the demands of a particular role may often be in complete contradiction to other roles. One such example are the requirements of tenure. In many cases, some Black faculty are torn between working to meet the requirements of tenure and advising and counseling disproportionately larger numbers of nontraditional students, as well as other duties, such as committee work (Aquirre, 1981). These activities are often encouraged by departments, but are rarely taken into consideration during tenure review. Furthermore, it often serves to penalize the faculty member for interfering with scholarly productivity (Valverde, 1981).

Rafky's 1972 research on Black scholars reveals that over one-quarter of Black respondents perceived they were required to have better credentials than Whites to be appointed and granted tenure at most institutions, particularly predominantly white institutions. Blacks at historically Black institutions were more likely to be tenured than those employed at PWI's (Logan, 1990).

In order to obtain tenure at most doctorate-granting four-year American colleges and universities--particularly at research institutions--faculty are required to consistently conduct quality research and publish in scholarly journals--preferably peer-reviewed journals. Some minority faculty have reported that majority faculty sometimes fail to recognize the actual quality of their research, and instead focus on their publishing sources (Fikes, 1978). Some minority faculty do not publish in predominantly white journals often considered "scholarly." As a result, many Black faculty have reported that the quality of their research is rarely considered (Sudarkasa, 1987). Furthermore, other reports indicate that research by minority faculty on minority populations are rarely considered 'relevant in the field' or are 'significant contributions to the academy,' and therefore not recognized as a scholarly piece of work (Epps, 1989; Wilson, 1987).

In support of this contention, Astin and Bayer found in a 1979 study of active male and female scientific scholars that women perceive to have less control over how work is judged by peers. This can often block tenure for Black and other minority scholars, thus leading to greater numbers of Black faculty leaving the academy.

In Tack and Patitu's (1992) comprehensive report on faculty job satisfaction, Silver, Dennis, and Spikes (1988) argued that "in the 'up to 5 years' category, 89.6 percent of the Black faculty have not been tenured; in the '5-10 years' category, 75.9 percent have not been tenured; in the '10-15 years' category, 49 percent have not been tenured; and in the '15 or more years' category, 49.1 percent have not been tenured. If there is a direct correlation between tenure and job satisfaction, most of the Black.... faculty.... possesses little or no job security" (p. 44, 51).

In a study of the National Research Council's Survey of Doctorate recipients, Brown (1988) found data that suggest that in 1981, 11.1 percent of Black faculty left academe, more often than any other ethnic group. Hispanic faculty accounted for 7.2 percent and Asian Americans 4 percent. In 1985, Blacks still earned the largest share among minority faculty leaving academe at a rate of 9.7 percent, as compared to 5.7 percent for Hispanics, and 7.4 percent for Asian Americans. Most faculty who were denied tenure were forced to leave. Those who did not leave, usually transferred to non tenure-track or non teaching positions at the current institution. In both 1981 and 1985, Black faculty had the least tenure of any group and were most likely to be on tenure-track without tenure.

According to Smart (1990), regardless of tenure status, younger faculty, those at institutions who had experienced decline and had more autocratic forms of governance, and those who had lower levels of organizational and career satisfaction, were most likely to leave the institutions. Being a man, spending more time on research, and having a stronger record of scholarly productivity were positive influences on the intentions of tenured faculty to leave the institution, while salary satisfaction was an influential variable only for non-tenured faculty (Smart, 1990). Of all groups, Blacks were least likely to be tenured (Maxfield, 1981). According to Moore and Wagstaff (1974) and Rafky (1972), whites were twice as likely to hold tenure than Blacks.

Today, African Americans make up roughly 23 percent of the 526,324 faculty who teach at American colleges and universities. Approximately 4.8 percent of the 23 percent of full professors are African American, 2.6 percent teach at the associate level, 7.7 percent are assistant professors, and 8.1 percent teach at the instructor or lecturer level (Snyder and Hoffman, 1995).

To summarize, the essence of the tenure system today is based on a process developed by and for an academy which was and presently is composed primarily of non minority men who may not share the same interests, needs, views, or experiences of Black women. It seems plausible to consider that Black women, as well as other minorities and women, may experience some degree of difficulty matriculating through the tenure process. Some explanations might include findings that indicate gender differences among women and men academics (Baldwin and Blackburn, 1985; and Ladd and Lipset, 1976), and differences in corresponding roles for women and men both in the home and in society at large. It follows that this conflict could lead to Black faculty women seeking alternative employment elsewhere, whether the reason is for failure to successfully meet the requirements of tenure at the current institution, or whether faculty members simply perceive they have little prospect of obtaining tenure, based on their experiences. In some cases, Black faculty women, when confronted with these issues, may have little choice but to voluntarily or involuntarily seek employment elsewhere.

Institutional Type

Institutions are often categorized by control (public or private), type (two-year or four-year), size, or quality (prestige). Prior to the *Brown vs. Board of Education* decision in 1954, approximately 96 percent of all Black faculty were employed at historically black colleges and universities (HBCU's) (Thomas, 1981). A gradual shift away from HBCU's to other types of academic institutions began in the mid-1960s (Pearson, 1985). Today, most Black faculty teach at two-year and four-year colleges which do not offer comprehensive doctoral programs, such as major research centers (Zimbler, 1990). Most "faculty are more likely to be employed by HBCU's, regardless of the type of institution" (Smith, 1992, p. 4). Approximately 44.2 percent of all full-time permanent faculty of HBCU's are Black, as compared to 4 percent at predominantly white institutions.

Numerous studies have indicated that women and minorities are heavily concentrated in two and four-year American colleges and universities. In 1987, for example, 37.9 percent of all faculty at two-year public American institutions were women, as compared to 19.5 percent of all faculty at private research institutions. Women accounted for 27.3 percent of all faculty in American higher education institutions, while only 3.2 percent of all faculty were Black. In private doctoral institutions, Black women made up less than one percent of all faculty, as compared to eight percent in liberal arts institutions.

Several studies indicate that women and minorities are more likely to be at less prestigious institutions (Bernard, 1964; Cole, 1979). Caplow and McGee (1958) found that for younger faculty, the degree of prestige an institution held was very important. However, for older faculty, a greater value was placed on job security and autonomy. The actual or perceived prestige of a certain institution may influence the decision of faculty to leave for alternate employment. Finkelstein, for example, argued that prestige was a factor in the decision of faculty to leave for two main reasons: (1) the quest for prestige was clearly secondary to the desire for satisfying work and stimulating colleagues (Brown, 1967; Ladd and Lipset, 1976; Nicholson and Miljus, 1972; Stecklein and Lathrop, 1960); and (2) prestige operates similar to salary as a 'nonuniform' motivator (1984).

Finkelstein (1984) found that the prestige of one's doctoral institution can have a "halo effect," giving the doctoral recipient "the aura of prestige" that can surround the doctoral department, program, or institution. The prestige a scholar may receive from the institution was found to be the most important predictor in determining the prestige of the first job. The prestige factor, however, appears to decrease as the number of positions increase (Breneman and Yuon, 1989; Burke, 1989); scholarly activity then becomes the most important factor of career advancement (Finkelstein, 1984).

Intention to Leave

During the past 35 years, numerous articles have appeared which examined job turnover (Steers and Mowday, 1981) and identified job attitudes (job satisfaction, commitment), and demographic variables (age, marital status, tenure) as important predictors of job turnover. Other studies have looked at the importance of alternative job possibilities (Mobley, Griffeth, Hand, and Meglino, 1979) and the importance of behavioral intentions (to look for a job or intend to change positions) as key determinants of actual turnover.

Many scholars contend that individual characteristics, such as one's occupation, education, age, tenure, family responsibility, family income level, personal work ethic, previous work experiences, and personality can influence job expectations and ultimately turnover (Mobley, Horner, and Hollingsworth, 1978; Porters and Steers, 1973; Hines, 1973). As a result of these factors, people consciously determine what they expect from a job, what they feel they must have, what they would like to have, and what they can do without. The greater the number of attractive job alternatives, the more demanding an individual may be when evaluating career alternatives. There may also be circumstances when an individual may not like his or her position, but does not seek alternative employment when, for example, they are due to family considerations (Porter and Steers, 1973). Steers and Mowday (1981) contend that turnover intentions are influenced by the extent to which an individual's expectations are met by the organization. Some of the organizational factors identified by Steers and Mowday include salary, promotion policies, job duties, relationship with fellow workers and supervisors, size of the work group, and opportunities to participate in decision-making.

The intent to leave may also lead directly to turnover (Muchinsky and Tuttle, 1979). Others may leave their jobs even if alternative employment is not available. Intent to leave may also influence actual turnover in an indirect way by causing the individual to initiate searches for more preferable job alternatives. Simon and March (1958) found that less satisfied people were more sensitive to job market changes. Search behaviors appeared to open potential candidates to a greater number of job possibilities, thereby increasing the likelihood of leaving. If there were no or few job opportunities, the person may be less likely to leave the organization. If the person desired to leave and was capable of doing so, the probability of turnover would increase substantially (Mobley, Horner, and Hollingsworth, 1978). March and Simon (1958) and Flowers and Hughes (1973) argued that the major elements involved in an individual's choice to remain in or leave his or her current employment situation were defined as: (1) an individual's ease in movement; (2) the perceived desirability of moving; (3) the contribution the individual has rationalized; and (4) the particular decision made by the individual to remain or leave.

Several scholars have cited the consistent and negative, although moderate relationship between job satisfaction and turnover. Mobley, Griffeth, Hand, and Meglino (1979) contend that the primary determinants of intentions are thought to be: (1) satisfaction; (2) attraction expected utility of the present job; and (3) attraction expected advantage of alternative jobs or roles. The relationships among satisfaction, attraction, turnover intentions, and behaviors are greater when non work values and interests are not primary to an individual's life values and interests (Dublin, 1979). Individuals have also been shown to associate significant non work consequences with quitting (Newman, 1974).

The length of time with the organization (Steers, 1977; Mangione, 1973), job satisfaction (Mobley, Griffeth, Hand, and Meglino, 1979, Porter and Steers, 1973), and organizational commitment have been found to be significantly, negatively related to turnover (Porter, Steers, Mowday, and Boulian, 1974; Steers, 1977), and have been suggested to be three of the best predictors of turnover. In support, Porter and Steers (1973) have found that "the intentions to remain [in the work setting] were positively related to salary, length of time in the organization, and tenure" (Pfeffer and Lawler 1980, p. 38). Although studies on gender have been found to be inconclusive, Marsh and Mannari (1977) have found that women have higher turnover rates, whereas Mangione did not find any gender differences in turnover rates.

Recent models of the turnover process (Mobley, 1977; Steers and Mowday, 1981) have acknowledged the importance of taking into consideration the availability of alternatives in understanding turnover, however, relatively few researchers include them in their studies. Turnover has been shown to be significantly influenced by age, tenure in the organization, overall job satisfaction, organizational commitment, perceived job security, and intention to search for alternative positions. Turnover was found to be more strongly related to intentions of searching for alternatives than on intentions of changing positions. Intentions of searching for alternatives were found to be highly predictable by a combination of age, job satisfaction, and organizational commitment. Results in a study of accountants, for example, suggested that the most powerful model of turnover behaviors contained four significant individual predictor variables: tenure; job satisfaction; perceived job security; and intention to search for an alternative position.

A handful of studies by scholars such as Cotton and Tuttle, Locke, Fitzpatrick, and White; McGee and Ford; Mobley, Horner, and Hollingsworth; Pfeffer and Lawler; and Smart have explored what factors influence the intentions of faculty to leave their current institution.

McGee and Ford (1987) examined 350 faculty members at four-year colleges and universities in the United States and Canada. The purpose was to evaluate influences of various contextual and work environment factors relating to faculty turnover intentions. After controlling for prestige of the employing institution, disciplinary area, academic rank, and work environment, they found that institutional prestige significantly contributed to predicting both research performance and intention to leave. Academic rank and discipline did not appear to make a significant contribution to predict leaving. Work environment factors, however, explained a significant amount of variance of intent to leave for all demographic variables; interpersonal relationships with colleagues and administration, extrinsic rewards, and faculty influence had a significantly negative effect on faculty members' intent to leave the institution. They found both intrinsic and extrinsic aspects of the work environment important for determining whether faculty members tended to leave an institution or not. Furthermore, they found that the level of the faculty members' teaching responsibilities were negatively related to faculty turnover intentions. Blackburn and Havighurst (1979) found that faculty who valued and were engaged in scholarly activities were more likely to remain at their institutions. Caplow and McGee (1958) have argued that individuals leave jobs mostly because of an internal push rather than an external pull.

Locke, Fitzpatrick, and White (1983) examined faculty intent to remain, and found that work achievement, work role clarity, and salary accounted for the variance in a faculty member's intention to remain. In a similar study, Pfeffer and Lawler (1980) studied over 4,000 faculty members and concluded that expressed intent to remain and satisfaction with the organization were positively related to the amount of salary, length of time in the organization, and tenure. These factors were also negatively related to the availability of job alternatives.

The work of Cotton and Tuttle (1986) illustrated a causal model of faculty intentions to leave their current institution. Cotton and Tuttle concluded "it is no longer valuable to simply link variables to turnover." The findings of Cotton and Tuttle clearly identified "intentions" as being the single best predictor of actual employee turnover in organizational settings (Mobley, Horner, and Hollingsworth, 1978). Most recently, Smart (1990) employed the causal model to explain turnover intentions among tenured and nontenured faculty, and produced similar findings to Cotton and Tuttle (1986).

Mobley, Horner, and Hollingsworth (1978) found that the intention to quit was the immediate effect of actual turnover (Locke, 1969, 1976; March and Simon, 1958; Mobley, 1977; Mobley, Horner, and Hollingsworth, 1978; Newman, 1974). Job satisfaction, on the other hand, had no direct effect on turnover. Both dissatisfaction and the probability of finding an acceptable alternative position contributed to eliciting thoughts of quitting, and such thoughts generated the intention to search. This intention appeared to be stronger when job satisfaction was lower and when the employee was younger and not tenured. Intention to search exhibited the strongest coefficient with intention to quit, with age/tenure showing a weaker but still significant coefficient. The probability of finding an acceptable alternative did not illustrate a significant direct effect. Intention to quit appeared to have the only direct effect on turnover. Thoughts of quitting and intending to quit were the effects of job dissatisfaction, rather than turnover itself.

Previous research has cited the internal push as more effective than being the external pull in an individual's decision, although both factors appear to play a role in the decision making process (Matier, 1988). Pushing and pulling could take place on the part of both the offering and incumbent institutions. For example, while an individual's current salary might constitute a push, the degree of autonomy experienced in his or her present position might be considered a pull. On the other hand, a generous salary offer from another employer may be considered a pull, but the offering institution's geographic location could be a push to remain. In this study, the internal push appeared to encourage individuals to give serious consideration to the external pulls available to them. In the Matier study, the majority of reported respondents pursuing firm offers did so because the pulls to go to another institution and the pushes to leave their present one were sufficient to move.

Blackburn and Aurand (1972) contended that faculty members' primary concerns were with the work environment. Intangible benefits appeared to be the most important. In contrast, Stecklein and Lathrop (1960) suggested that intangible and non-work related benefits were not extremely important in the decision making process. Yet, Matier (1986, 1988) found exactly the opposite to be the case for a limited group of faculty in his study.

Pfeffer and Lawler (1979) reported that the availability of alternative jobs were negatively related to job attitudes among a large sample of university faculty. However, Mowday and McDade (1979) found that the mere availability of alternative jobs were less of an important influence on job attitudes than the relative attractiveness of the alternatives. In addition, they found that the influence of attractive alternative jobs on attitudes changed over time. Faculty were most likely to consider leaving an academic institution for another faculty position or a position outside of academe when: (1) just before coming up for tenure; (2) just after promotion; and (3) just before coming up for promotion to full professor. While 17 percent considered leaving academe, only 1 percent actually left (Finkelstein, 1984).

In summary, numerous studies suggest that the intention to change positions can directly influence turnover. In academia, several factors such as the work environment, salary, tenure, personal factors, and external barriers have been found to positively influence faculty turnover intentions, which may lead to actual attrition.

Marital Status

Although there are currently no complete studies on the influence of marital status on the career mobility of Black women professors, a number of studies do exist, which examine the relationship between careers and marital status of professional women, academic women, and Black professional women. The examination of this research might provide insight into the factors that contribute to the decision patterns of Black faculty women.

The major changes in a woman's life, such as completion of school, marriage, birth of a child, change of employment, employer status of self or spouse, and a physical move all constitute important changes in an individual's life. The life-cycle of an adult, for example, typically begins with the completion of college and acquisition of the first professional job or, in some cases, marriage. The career life cycle generally ends with retirement. These stages are important to recognize because they can affect the relationship between work and family in several ways, depending on what stage an individual is in the life cycle. Rapoport and Rapoport (1965) have argued that the outcomes of a person's life cycle depends on the ability of the person and his or her family to cope with the issues which confront them at each stage.

The division of family work has been found to be an important issue because of its implication for professional women managing both career and family. In egalitarian relationships, dual-career couples compromise by sharing the parental and family responsibilities within the household. Typically, husbands take on greater responsibility by assuming some of the household and child care responsibilities, which in a traditional marriage, would generally be the exclusive task of the wife (Yogev, 1981).

In a traditional household, the family follows the man because he is usually the principal wage-earner (Aisenberg and Harrington, 1988). Sometimes this can cause women to postpone advancement because of geographical immobility (Marwell, Rosenfeld, and Spererman 1979; Sagaria, 1988). "If women are unable to relocate, their chances of increased job satisfaction and career advancement diminish substantially" (Tack and Patitu, 1992, p. 47). Crawford contended that "marriage is bad for women's careers" (1982, p. 90) and can often create conflict for professional women (Amatea and Cross, 1981; Benton, 1986; Crawford, 1982; Villadsen and Tack, 1981). Some research suggests that women often compromise advancement in their careers (Marwell, Rosenfeld, and Spererman, 1979; Sagaria, 1988) to minimize conflict with marriage and family.

Felmlee argues that individual constraints, such as marital status, can affect a women's job mobility (1980). Furthermore, being married, Felmlee contends limits the rate of job changes for women because having a husband decreases a woman's flexibility. Married women, she argues, must often coordinate work choices with her husband, making geographical moves required by job transfers or advancement opportunities very difficult. Reoccurring discrimination against married women may also negatively impact them. Studies have suggested that employers sometimes hesitate before hiring a married woman because they expect the commitment to her family to take priority over her career.

In contrast, Amatea and Fong (1991) found that the number of roles a woman played were negatively related with role strain. In fact, women who served in multiple roles reported better physical and psychological health than those women who reported fewer role participation (Cooke and Rousseau, 1984; Crosby, 1982; Thoits, 1983; Verbrugge, 1983). Furthermore, women who reported higher levels of personal control and social support in tandem with greater numbers of roles, reported lower levels of role strain.

In an early 1964 study, Simon, Clark, and Galway sought to explain the professional characteristics of women Ph.D.'s who were married and unmarried. They found that married women were less likely to be promoted to the rank of associate professor and were generally less likely to be tenured than unmarried women. In addition, unmarried women were more active in professional and community organizations than married women. They concluded that women earned less than men, and were less likely promoted or given tenure, particularly if they were married.

Many scholars contend that the relationship between turnover rates and gender differ among academic and nonacademic organizations. For example, Cotton and Tuttle (1986) reported that turnover rates in the general population were higher for women, whereas Brown (1967) and Finkelstein (1984) argued that turnover rates in academia were higher for men. Employee turnover was also found to be negatively related to age and higher for single persons (Cotton and Tuttle, 1986; Finkelstein 1984).

Simeone (1987) has argued that marriage and family were beneficial and had positive effects on the careers of academic men, but had a negative impact on the progress for career women. In one study (Centra, 1974), when asked for reasons of current unemployment, 40 percent gave reasons related to marital status ('spouse did not want me to work,' 'anti-nepotism policies,' and 'not suitable job for spouse').

On average, academic men had more children than academic women. Furthermore, married women, particularly with children, were more likely to have dropped out of graduate school, had interrupted or abandoned their careers, were under-employed or unemployed, and held lower academic rank. In some cases, married women were taken less seriously and their careers were assumed to have less priority than family matters.

Although many scholars argue that academic women face numerous difficulties carrying out scholarly work and domestic activities, most data does not show any differences in productivity between married and single women. Astin and Bayer have found that married women were more productive than single women (1979). In contrast, when studying faculty in the sciences, Cole (1979) concluded that after controlling for all factors, neither marital status nor the number of children, had an effect on productivity. Academic women who were successful were often "able to make arrangements that had been workable for themselves and their families, and they had achieved a high level of professional success. Yet the success had been based on their own individual abilities to cope, adapt, and arrange their lives, and on at least some measure of cooperation from those around them, including husbands, department heads, advisors, and children" (Simeone, 1987, p. 133).

Hensel (1991) has argued that "the professoriate can often times be considered a two-person career. When a woman is in the position, it is a one-person career and the one person may be psychologically divided between home and career" (1991, p. 9). A common problem often reported by professional career women with families is that when a woman is at work, she feels she should be home with her children and when a woman is at home with her children, she feels she should be at work. While academics have been found to have more flexible work schedules, academic women were less likely to be able to leave their work at the office (Biernat and Wortman, 1991). Burke (1987) has contended that emotional exhaustion was the primary cause of burnout among faculty women. Few studies are available on the stresses of faculty women in higher education, but most of them completely ignore the relationship of work and family on their careers (Burke, 1987).

In some cases, choosing both work and family requires one spouse to commute. While this has often led to emotional and financial stress, it has also, at times, proven beneficial to both spouses and their careers. In 1982, approximately 700,000 couples were involved in commuter arrangements, and more than half involved academic men and women (Hileman, 1990). Most couples in commuter marriages maintained both a family and career by focusing solely on work when they were apart and exclusively on each other when they were together. Hileman (1990) has found that women were likely to be more satisfied with commuter marriages than men.

In Robert Merton's prominent article on role-sets (1957), he defined a "role-set" as a "complement of role-relationships in which persons are involved by virtue of occupying a particular social status" (p. 110). A Black woman professor, for example, may have an array of academic roles such as teacher, colleague, advisor, committee member, and community advocate. Other non-professional roles that Black women hold may include those of wife and mother. Merton suggests that conflicts may arise from managing multiple role-sets and integrating the expectations of others.

Merton contends that certain roles often have priority over others. For example, Merton argues that the obligations of family and career are valued more highly than professional or social organizations. Furthermore, the presence of a supportive spouse can help to relieve conflict that may arise in multiple role-sets. In the absence of a supportive spouse or significant other, social support--or what Merton (1957) terms "coalitions of power"--can serve to balance the conflicting roles and enable the individual to continue a desired plan.

According to Merton, Black professional women are special because they hold two ascribed statuses. In his 1948 book, *Social Theory and Social Structure*, Merton explains that a status is dominant when it determines the other status one is likely to acquire. Gender and ethnicity statuses, in the case of Black women, are dominant and they "are visible and immutable, and impose severe limits on an individuals' capacity to alter the dimensions of their work and the attitudes of others towards them" (Epstein, 1973, p. 913). However, for successful professional Black women in the higher income brackets, the effects of this status set do not always result in a negative status set, because of the gender status. The hierarchy of other status sets, such as career, mother, and wife, vary from individual to individual.

Black women and their families have traditionally developed alternative family patterns to survive (Billingsley, 1968; Hill, 1972).

For example, some Black women, while continuing to marry, are doing so at a later age. Furthermore, college educated Black women continue to combine marriage, children, and a full-time career (Higginbotham, 1981; Fichter, 1967). Studies indicate that Black women as a group are remaining single at a greater rate than whites (Higginbotham, 1981; Staples, 1981). "Personal issues were often better resolved once the [African American] women had secured their social class positions by completing college and moving into work situations" (Higginbotham, 1981, p. 265). "Even though remaining single can be a successful mobility strategy, it is one with many costs" (p. 266).

Studies on professional women, academic women, and Black professional women suggest that marriage can often limit career mobility. Also, the combination of marriage and career may produce conflicting role strains which, if left unmediated by personal control or social support, can influence the decisions of Black faculty women to leave their academic positions for alternative employment.

Number of Dependents

As in the case of marriage, there are currently no existing studies on Black faculty women which examine the relationship between career and motherhood. There are, however, an adequate number of studies available that focus on the effects of motherhood on labor force participation, job satisfaction, role conflict, and job mobility, which may provide valuable information on factors influencing mobility decisions of Black faculty women.

In 1980, Felmlee studied the job mobility constraints of women, such as marital status, number of children, and husband's income. Felmlee found that marriage, in general, had a negative effect on the job mobility of women. Although raising children had a significant effect on the labor force participation rate of women, its effect on the job mobility rate for women was small and relatively inconsistent. Children often reduced the time flexibility of women, and childcare responsibilities also influenced women to change jobs more frequently. The income of the husband typically had a large negative effect on women's job mobility rates, because a higher income on the part of the husband rarely influenced the wife to change her position since her family was financially secure.

Numerous studies suggest that women receive lower returns to their human capital than men.   Many often assume that these disparities in wages are due to family circumstances (Rosenfeld 1978, 1981; Spilerman, 1977).   A study by Sorensen (1983) examined the effects of motherhood and found that although children may affect the timing of a woman's career, children cannot account for gains in status once a woman decides to return to the labor force. However, family responsibilities of women as wives and mothers have generally been associated with decreased turnover (Federico and Lundquist, 1976; Marsh and Mannari, 1977; Mangione, 1973).

Many studies suggest that women who combine work and have a family may feel dissatisfied or guilty because "employed mothers feel a more intense sense of responsibility or guilt with respect to their children's problems" (Baruch, Biener, and Barnett, 1987, (p. 172). Also, women were most likely to be more critical of their performance as wife and mother than men (Biernat and Wortman, 1991). Others argue that women must often choose between "the life" or "the work" (Aisenberg and Harrington, 1988), or struggle with competing demands. Choosing both, according to Aisenberg and Harrington (1988), can often mean that women will "be forced to lead two separate entire lives simultaneously.... squeezing two lives into one through superhuman effort" (p. 117).

In contrast, Thois (1983) has argued that multiple roles do not necessarily mean role conflict. In fact, some studies indicate that the "lowest levels of stress are found among women who have the most complex role configurations" (Kandel, Davies, and Ravies, 1985), such as married mothers working full-time.   Other studies support this contention, and indicate that "multiple roles actually increase opportunity for satisfaction" (Hammond, 1988, p. 17).

Many studies on academic women point to motherhood as the primary cause of career mobility among faculty women, but the findings vary. In a study of professional career women, Amatea and Cross (1981) found that some women reported they "view the joint commitment to the roles of wife and mother and professional career women as a barrier that will prevent them from moving into and through the occupational world as equals with men" (p. 5). Seeborg (1990) argued that in the case of academic scholars, children tended to reduce a faculty member's research productivity. For women, the pressures, challenges, and consequences of marriage and motherhood are greater than men (Glowinkowski and Cooper, 1987) because women are still considered primarily responsible for the family. Hensel (1991), for example, has found that few successful women were married with children. However, most successful men maintained both marriage and family.

In contrast, Cole and Zuckerman (1984) found a positive relationship between marriage, motherhood, and research productivity when studying men and women scientists. Cole and Zuckerman contended that married women published more than single women, and mothers published more than childless women. Furthermore, they argued that the publication rates for women did not decline following childbirth, nor did they decline during the years in which they raised their children. They concluded that, although marriage and children may add considerable responsibility on women scholars, many women produce more research and successfully manage both career and family obligations. The determinants of success appear to be the number and compatibility of obligations. Cole and Zuckerman (1984) found that 100 percent of the women scientist scholars who were married mothers, reported that they relied on some sort of household assistance to maintain family and work. In a similar study, Hensel's (1991) research supported the work of Cole and Zuckerman, and found that although marriage and motherhood presented numerous concerns regarding research and careers of academic women, it did not affect the rate of publication. Successful academic women appeared to engage in what Cole and Zuckerman termed "status-set management" strategies to maintain research. Cole and Zuckerman concluded that there was a more significant positive relationship between the rate of publication and research practices and environments, and a smaller correlation between marriage and motherhood.

Recent studies report that tenure probationary periods often begin as faculty women are entering the prime of their childbearing years. This would suggest that women may be promoted less often due to the constraints of tenure (Finkel, Olswang, and She, 1994). "Although some women have been able to balance careers and families, many women have had to leave academia or settle for positions on the periphery" (p. 260). Finkel, Olswang, and She concluded that institutions should consider offering deferrals for tenure to all faculty members who become parents. Such deferrals, they argue, would give faculty members reasonable time to achieve tenure. "Women should not be denied the opportunity to progress in academia because they have decided to have a family while pursuing their careers" (p. 268). Hensel (1990) has also argued that some women who are not as successful in managing both family and career may feel pressured to leave the academy indefinitely after the birth of a child.

In one of a few available studies on the family lives of academic women (Levinson, Tolle, and Lewis, 1989), a national survey was conducted to examine how academic women in medicine combine career and family responsibilities. Most academic women in the study were satisfied with their decision to combine children and career, even though most (78 percent) perceived that motherhood slowed down their career progress.

Studies also indicate that many faculty women and men spend at least 50 hours a week at work (Clark, Corcoran and Lewis, 1986), while academic women spend closer to 80 or more hours each week between work at home (Hensel, 1991). Approximately 35 of these 80 hours are spent doing housework and caring for the children, as compared to an average of 7 hours per week for academic men working in the home (Hensel, 1990). Studies indicate, however, that the higher the education and income level of academic women, the less amount of time is spent on household chores by both spouses (Seeborg, 1990).

Research suggests that family obligations, such as caring for a child, may explain the greater length of time it takes for faculty women to be promoted (Long, McGinnis and Allison, 1993). In contrast, Cole and Cole (1973) and Bayer and Astin (1975) have found a negative correlation between having young children and academic rank for women. However, in a 1981 study, Ahern and Scott contended that the presence of children, combined with fluctuations in the job participation rates of academic women, did not account for sex differences in rank. Bailyn has further found that the absence of children increased the likelihood that women would work. Bailyn (1975) has argued that the age of the children in the household often influence career continuity.

The research findings regarding simultaneously managing the demands of marriage, motherhood, and career appear to be conflicting, particularly for academics who both teach and conduct research. However, the wealth of research on faculty and Black professional women suggests that, while Black women can be successful professors and mothers, the costs are potentially high. Whether Black women choose work will depend greatly on the nature of the roles, the ability of coping at each stage in the life cycle, the value they place on choices made with regard to career and family, and the support or lack thereof received from the academic institution, family, friends, and community. In summary, the mobility decisions of Black faculty women depend on these factors and ultimately determine which life path they choose.

Support Systems

Numerous studies indicate that interpersonal relationships and support systems are important factors for a successful career. As mentioned earlier, no studies are currently available on how primary and extended Black family networks can affect career mobility. However, numerous findings clearly indicate that many successful Black women are more likely to rely on household support (Cole and Zuckerman, 1984), be involved in professional networks and associations (Merriam, 1983), have extended support networks (McAdoo, 1988), and attend church on a regular basis (Taylor, 1988). In an academic setting, supportive networks and hospitable academic environments are particularly important for Black faculty women, who often seek various types of professional, social, and religious networks. These networks provide a source of support, strength, and encouragement to persevere in an often stressful and competitive academic environment.

Merton (1957) has contended that professional and social institutions often help to cope with conflicts which may arise from competing demands in a "role-set," such as professor, wife, and mother. According to Merton (1957), "this function becomes all the more significant in the structural circumstances when status occupants are highly vulnerable to pressures from their role-set because they are relatively isolated from one another" (p. 117). The lack of a critical mass among Black professors and women, and the reports of cultural, social and intellectual isolation among Black faculty women, suggest they may be particularly susceptible to conflicts within the multiple role-set.

In the professional academic environment, Black faculty women may rely on professional associations, networks, or mentoring-type relationships to provide support and guidance. Black faculty women are still considered "outsiders" because they are rarely invited to participate in university networks. Many, therefore, seek intellectual stimulation through participation in professional organizations and associations, both within and outside the discipline. These professional networks provide numerous advantages in obtaining a position, becoming successful, and perhaps even achieving tenure and promotion. First of all, professional networks can serve as a vehicle for professional mobility by helping one access greater information regarding job opportunities. Many emphasize the importance associates play in obtaining a professional position. Knowing the right people and being told about the right job at the right time, greatly enhances opportunity. Secondly, once a position is secured, professional networks can help affirm oneself and one's abilities, enhance one's social network, enable one to share ideas and collaborate on projects, offer peer evaluation of scholarship and intellectual stimulation, teach the proper protocols, and offer greater professional visibility. Finally, professional networks can help enhance the opportunity for promotion by sharing information on unwritten criteria for promotion and tenure, and offer letters of support, particularly if members are in the same professional discipline.

Professional relationships and friendships with other academic women on and off campus are very important because they serve several purposes. First, they can assist her in shaping her own identity as a legitimate scholar. Second, they can collaborate and help each other develop effective research strategies. Third, they serve to alleviate the feeling of isolation. In a 1997 study of collaborative relationships among faculty women, Dickens and Sagaria found that these personal and professional relationships were formed by women who wanted to share their ideas and scholarly lives with close friends, life partners and other family members. Some of these women sought friendships with other women from the same ethnic or racial group and expressed that shared identity in their work, but all of the women expressed the need and importance of a shared understanding, mutual respect, trust, and support.

In a 1978 study of structural barriers, Kaufman examined collegial friendships and concluded that women's exclusion from male networks isolated them from important informal contacts, leaving them at a professional disadvantage. Similarly, Menges and Exum

(1983) argue that women and minority faculty progress more slowly through the academic ranks because of the array of problems they experience in understanding and matriculating through the peer review process that favors publications in conservative, mainstream, referred journals.

Mentoring, which is often confused with role modeling and sponsorship, has often been referred to as a method used to develop and advance an individual's career (Merriam, 1983). Levinson (1978) states in the *Seasons of a Man's Life* that "support can facilitate the realization of the Dream" (p. 98), referred to by Levinson as an individual's vision concerning the kind of life he or she desires. In *Effective Teaching and Mentoring,* Daloz (1986) contends that "mentors are guides. They lead us along the journey of our lives. We trust them because they have been there before. They embody our hopes, cast light on the way ahead, interpret arcane signs, warn us of lurking dangers, and point out unexpected delights along the way" (p. 17).

Hundreds of descriptive articles have been published on academic and professional mentoring, but very little empirical research is available on mentoring relationships between senior and junior faculty. Queralt (1982) examined the benefits of assigning mature and experienced faculty with less experienced junior faculty. Melillo (1981) has explored the influence of mentors on the career development of academic women. Little research is available on what factors, if any, influence the career paths of faculty men and women.

Queralt studied 430 faculty and administrators holding academic rank and found that faculty with mentors appeared to have a significantly higher level of career development than those without mentors. Furthermore, faculty with mentors published more, and received a larger, more competitive number of grants than those without mentors. Long-term mentoring appeared to have a more significant impact on academic careers than did shorter mentorships, and faculty who had numerous mentors or mentors early in their careers, appeared to progress more rapidly and out perform those who acquired mentors later or only had one. Melillo (1981) surveyed 175 women doctorate recipients from California institutions and found that having a mentor helped them achieve higher career goals.

While examining the literature on mentoring, several factors are of significant importance. There are numerous definitions of mentoring which vary from study to study. For example, some are specific and yield fewer responses, and others are more broadly defined and receive greater reports. Also, the methods of data collection seem to affect the reports of mentoring. For example, in-depth interviews on mentoring with smaller samples tend to produce more reports than larger surveys. These two factors alone make it very difficult to assess the extent, if any, to which mentoring has on the impact of career paths (Merriam, 1983).

Dodgson argues that mentoring is a method women often use to enhance career mobility. Dickens and Dickens (1982) state in *The Black Manager* "the recognition of black role models can open doors and make opportunities available for other blacks, thereby allowing fuller utilization of existing talent. Younger blacks need to see that they can make it in the organization, and they can do this by looking up the hierarchy and seeing that there are successful blacks in the organization...Black role models can make other blacks feel as though they can succeed, and this in turn makes these blacks productive" (pp. 307-308).

Blackwell contends that the presence of Black faculty is the most powerful predictor of enrollment and graduation of Black students from professional schools. "Black students want and need black mentors" (Blackwell, 1983, p. 359). Studies have consistently cited the lack of mentoring as one of the major reasons colleges and universities have had difficulty recruiting and retaining Black and other non Asian American students (*Black Issues in Higher Education,* 1987; Blackwell, 1983; Brown, 1988; Hochscild, 1974; Mommsen, 1974; Pruitt, 1981; and Wilson, 1982). Other studies have found that just the mere presence of Black and minority faculty provide evidence to minority students that they can complete their degrees and become competent, successful professionals (DeFour & Hirsch, 1990). Due to the current lack of minority faculty representation, few minority role models exist for talented minority students.

Social supports are also essential for many Black faculty women. In one study of Black faculty, the lack of opportunity for association with other minorities was the greatest source (43 percent) of dissatisfaction. The majority of Black faculty (68 percent) agreed with the statement "I need contact with other black faculty and black students to make my job environment more satisfying" (Elmore and

Blackburn, 1983, p. 12). "From predominantly white institutions, black women were more likely to encounter barriers to mobility and little support for the emotional aspect of the experience" (Higginbotham, 1981, p. 264).

In a 1989 study of role strain among Black women, Lewis examined the economic and other pressures in the lives of 592 Black mothers (half lived with a spouse and half were single mothers) living with their small children. The study expected to find tremendous difficulty among these women in carrying the multitude of tasks required of a working mother. Of the 592 Black women, 65.4 percent reported economic strain, 54.1 percent reported household maintenance strain, and most reported having sufficient network support. Three-quarters of the women reported having significant kinship or partner support. Over two-thirds reported high religious community and church support. Lewis concluded that older women who had higher levels of support were less likely to report role strain and the presence and support of a partner provided the greatest relief from role strain. The younger the women, the more likely they were to report role strain.

An essential aspect of social supports is the role of the Black community. The Black community serves as an extended network that helps provide a source of strength (Hill, 1972). Black women who were married often received support from their spouses. Lloyd contended that married women who were in a supportive network, tended to be more satisfied with their marriage. However, if a married woman did not receive support from her spouse, Lloyd argued that "perhaps the presence of the networks support helps to "makeup" for this decreased spousal support from the husband and thus helps to enhance her feelings of satisfaction" (1982, p. 11).

The third, yet very important support system, is the Black church, which has traditionally provided tremendous strength in the Black community. Billingsley has argued that "in the African American community, the church is more than a religious institution" (Billingsley and Caldwell, 1991, p. 423). The Black church is often the primary source of spiritual, emotional, educational, social, and political support, and is often the focal point of the Black community where the common belief that "we are all in this thing together" helps to build a strong and cohesive bond among group members. According to data from the National Survey of Black Americans,

Taylor and Chatters (1988) argued that the Black church was the greatest source of support in the Black community. The study clearly indicates that two-thirds of all Black respondents are active members of a church and attend regularly. Furthermore, contrary to previous studies, Taylor (1988) found that better educated, higher salaried, and more married Black women had higher levels of church participation.

In summary, professional, social, and religious support systems are essential elements for the success of many Black women scholars because they are coping strategies that help to mediate stress often encountered by them from the numerous barriers of a successful academic career. The lack of such supports could lead to fewer numbers of Black faculty women leaving the academy, and thus increase the difficulty in recruiting and retaining Black and other minority students.

External Barriers

External barriers are often described as those that an individual can only exercise minimal, if any, control over (Biklen and Brannigan, 1980). Research on Black faculty women have cited several external barriers which often stifle the success of Black women scholars (Austin, 1969; Austin and Gamson, 1983; Clark and Corcoran, 1986; DeFour, 1980; Dodgson, 1986; Elmore and Blackburn, 1983; Epstein, 1970; Exum, 1983; Finkelstein, 1984; Freeman, 1977; Frierson, 1990; Graham, 1973; Harrigan, 1977; Harvey and Scott-Jones, 1985; Henning and Jardim, 1977; Malcolm, Hall, and Brown, 1976; Mayfield and Nash, 1976; Merriam, 1983; Moore and Salembine, 1980; Moore and Wagstaff, 1974; Moses, 1989; Swoboda and Miller, 1986; Theodore, 1971; Walker, 1973).

Numerous scholars have suggested that conflicting and excessive academic demands often placed on Black faculty women are the most significant external barriers to career development and faculty mobility. Austin (1969) argues that "highly educated women often find themselves unhappy and frustrated because of the barriers they encounter in their career development." According to Graham (1973), "when there are but a few women on a faculty, excessive demands are made upon them; not only must each fulfill the usual academic requirement, but she must serve as a token woman on all kinds of committees" (1973, p. 733). If the faculty woman is Black or minority, the demand can become even more burdensome.

Walker (1973) describes a "double-consciousness among black university professors as they struggle to reconcile the demands of the academic and black communities. Incompatibilities between action-research oriented towards the Black community and the academic research oriented demand by promotion and tenure committees. The double consciousness is reflected in the goals black faculty pursue in their teaching and involvement in counseling black students, serving on disproportionately high numbers of committees, attending black events on and off campus, and maintaining strong relationships with the black community" (p. 69).

Moses claims that "because there are so few Black faculty women members...there is a tendency for the majority to see these women as spokespersons for all Blacks rather than as individuals with other qualifications. Black women are often asked to sit on committees as experts on Blacks, and they are asked to solve problems or handle situations having to do with racial difficulties that should be dealt with by others. There is often no reward for this work; in fact, Black women may often be at a disadvantage when they are eligible for promotion or tenure because so much of their time has been taken up with administrative assignments" (1989, p. 15).

A second external barrier of academic success for Black women scholars is the lack of support groups. Although, there has been much debate about the impact mentoring has had on career success for both faculty and students, many studies confirm that mentorship and sponsorship type programs can provide greater access to resources for research, advice, and collegial networks, which can often lead to greater academic productivity (Clark and Corcoran, 1986). White faculty men have traditionally benefited from this type of sponsorship, but it has been absent for most women and minorities (Merriam, 1983). Harvey and Scott-Jones (1985) have argued that often "in the absence of a support group... black faculty members are subjected to the aggravating aspects of the academic milieu without enjoying some of its compensating benefits: contemplation, independence, and social and intellectual stimulation from colleagues sharing the same interests and outlook "(p. 70).

Dodgson (1986) has contended that mentoring has often been a vehicle for upward mobility in the careers of women. Many Black faculty have reported a feeling of isolation. Mentors can often nurture a sense of belonging for minorities in the profession (DeFour, 1990). The shortage of Black faculty women appears to support the need for some type of mentoring and support networks (Swoboda & Miller, 1986).

A third external barrier is what many consider discriminatory practices against women and minority scholars. In 1985, for example, Moore and Wagstaff surveyed over 3,000 Black women scholars working with or in predominantly white institutions. Moore and Wagstaff found that 95 percent of all Black respondents reported some discriminatory activity by persons within their institutions. Black professionals from two-year colleges have reported similar experiences (Moore and Wagstaff, 1985).

Theodore (1971) defines discrimination against women professionals as "when women of equivalent qualifications, experience, and performance do not share equally in the decision making process or receive equal rewards, such as salary, promotions, prestige, professional recognition, and honors" (p. 27). In the academic workplace, Black faculty often encounter prejudice and discrimination which can often create major obstacles to the academic success of faculty (Frierson, 1990).

According to Tack and Patitu (1992), "black women who have gained access to higher education and higher-paying positions, often find themselves in less than optimal work environments. The racist and sexist attitudes of colleagues can often result in less than satisfactory work conditions and increased stress in the life of a Black female professional" (Steward, 1987, p. 3). Epstein contends that Black professional women are caught in what she terms a "double bind" between discriminatory racism and sexism, which can cause tremendous stress for Black women scholars (Epstein, 1970). For example, some women who choose to concentrate on scholarship to further the research of Blacks often report that the majority of faculty peers and superiors do not consider such work relevant or worthwhile.

A study from Mayfield and Nash (1976) found that roughly one-third of faculty women perceive themselves to be victims of discrimination in salary and one-fourth discrimination in rank. Also, one-fourth indicated that performance standards were higher for them than their male counterparts. When gender and ethnicity were combined, Black women professors were less satisfied than both white women and Black men colleagues.

In 1995, Stokes, Riger and Sullivan conducted a study on the climate for women in corporate settings and found five barriers to a women's career. The first, which they call dual standards and opportunities, occurs when women find that they have difficulty finding mentors because senior male faculty may be uncomfortable mentoring women (or may see them as higher risks than junior males) and few senior women may be available to serve as mentors. The second are sexist attitudes and comments, which comes from McKinney's 1990 study which indicated that 20 percent of the women reported being harassed by another faculty member and the majority of harassers held a higher academic rank than the targeted person. The third is internal socializing, where most social networks among colleagues tend to exclude women, cutting them off from sources of information and support that may be important for career advancement (Moore and Sagaria, 1993). The fourth is balancing work and personal obligations that are critical for women since we still are primarily responsible for child rearing. The final barrier they found involved remediation policies and practices, which in this case was the extent to which academic departments were supportive or hostile and perception of discrimination by individual faculty women.

The obstacles created by external barriers are important to examine because they may influence the decisions of Black scholars to leave academic employment for careers in business or industry. In some cases, non academic careers may allow Black scholars to compete on a more level playing field, have a clearer understanding of what is expected of them, avoid isolation by working among a critical mass of other Black, minority, and women professionals with similar interests, and receive greater monetary rewards for their energy, effort, and time.

V. *Results of the Study*

COMPARISON OF BLACK WOMEN PH.D.'S: 1981 and 1994

This chapter provides a comprehensive description of the inferential analysis and is divided into four sections. The first section is a descriptive comparison on Black women faculty from 1981 and 1994. The next section is the descriptive analysis that provides an overview of the three decision groups compared against a 1988 study which is included in the inferential analysis. The third section is the inferential analysis of the statistics. And the final section is the decision model describing the characteristics of career mobility among Black women faculty.

In order to conduct a meaningful analysis, the researcher compared the descriptive findings in this study to one of the few studies available on Black women faculty Ph.D.'s (Tobin, 1981). It is important to mention one primary difference between Tobin's 1981 study and the one in this document before beginning the analysis. Tobin's study (N=118) focused specifically on all Black women doctorates from Black public (state-supported) colleges and universities who were employed during 1973-74. Ninety-eight percent (or 116) of all women respondents were professors, associate professors, or assistant professors at the time of the study. Twenty years ago when Tobin's study was conducted, only a handful of Black women full-time faculty were teaching at four-year American colleges and universities other than HBCU's. Despite this limitation, Tobin's study remains to be the only adequately comparable study in existence which includes comparative data on family background, marital and family status, career history, community life, household responsibilities, and career development of Black women Ph.D.'s.

Of the 182 women in this study, 42 percent were married, as opposed to 57.6 percent in Tobin's study (See Table 5.1). Nearly 18 percent of the women sampled had never been married, compared to 22 percent in Tobin's work. Furthermore, the age of the women were slightly higher at 50 years of age in this study as opposed to 48 years of age in Tobin's study. This would appear to suggest that fewer Black women educators are marrying today than 20 years ago, and roughly one-fifth of Black women continue to remain single without ever marrying. Less than half the women in this study were married, as compared to more than half 20 years ago. This data supports previous research like Tobin's, which indicates that greater numbers of highly educated Black women are unmarried and a relatively significant number never marry.

TABLE 5.1:
Descriptive Statistics of Independent and Other Variable Attributes: A Comparison of ABWHE and the Findings in the Black Female Ph.D.

	ABWHE N = 182	Black Female Ph.D. N = 118
	Mean	Mean
Independent Variables		
Salary	57,328	17,000
Intention to Leave	20	****
Marital Status	.42	.576
Number of Dependents	.41	.458
Other Related Variables		
Age	50	48
Never Married	.177	.22
Job Satisfaction	.62	****
Hrs of Work in Household	20.72	22.4
Hrs of Work Responsibilities	51.27	****

**** - not available in the study.

Source: Tobin, McLean. 1981. *The Black Female Ph.D.: Education and Career Development.* University Press of America.

Job satisfaction and the intention to leave have often been suggested to be related to turnover. In this study, job satisfaction had a high mean of .62 on a scale from "1" being very high to "0" being very low. A mean of .62 would appear to suggest that most women working in the academy at that time had an above average or high job satisfaction rate and would tend to be more inclined to remain at their current institution, therefore becoming less mobile. For women working outside the academy, a mean of .62 would suggest a very high satisfaction rate in the current nonacademic position. The intention to leave among respondents obtained a mean of .20 on a scale from "1" being very likely to "0" being not likely to intentionally leave. This finding further suggests that most of the women sampled only possibly or not likely intended to leave their current position in the next 2-5 years, possibly due in large part to the relatively high job satisfaction rate.

The number of hours women spent working on household domestic activities appear to be related to the number of dependents. One distinguishing difference between these two studies is that, in this study, the number of dependents included two combined categories: one for dependent children in the household ages 0-17, and the other for dependent elderly parents. For comparison purposes, dependent parents were excluded from analysis because Tobin's study focused entirely on children, (ages 0-17) living in the household. In this study, the average number of dependents was .41, as compared to .458 in Tobin's study. While the smaller number of dependents could conceivably be attributed to the fewer number of married women, a relatively small number of unmarried women also had dependents. Most women with children in both studies had only one child. This finding tends to support research indicating that many highly educated Black women have fewer children than most other women. The fewer the number of dependents and the greater the salary, the less time reported engaging in domestic activities in the home. In this study, women spent on average 20.72 hours working in the household, as compared to 22.4 in Tobin's study.

The annual salary for the women in both studies appear to be greater than the average reported in other national studies. In this study, the mean for annual salary was $57,328, as compared to $17,000 in Tobin's 1981 study. The United States Department of Education's National Council on Education Statistics (1994) reported that the average annual salary for all women faculty at all ranks in

1991 was $35,564. Although this figure has increased slightly to keep in line with the consumer price index, the average salary reported in this study is still significantly greater than the national average for all women faculty at all ranks.   In 1981, the National Education Association's Salary Report indicated an average salary ranging from $9,032-$17,399 for doctorates in public higher education.   The average salary in Tobin's study was also at the highest end of the range reported at $17,000 for all doctorates in public higher education institutions.   In Tobin's study, 90 percent of these women were clustered in the professor and associate professor rank, which may account for the higher reported salaries.   In this study, 45 percent of the women held administrative positions as their primary work activity at their current institution.   A small number held an administrative position as their primary work activity and teaching as their secondary one.   Although 54 percent of women held faculty positions, most were clustered at the assistant rank, where a significant number may have been off tenure track.   The remainder of the faculty were fairly evenly distributed between the associate and professor ranks.   In this study, the significantly higher reported salaries may be largely due to greater salaries differentials between faculty and administrators, with administrators earning relatively higher wages, and less the result of greater salaries offered to Black women faculty.   Salaries also appear to correspond with the number of hours worked.   The higher the salary, the greater the number of hours a woman tended to work on activities associated with her primary place of employment.   The average number of hours spent on work activities reported in this study was 51.27.

DESCRIPTIVE ANALYSIS: 1988 AND 1994

The descriptive analysis included each of the three groups in the inferential analysis and were restricted to those remaining in, returning to, and voluntarily leaving the academy.   Those who did not voluntarily leave (as defined in the Appendix) were removed from the analysis, leaving a total sample of 180 out of 182 respondents.   Of the 180 sample, 96 (or 53.33 percent) of the women had remained exclusively in academic employment since the completion of graduate training.   Fifty-nine (or 32.77 percent) of the women had worked outside of the academy since the completion of graduate training but had returned and were currently working in a two or four-year American college or university. The third group of women, totaling 25 (or 13.88 percent), were those who voluntarily left the academy and did not return (Table 5.2).

TABLE 5.2:

Decision Pattern Composition of Sample
(n=180)

Category	Number	Percent of Sample
Remain in the Academy	96	53.33%
Return to the Academy	59	32.77%
Voluntarily Leave the Academy	25*	13.88%

* *Because there were only 25 observations for those who voluntarily left the academy, the maximum number of independent variables could only be 21. The program default stepwise selection procedure was employed.*

Currently, no other studies exist on the decision patterns of Black women faculty. Consequently, a comparative reference for all three groups were unfortunately not possible for this study. However, a limited and similar comparison was possible on the number of Black faculty who voluntarily left the academy and for those who remained over a nine-year period.

In the 1988 Brown study discussed in Chapters Two and Three, the career patterns of minority faculty were examined from the National Research Council's Survey of Doctorate Recipients between 1975-1986. The study included science, engineering, and humanities doctorates, and excluded the field of education. The study assumed that those respondents who did not receive tenure and did reply to the follow-up study in 1985 were no longer in academic employment, and were therefore excluded from the analysis. In addition, the study assumed that respondents who were in the academy in 1977, 1981, and 1985, had consistently remained in the academy and had not left and then returned within the nine-year period. This method of separating voluntary from involuntary movement was relatively consistent with the operationalization employed in this study. For purposes of this comparison, it was assumed that the respondents in the 1988 study who were in academic employment in 1977, 1981 and 1985 had remained, and that those who had involuntarily left the academy were excluded from the analysis.

The 1988 Brown study indicated that of 241 Black doctorate recipients who were non-tenured full-time faculty in 1981, 82.5 percent were employed in academe, while 17.5 percent were employed in nonacademic institutions. Of the 116 who responded nine years later in 1985, 87.8 percent (See Table 5.3) were employed in academe, while 12.2 percent opted for nonacademic employment (business, industry, government, and others). In comparison to other ethnic minorities, Brown found that Asian Americans (40.7 percent) were the largest group to leave the academy after nine years, followed by Blacks with 27.9 percent, and Hispanics leaving at a rate of only 18 percent. Brown concluded that more non-tenured Blacks are choosing to remain in the academy as non-tenured faculty, although a smaller percentage of Black doctorate recipients are choosing academic employment.

TABLE 5.3:

Decision Pattern Comparison

Category	ABWHE (n=180)		Brown (n=82)	
	Number	Percent	Number	Percent
Remain	96	53.33%	72	87.8%
Return	59	32.77%	na	na
Voluntarily Leave	25	13.88%	10	12.2%

When comparing the numbers of Black faculty who remained in and voluntarily left the academy, it is important to note several distinguishing differences. First, the Brown study examined the number of non-tenured full-time Black faculty who remained in and left academe between 1977 and 1985. While comparing these numbers with the ABWHE sample may provide some insight into the patterns of mobility, it cannot explain the numbers who remain in or leave the academy over a life span since graduate training nor can it provide evidence of why Black faculty remain in or voluntarily leave the academy. It can, however, provide a relatively adequate comparison between the mobility patterns over nine years (Brown) and approximately 20 years (ABWHE). Also, the sample characteristics are not the same. The Brown study included both Black men and women full-time faculty, excluded tenured faculty, and excluded faculty in education and the professions. While these differences limit the accuracy of comparison, it still provides useful information for an adequate comparison.

A comparison of the numbers from the data shown in the previous table indicates that, although the samples differ, the results are quite similar. There appears to be a strong propensity to leave and return, as compared to the propensity to leave. The relatively small percentage of those who leave the academy in the Brown study were 12.2 percent as compared to 13.88 percent in the present one. In addition, if the numbers of those who were currently in the academy are combined [those who returned (32.77) with those who remained (53.33)], there is little difference between the two studies for those currently working in the academy (87.8 percent as compared to 86.1, respectively). The Brown study covers a nine-year time period for new doctorates, and in this case one's career (average 25 years). Given a more equitable and comparable time frame to show career mobility patterns, it is likely that a good percentage of those who appear to remain in the Brown study would actually leave at some point and return to the academy.

The relatively smaller percentage of faculty choosing to remain in the academy as compared to the greater numbers who chose to remain in Brown's study may also be due to a number of other factors. First, the Brown study examined the mobility of faculty who were also recent doctorate recipients. This sample population had a mean age of 50.9, and in all likelihood were older than the new doctorates in the Brown study. Due to disparities in age, the ABWHE sample were more likely to have had longer career histories with greater opportunity to seek alternate employment and either later return to the academy, or never return. Secondly, the absence in the Brown study of those faculty who returned to the academy most likely explains the large number of those who remained. Because the Brown sample was more likely to be younger in age, making a return category inappropriate, it is plausible to consider that a fair number of these younger faculty in the "remain" category--if given an adequate period of time to show a career mobility pattern--would likely fall into the "return" category. The percentage of those who choose to voluntary leave the academy were remarkably similar in both studies. This study indicates that 13.88 percent of the sample voluntarily left, as compared to 12.2 percent in the Brown study.

Although there are a number of similarities in the data, a number of differences exist as well. First, the Brown study included Black men and women. Second, it focused exclusively on non-tenured full-time Black faculty, whereas this study focused on both tenured and non-tenured faculty. This may not have been as great of a concern had it not been for the fact that a significant number of faculty (43 percent) in this study were tenured, possibly explaining the smaller numbers of Black women faculty remaining.

Third, the Brown study represented a very different time period than this one. For example, this study focused on the decisions of Black women to leave the academy over the lifetime of their careers since completion of graduate training. The average age of respondents was 50.9 years old, indicating a stronger likelihood of having had experienced the women's movement, segregation, civil rights, and other historical periods which may have influenced their choice to remain in or voluntarily leave the academy. Also, the older the respondents, the greater possible number of positions they may have held, and therefore, the greater likelihood they may have been married or have dependents, which could significantly influence this decision as well. While at first glance a comparison of 53 percent of respondents remaining in the academy, as compared to nearly 88 percent in the Brown study, might appear to be highly significant, it lessens with the knowledge that ABWHE was studied over the lifetime of their careers (being on average a 20-year career), while the Brown study was a relatively brief nine-year period. Fourth, the sample size of Black faculty in this study was more than twice the size of the

Brown study. Typically, the larger the sample size, the more likely the instrument will measure accurately.

The similarities between the Brown study and this one provide an opportunity for comparison, although the researcher cannot accurately provide additional support for the model. As mentioned earlier, the Brown study was concerned with the characteristics and career choices of new minority doctorates. Therefore, no comparative evidence was available to predict what the pattern of mobility would be among Black women faculty. The Brown study does, however, offer initial insight into where minority faculty are going, albeit failing to indicate why Black faculty are leaving.

INFERENTIAL ANALYSIS OF STATISTICS

The inferential statistical technique employed for this study was a discriminant analysis applied to the data in order to determine at what degree each of the designated independent variables would prove significant in predicting the decision (dependent variable) of Black women professors to remain in, return to, or voluntarily leave the academy.

A regression analysis was not possible because the dependent variable was categorical. Although there were several ways to examine discrete dependent variables, such as a multinomial logit model, the discriminant analysis was fairly robust with regard to violations of normal distribution assumptions. In all likelihood, it only existed when the probability of group membership was extremely large (or extremely small); when it might have been more appropriate to use logistic models. Because the probability of group membership was not extreme (See Table 5.2), the discriminant analysis was deemed the most appropriate and effective means of distinguishing the differences in the characteristics of women who remain in the academy (group one), return to the academy (group two) and voluntarily leave the academy (group three).

This study included three different operational definitions of the "decision" variable for the discriminant analysis. Each of the three decision categories (to remain in, return to, or voluntarily leave) were represented in the mobility model and then classified within the predicted memberships, along with the actual number in the group. The classification indicated the "goodness of fit" associated with each of the groups in the model, which accurately predicted the majority of the cases. This model was employed to provide the analysis discussed in the remainder of this chapter.

The discriminant analysis was employed for each of the three groups and for the model. Two discriminant functions were required. Function One was statistically significant and accounted for the greatest degree of variance between the three groups. The first function separated those who remained in the academy (group one) and those who returned to the academy (group two) from those who voluntarily left the academy (group three), and accounted for 76.76 percent of the variance. The first function displayed a positive direction of the first (remainers) and second (returners) coefficients, separating them from the negative direction of the third coefficient (voluntary leavers).

A stepwise discriminant analysis was applied to the data to identify and select from 21 possible variables those with greatest statistical significance ($p \leq .05$) of the decision to remain in, return to, or voluntarily leave the academy. Of the 21 possible independent variables, 5 were selected in the discriminant stepwise procedure and were presented in order of significance. The primary goal of the stepwise discriminant analysis was to determine to what degree each of the designated independent variables would prove significant in predicting the decision patterns (dependent variable) of Black women faculty to remain in, return to, or voluntarily leave the academy.

The binomial variables tenure status and academic employment offers were by far the most important of these five independent variables. The standardized discriminant coefficients for tenure status (.51) and academic employment offers (.50) both represented 2 times the weighted value of other barrier (discriminant function coefficient of .22) and was significantly greater than the weighted value of job satisfaction (discriminant function coefficient of -.47), and institutional type (discriminant function coefficient of -.53).

Tenure status was indicated as the single most important (discriminant function coefficient .51) binomial variable of the five. The positive direction of the coefficient suggested that those who remained in or returned to the academy were more likely to hold tenure, as compared to those who voluntarily left the academy. The descriptive statistics (See Table 5.4) indicate that the mean tenure status for those who voluntary left was 20 percent, as compared to 54 percent for those who remained and 37 percent for those who returned.

TABLE 5.4:

Descriptive Statistics

	Remain Mean	Return Mean	Leave Mean
Tenure Status	0.54	0.37	0.20
Academic Offers	2.75	2.39	1.04
Other Barrier	0.05	0.15	0
Job Satisfaction	0.65	0.64	0.48
Institutional Type	3.46	3.39	4.00

This further substantiates the claim that those who remain are more likely to hold tenure than those who return. And those who return are more likely to hold tenure than those who voluntarily left.

The continuous variable academic offers demonstrated the second most important positive discriminant function coefficient (.5) in the model. The positive direction of the coefficient suggested that those women who remained in or returned to the academy were more likely to receive the greatest number of academic employment offers. In comparison, those women who voluntarily left the academy were more likely to receive the fewest number of academic employment offers. The descriptive statistics indicate that the mean value for academic offers was 1.04 for those who voluntarily left, as compared to 2.75 for those who remained, and 2.39 for those who returned.

Of the thirteen factors listed as barriers toward academic career advancement, the binomial variable other barrier demonstrated a positive coefficient (.22) in the model. External barriers indicated by respondents in the "other barrier" variable fell into four main categories: 1) limited upward mobility opportunities within the current institution; 2) unrealistic expectations of time to do the work; 3) inability to manage the role-set; and 4) other personal interests. The positive direction of the coefficient suggested that those who decided to return to the academy were more likely to experience other barriers than those who decided to remain. And those who decided to remain were more likely to experience other barriers than those who voluntarily left. The descriptive statistics indicated that the mean value for other barriers for those who remained was 5 percent, as compared to 15 percent for those who returned. In comparison, the mean value for those who voluntarily left the academy was 0 percent.

The negative direction of the coefficient job satisfaction (-.5) suggested that the women who voluntarily left the academy were least likely to be highly satisfied in their current nonacademic position than those currently employed (remainers and returners) in the academy. The mean score provides further evidence of this interpretation. The mean rate of job satisfaction for those who left the academy were 48 percent, as compared to 65 percent for those who remained, and 64 percent for those who returned. This would appear to suggest that slightly less than half the women who voluntarily left the academy had a high job satisfaction rate, whereas, nearly two-thirds of the women who remained in or returned to the academy were highly satisfied with their current academic position.

The institutional type variable demonstrated a negative discriminant function coefficient of (-.5) in the model. The variable institutional type was coded as "2" to indicate a two-year institution and "4" to indicate a four-year institution. The negative direction of the coefficient suggested that those who voluntarily left the academy were most likely than the other two groups to leave from four-year American colleges and universities. The descriptive statistics indicated that the mean value for institutional type for those who voluntarily left were 4.0, as compared to 3.46 for those who remain, and 3.39 for those who return. The value of the similar means for institutional type indicate that all three groups were more likely to be employed by a four-year institution as opposed to a two-year institution. However those who voluntarily left had been employed exclusively by four-year academic institutions.

DECISION MODEL OF CAREER MOBILITY

Referring to the variables described in Table 5.4 and the inferential analyses presented in the previous section, the following is a generalized description of the decisions that are represented in each of the categories. In general, the respondents fell into two distinct groups: those who were currently working in the academy (remainers and returners), and those who were not (voluntary leavers).

Those who remained or returned to the academy represented a total of over 86 percent of the sample and had two major characteristics.

First, the members of this group were successful intellectual Black women scholars. They were most likely to hold tenure (.54 for those who remain and .37 for those who return, as compared to .20 for those who leave), and received the greatest number of academic employment offers (2.75 for those who remain as compared to 2.39 for those who return and 1.04 for those voluntarily leave) from other four-year colleges and universities. Because of the demand for these academic women, many tended to have a high rate of mobility as they moved from institution to institution, as they received numerous attractive career opportunities. This group of academic women, however, were most likely to seek alternative employment opportunities within the academy.

Second, these academic women were not only successful, but also tended to be highly satisfied (.65 for those who remain, and 64 percent for those who return, as compared to 48 percent for those who leave). Apparently, nearly two-thirds of these academic women were happy despite the perceived barriers to career advancement. Some of the reported barriers included: limited upward mobility opportunities within the current institution; unrealistic expectations of time to do the work; inability to manage role sets; and other personal factors. These barriers may have often influenced these women to seek other opportunities either within or outside the academy. Many women appeared to become more mobile because they perceived that the academy had limited opportunities for advancement and, therefore, sought more attractive career opportunities elsewhere, but still most often within academia.

Those who were no longer working in the academy and had voluntarily left displayed a number of distinct characteristics. They were twice as likely to be non tenured and had the lowest job satisfaction rate of all three groups. Tenure status for those who left was the most significant of all five variables identified in the stepwise discriminant analysis. Those who left the academy: 1) were most likely to hold a non tenured position; 2) voluntarily left exclusively from a four-year college or university as opposed to a two-year institution; 3) most likely received the fewest number of academic employment offers; and 4) were least likely to experience other barriers which interfered with academic career success.

VI. *Summing It Up*

The focus of this study was on the effects of economic and psychosocial variables on the decisions of Black women professors to remain in, return to, or voluntarily leave the academy. The primary purpose was to determine the factors that attributed to success and achievement. Findings confirmed that the model that most accurately predicted the mobility decisions of Black women faculty was to voluntarily leave. Furthermore, the stepwise discriminant analysis indicated that five out of 21 independent variables (tenure status, academic offers, other barrier, job satisfaction, and institutional type) were significant ($p<.05$) factors. These correlations, along with the study results presented in Chapter Five, provide the basis for addressing the following research questions.

MAJOR FINDINGS

1) *What was the primary factor associated with the decisions of Black women to remain in the academy?*

The primary factor associated with the decisions of Black women faculty to remain in the academy was tenure status. Those who remained were most likely to hold tenure, be employed by a four-year academic institution, and receive the greatest number of academic employment offers. The women who remained also had the highest rate of job satisfaction, as compared to those who returned and those who voluntarily left, and were more likely to experience other barriers than those who voluntarily left, albeit less than those who returned.

"Other barrier" was the last of 15 questions asking respondents to specify any other barrier (other than the 14 previously asked) that may have interfered with academic career advancement. Most of the seventeen responses indicated external barriers in four main categories: 1) limited upward mobility opportunities within the current institution; 2) unrealistic expectations of the amount of time it takes to do the work; 3) inability to manage role sets; and 4) personal factors. In general, these women faculty remained in the academy because they were relatively happy and held tenure, which provided job security. Furthermore, the enticement of a relatively greater number of academic employment opportunities, did not provide a strong enough force to encourage these academic women to seek alternate employment outside the academy.

2) *What are the primary factors associated with the decisions of Black women to return to the academy?*

There were four factors most associated with the decisions of Black women faculty to return to the academy. The two factors of greatest association with the decision to return were job satisfaction and other barriers. These academic women were most likely to experience other barriers to academic career advancement than those who remained or those who voluntarily left. Of all these three groups, those who returned were least likely to be employed by a four-year academic institution and were more likely to have a higher job satisfaction rate as compared to those who left voluntarily. This group was also more likely to hold tenure than those who left, but was less likely than those who remained.

Overall, faculty who returned to the academy appeared to do so more out of personal choice than necessity. The majority of those who returned were unmarried and had received the greatest number of nonacademic employment offers, yet they still chose to work even though they were more likely to work at a two-year institution, be non tenured, and experience a greater amount of other barriers than the other two groups combined.

3) *What are the primary factors associated with the decisions of Black women to voluntarily leave the academy?*

Those who voluntary left the academy were most likely to have the lowest job satisfaction rate of all three groups. These women voluntarily left exclusively from a four-year college or university--as opposed to a two-year institution--and were least likely to experience other barriers which interfered with academic career advancement.

Tenure status and academic offers also played a role in the decision to voluntarily leave. Those who left were most likely to receive the fewest number of academic employment offers and most likely to hold a non tenured position. In general, those who left had the lowest job satisfaction rate in their current nonacademic position than both the remainers and returners employed in the academy. Although those who left were least likely to experience other barriers, they were more likely to have an unsupportive spouse and hold a relatively less secure non tenured faculty position, as compared to those who remained and those who returned to the academy.

4) *Is there a significant relationship between salary and the decision to remain in, return to, or voluntarily leave the academy?*

Given the way in which salary was operationalized in this study, there appeared to be no evidence to support the hypothesis that salary was a significant factor in the decision to remain in, return to, or voluntarily leave the academy. However, this contradicted a number of studies which more clearly defined salary differentials. This would appear to suggest that, while salary may not have been a significant factor in the decisions of Black women faculty to voluntarily leave the academy, it is not insignificant; it may be due to the existence of alternative employment opportunities in either academic or nonacademic institutions, and the greater importance placed on tenure, as opposed to salary.

5) *Is there a significant relationship between marital status and the number of dependents on the decision to remain in, return to, or voluntarily leave the academy?*

Generally, marital status and number of dependents did not appear to play a significant role in the decision to remain in, return to, or voluntarily leave the academy. One reason for this finding may have been the relatively small numbers of respondents who were married or had dependents. Less than half of all respondents from the three decision categories were married, and fewer still had dependents. Of those who had dependent children or elderly custodial parents living in the household, only half had greater than one, and only three of those respondents had more than three.

6) *What are the primary barriers that impede progress towards academic success and achievement?*

Of the 15 barriers presented in the survey instrument, only "other" barrier proved to be statistically significant. The four main external barriers reported in the "other barrier" category were: 1) limited upward mobility opportunities within the current institution; 2) unrealistic expectations of amount of time it takes to do the work; 3) inability to manage role sets; and 4) personal/family factors. This suggests that the most significant barriers interfering with career advancement primarily involve relationships with family, time constraints, management of multiple roles, and lack of institutional mobility opportunities. These barriers further suggest that some Black women faculty, if given a greater range of mobility opportunities within the institution, will be less likely to voluntarily leave the academy.

COMMON BARRIERS TO SUCCESS AND ACHIEVEMENT

In addition to the five external barriers discussed above which were selected by the discriminant analysis as being statistically significant, several other barriers were identified to varying degrees.

The information presented in this section was taken from a question in the survey instrument which asked respondents to rate 15 given factors (major problem "3", minor problem "2", or not a problem "1" which most frequently interfered with academic career advancement and achievement. The 15 items included: (1) academic support at home; (2) spouse's job mobility; (3) spouse's negative views toward spouse's academic job/career; (4) qualifications challenged unfairly; (5) salary differentials; (6) differential policies/practices toward tenure and promotion; (7) lack of appointment to important committees; (8) academic climate; (9) teaching inequities; (10) research inequities; (11) service obligations within the institution; (12) service obligations outside the institution; (13) discrimination/racism;

(14) inflexibility/inability to accommodate family needs; and (15) other barriers. All questions in the study originated from a modest pilot survey conducted by the author in 1993. This survey asked Black, White, Latino, and Asian men and women faculty and administrators to list up to 5 factors they had experienced or witnessed which interfered with career advancement in a present or past position. The 15 items in the question and others, were based on the responses reported in this pilot study and additional factors reported from other studies.

Due to the method of coding, the factors with the highest mean (on a scale from 1-3) indicated those areas where respondents most frequently experienced the greatest interference with advancement and achievement. Table 6.1 indicates the corresponding means for each of these 15 external barriers listed in order of significance.

TABLE 6.1
Most Common Barriers to Career Advancement

Barrier	Mean
Undefined Other	2.58
Discrimination/Racism	1.35
Academic Climate	1.17
Service Obligation with Institution	1.14
Salary Differentials	1.04
Differential Policies/Practices Regarding Tenure & Promotion	1.01
Teaching Inequities	1.01
Research Inequities	.98
Service Obligation Outside Institution	.96
Spouses Job Mobility	.95
Qualifications Challenged Unfairly	.95
Spouses Negative Views Towards Academic Job/Career	.88
Inflexibility/Inability to Accommodate Family Needs	.86
Adequate Support at Home	.85
Lack of Appointment to Important Committees	.75

The variable of greatest value was 'undefined other' and was also identified in the stepwise discriminant analysis as a significant factor interfering with career advancement and success. This 'undefined other' category was composed of the additional responses of 18 women faculty, who felt the 14 items presented in Table 5.1 did not adequately reflect all of the factors which they had experienced.

In the majority of the cases, respondents indicated personal and family factors as being the greatest obstacles, such as child or spouse not wishing to relocate, personal interests, not wanting to leave older parents or relatives, lack of financial and household support, and the inability to accept added responsibility due to multiple role sets. Over a dozen women faculty cited numerous institutional factors they felt impeded career advancement. For example, four women reported gender discrimination from an immediate supervisor or chair, lack of funding and resources to conduct research needed for tenure and promotion, and one women stated, "the unwritten rules and politics of the white boy's administrative club" was her greatest barrier to advancement and achievement.

The most common responses indicated in the 'other category was lack of opportunity for advancement, promotion, and tenure. Today, many colleges and universities are downsizing and freezing salaries, thereby limiting the number of faculty promoted and awarded tenure. Because of limited opportunities for inteinstitutional mobility, some Black women faculty were increasingly seeking employment outside of the academy. Despite the lack of opportunity and extraordinary time constraints limiting research potential, a handful of women reported being reluctant to venture into the non-academic arena because of the fear that they would lose their security as tenured faculty.

In addition to the 'undefined other' category, the first 6 variables in Table 6.1 illustrates those which were most often selected as interfering with career advancement and success. They included discrimination and racism, academic climate, service obligations with the institution, salary differentials, differential policies and practices regarding tenure and promotion, and teaching inequities. These findings support the research of Moore and Wagstaff (1985), Harvey and Scott-Jones (1985), Tack and Patitu (1992), and numerous others.

A 1998 study from Thompson and Dey suggests that the greatest sources of stress for African American university faculty are time constraints (lack of personal time, time pressures, and teaching load), promotion concerns (review and promotion process, research and publishing demands, subtle discrimination-prejudice, racism, and sexism) and overall stress. Faculty in four-year colleges experienced the greatest stress as opposed to those in two-year colleges and the more the particular type of stress experienced the lower the job satisfaction. The more stress African American faculty experienced related to job promotion, the less likely they are to be satisfied in their relationships with other campus professionals. Because African American were most likely to have lower professional status, they tend to have greater vulnerability to particular types of stress, such as promotion concerns, overall stress, and marginality. In addition, women are must likely to be primarily responsible for household chores and therefore experience greater stress related to time constraints at work. Single women, however, experienced lower levels of stress then married women with children and having adolescent children positively contributes to greater stress.

The only work-related experience that women experienced more was often than men was sexual harassment, which also may be one of several reasons for lower research productivity. Dey, Korn and Sax (1996) found that African American and minority faculty women are more likely to be harassed because of their lower status, but are less likely to report sexual harassment because of the personal and professional cost to themselves (Boyd, 1993). When one African American faculty woman was asked why she had remained silent for so long after continually being harassed, she said, "When the president of the United States gets on national television and discredits the credibility of an educated professional... like Anita Hill, what chance do I have the somebody is going to believe me?"(Boyd, 1993, p. 11). Finally, many African American women reported concerns about maintaining the integrity of their work while finding sources for publication and validation during promotion. One of the greatest sources of stress, according to Thompson and Dey (1998), is being an African American woman.

West (1993) contends that if African American faculty are going to secure their position in academe, they must imitate dominant paradigms using African American culture and subject matter. He further argues that conflict between these paradigms can lead to experiences for African American faculty that can be demoralizing and stifling to their intellectual creativity. Often, multi-marginality can be experienced based on one's scholarly research agenda (Harvey, 1996). These agendas are often misunderstood by the dominant culture and therefore not treated as quality research. Bell (1994) argues that successful African American faculty must maintain a "tightrope act" where the role of race cannot be denied regardless of successes and failures. We need to understand the work conditions and sources of stress for African American faculty if we are to truly understand their decisions to leave or remain in academe.

PERSONAL LIFESTYLE CHOICES OF BLACK WOMEN FACULTY

The information contained in this section was derived from the personal comments made by the women in this study; much of which was not captured in the statistical data presented earlier. This section will focus on the personal characteristics of Black women faculty and how their values and lifestyle choices served to define their identity, and influence their personal and professional success. The personal areas most often cited include family background, discretionary activities, personal values, success and achievement factors, support systems, mentors, home life, and mobility factors.

The family backgrounds of these women centered primarily on marital status and history. Forty-one percent of the women were married; the majority had only one child. Most women married just after receiving a baccalaureate degree, and only 22 percent married after completing their graduate studies. More than half who were married had a spouse who held graduate degrees, 22 percent baccalaureate degrees, and 14 percent held high school diplomas. The most often cited occupation for a spouse was teaching, followed by the professions, educational administration, business management, professional counseling, and engineering, respectively. Approximately 10 percent of all women reported having household assistance.

Women faculty were asked to select which of the following discretionary activities they most often chose to participate in: family, religious, social, professional, volunteer, educational, neighborhood, and political. The majority of the women reported to participate most often in religious activities, followed by social, family, professional associations, and volunteer work. The findings support the 1987 National Survey of Black Americans, which reported that Black women have traditionally been the primary activists in the Black church, although their role has historically been one of subordination rather than of leadership. Since less than half of the women in the study were married, it is not surprising to see participation in social activities of greater value than that of the family, especially since only 42 percent of the women had a child under the age of 17 living in the household.

To determine the personal values of greatest importance, women were asked to rate the following six choices on a scale of 1 to 3: time for personal/family life, income for personal/family life, quality of personal/family life, opportunity for family, fulfilling social/community obligations, and other. The value of greatest significance was the 'other' category. Women most often cited personal and professional growth, truth-seeking, personal integrity, relationship with God, professional prestige, and quality time with family as those personal values of greatest importance in the lives of Black women faculty.

The factors women selected as those most important for success and achievement were God, early mentorship, personal and professional autonomy, research to advance the lives of Black people, adequate budget, public service, commitment to community, and family life, respectively.

Support systems in the lives of Black women faculty have been found to be important because guidance, strength, and encouragement in an academic setting is often unfriendly and isolating. Support systems become even more significant for women trying to maintain the demands of marriage, family, and career simultaneously. The support systems women most often relied upon were spouse, parents, friends, relatives, minority mentors, non-minority mentors, children, and professional Black associations. Women who were married most often reported a spouse and children as the greatest sources of support, whereas single women reported parents and friends as being the most supportive.

The presence of mentors was reported to enhance one's opportunity for promotion and tenure, and provide important information needed for professional mobility. Interestingly, 100 percent of the women faculty in this study reported having at least one mentor during their academic career, either in an informal or formal relationship. Mentors ranged broadly in gender, profession, discipline, and ethnicity. The majority of women faculty reported having several mentors, often simultaneously, in disciplines and professions different than their own. Eighty-seven percent of the women reported serving as a mentor for countless men and women from numerous cultural and ethnic backgrounds. And although most reported the mentoring relationship professionally rewarding, many reported being given disproportionately greater numbers of students to advise and counsel because of their visible concern and commitment to students.

Forty percent of the women reported living in the suburbs, while 39 percent resided in major metropolitan cities. Approximately 20 percent reported living in small towns, and research suggests that more professionals are migrating to smaller towns and cities, particularly young families with small children.

Women were also asked to indicate the primary factors that influenced the decision to leave their last place of academic employment. The factors of greatest significance were personal, followed by salary, lack of professional support, lack of a critical mass, and family. Nearly 10 percent of the women reported leaving a tenured position because of better pay, better opportunity for advancement, change of career/professional interests, or movement due to a spouse's job.

Some successful African American faculty women in the study found greater success when integrating teaching with faculty research. Many of them found it to be especially helpful when they had the ability to choose their own teaching assignments, which enhanced opportunities to integrate teaching and research. In Getzel and Guba's classic 1954 book, they discussed the severity of role conflict theory where the differences in rigor and compatibility with respect to role expectation definitions tended to correspond to differences in levels of teaching-research integration. In contrast and more recently, Boyer (1990) argues for a more broad definition and suggests scholarship can be in the form of inquiry, application, integration, and/or teaching. In some disciplines, integration may be more appropriate than in others. However, integration also makes it difficult to determine the amount of time you spend in any one area. In light of recent state laws in some areas (Hines and Higham, 1996) that require faculty to report the time they spend on accomplishing teaching, research, service, and other goals, policy decisions about the integration of faculty work may be more difficult to determine since information on the benefits and costs are ambiguous (Ludwig, 1996).

VII. *Changing the Rules of the Game*

TRANSFORMING TENURE AND PROMOTION

The primary factor most associated with those who remain in the academy is tenure status.   Since securing tenure at a four-year institution is most significant in the decision to remain, institutions should revisit the policies and practices surrounding tenure to ensure that requirements are equitably decided and policies are clear, appropriate, realistic, and fairly weighed. Also, recognizing that those who remain are most likely to receive the greatest number of academic employment offers, institutions should develop strategies to help reduce the rate of attrition.   Institutions can begin by providing rewards structures to encourage faculty success, and offer support systems to reduce isolation.   And administrators should help ensure that Black faculty women have the necessary tools required to succeed in the academy.   American colleges and universities need to provide a conducive research environment and help minimize the number of undue burdens placed on many Black women scholars which tend to detract them from scholarship.

Furthermore, the job satisfaction rate for those who remained in the academy was comparably higher than any of the other two groups. Tenured faculty who remained in or returned to the academy were apparently more happy than those who voluntarily left, which suggests that tenure is an important factor influencing job satisfaction.

Florence Mood (1971) has cited the tenure system as "the major barrier to the female scholar" after receipt of the doctorate degree (p. 983). She argues that the way to alleviate the problem is to eliminate the tenure system as it is today and rethink alternative measures. According to present research, nearly 85 percent of all American colleges and universities use the tenure system, as defined by the AAUP.   According to Finkelstein (1990), these institutions that maintain the tenure system employ approximately 95 percent of all full-time faculty.

The debate over the tenure system has existed for quite some time, yet little has been done because few viable alternatives have been proposed. In the early 1960s, over 20 states proposed legislation for the first time to reform or abolish tenure for new prospective faculty. The community colleges of Virginia was the only bill which passed of the 20 submitted for legislation (Finkelstein, 1990).

In his book, *Scholarship Reconsidered* (1990), Boyer examines the movement from teaching, to service, to research, and its implications on the roles of faculty. He begins by illustrating the renewed concern for undergraduate education, teaching, service, and the core curriculum. He states: "at no time in our history has the need been greater for connecting the work of the academy to the social and environmental challenges beyond the campus.... We need a renewed commitment to service" (p. xii). Since scholarship is most often the primary requirement for tenure, it is important to explore ways to redefine scholarly activity.

Boyer introduced four major, overlapping components of scholarship: discovery, integration, application, and teaching. He argues that "scholarship means engaging in original research. But the work of the scholar also means stepping back from one's investigation looking for connections, building bridges between theory and practice, and communicating one's knowledge effectively to students" (p. 16).

Discovery, according to Boyer, is the act of investigating and discovering new knowledge. "Commitment to knowledge for its own sake, to freedom of inquire and to the following in a disciplined fashion, an investigation wherever it may lead" (p. 17). Integration, on the other hand, is connecting that knowledge across disciplines to see the big picture. It also involves the reinterpretation of research, into a larger intellectual scheme. Integration, he asks, "what do the findings mean?" (p. 19). Boyer argues that application, the third element, refers to "how can knowledge be responsibility applied to consequential problems?" (p. 21). He states that some service activities can be considered scholarship if the scholar's field experience is directly related to the professional activity. The final element is teaching. Aristotle once said "teaching is the highest form of understanding." A good teacher transmits knowledge in numerously creative ways such as group activities, assignments, reading, and discussion, so as to more fully capture the attention of his or her students.

Tenure is said to serve as a lifetime guarantee that professors will receive due process within the context of the academic institution, although interpretation of academic freedom and protection vary. Tenure, in all fairness, is a process of exclusion. Many institutions argue against tenure because of the financial obligation, but numerous scholars have suggested workable alternatives mentioned earlier. Another might be imposing a post-tenure review process (Finkin, 1996) to increase the flexibility of institutional to hold tenured faculty accountable for performance.

> The custom on individual salary negotiations has been shown to place women at a disadvantage, particularly those who had not been mentored as graduate students and instructed on negotiation rituals and courtship customs that are common in hiring practices in the academy. Women often receive starting salaries that are lower than those of their male peers because they don't know what to ask or how to negotiate (Tierney and Bensimon, p. 79).

These shifts in scholarly activity, combined with the findings in this study, raise some additional questions regarding the distribution of tenure policies and practices. The policies concerning the requirements of tenure, the weight of responsibilities, the reassessment, and other issues need to be reassessed. Boyer has provided a new beginning for the possible transformation of scholarly activities considered for tenure and promotion. Given that most Black women and minority faculty often participate in greater numbers of service activities and prefer teaching to research, new guidelines such as these proposed by Boyer deserve further examination. Since tenure was the strongest factor influencing Black women to remain in the academy, ignoring its implications would be inadvisable and unfortunate.

DEVELOPING CAREER LADDERS

It is evident that the women in this study were career-oriented and valued the importance of achievement; those who left sought better career opportunities offering fewer external barriers, yet those who remained were predominantly tenured, indicating a high level of job security. However, it is also apparent that faculty women who remain in and return to the academy face external barriers to career advancement.   Numerous respondents indicated the lack of institutional career mobility as a factor interfering with advancement. It is clear that policies are not working as well as they should be to help retain Black women scholars. Institutions of higher learning need to take a closer look at the career opportunities for those already in the institution and explore advancing their own faculty prior to searching outside for new candidates.   Furthermore, institutional leaders should consider providing additional funds to develop career ladders within institutions, where appropriate, allowing for greater institutional mobility and possibly fewer attrition rates.

Most theories support the notion that career development is an evolutionary process rather than a static phase in one's life (Hall and Noughaim, 1968). When embarking on a career, a person experiences numerous successes and failures, which can serve to either undermine or encourage his or her ambition and drive. Kanter (1979) describes this phenomenon as 'vocational stuckness.'   She suggests that by providing opportunities for career growth and development, institutions can limit or postpone this behavior. Institutions can also take advantage of the desire many faculty feel to contribute more to their field of expertise. By investing resources, taking risks, and experimenting with new, innovative ideas, colleges and universities can capitalize on the knowledge, interest, and personal needs of senior faculty, while nurturing growth and development.

The overwhelming majority of remainers and returners in this study are faculty women in the field of education. Previous research has indicated that many faculty come from diverse backgrounds and often teach in fields other than their doctorate field (Brown, 1988). Institutions should consider a career profile bank for full-time tenure-track nontenured and tenured faculty who are in disciplines most likely to be down-sized or eliminated, and in those departments that are less likely to receive adequate funds to ensure future employment. Institutions could use computer databases to help plan for future needs, as well as provide greater opportunities for their faculty, while at the same time enhancing their own pool of available talent.

Advancement in the academy should not always have to mean alternative employment. But unfortunately it often does. The results of this study as well as other research, has pointed to the lack of opportunities for inter-institutional career mobility as a primary factor of faculty attrition. Research indicates that career mobility patterns differ with administrative area. For example, most academic administrators previously served as faculty members. Some academic affairs administrators were initially first hired by their own doctorate granting institution (Scott, 1978). Although the majority of upward mobility appears to have most often occurred within a particular specialty area, this movement has increasingly occurred both within and between academic and nonacademic institutions.

Boyer argues in *Scholarship Reconsidered*, that the years of greatest productivity for scholars vary significantly by discipline. For example, he states that mathematicians and physicists are most productive before the age of 35. Whereas philosophers and historians tend to be most productive much later in life. He suggests that because of these differences colleges and universities should consider alternative career options, such as what he calls 'creative contracts,' which would allow scholars to define their academic goals over a three to five-year period. He argues that this would not only individualize one's contributions, but help maintain productivity and facilitate interminable evaluations of one's performance as well. Creative contracts could also enhance professional development and entice faculty to remain in the academy by giving them equal say in how they define their roles and responsibilities. In light of the findings that Black faculty women value the security of tenure more than salary, the opportunities for retention would appear to be greater.

Career development is an important issue because it may well be the primary means to retain Black faculty women and other scholars. Institutions need to be willing to take risks. Several scholars have offered a few suggestions, such as more flexible leave policies, experimentation with administrative internships, early retirement programs, and retraining faculty where appropriate. A better understanding of the needs and desires of faculty at each stage of their careers, would shed light on the factors which may help to better retain and advance Black faculty women.

Finkelstein argues that there are several distinct characteristics of most faculty by rank. New assistant professors, for example, are often enthusiastic yet idealistic about their career, and are most concerned about teaching effectively and publishing. Given these characteristics, Finkelstein suggests that institutions encourage junior faculty to pilot new courses to capitalize on their new ideas and familiarity with the latest research techniques. Associate professors are better integrated into the system and enjoy working together with peers. At this point in their career, they are concerned most about obtaining tenure. In the instance of associate professors, institutions may wish to capitalize on this fear of not getting tenure and interest in working with colleagues by encouraging collaborations within and among institutions, and offering funding, secretarial support, and time for research.

According to Finkelstein, the characteristics of full professors differ depending upon whether or not they are five or less years from retirement. Some professors who are greater than five years from retirement often become disenchanted with teaching and research. They may often change the number of hours devoted to certain work responsibilities and participate in more external professional activities, such as consulting. Full professors within five years of retirement are more removed and isolated from others in the institution. They may begin to question their effectiveness and ability to keep abreast of recent developments in their area of expertise. Given these characteristics, institutions should encourage and provide funding for full professors to spearhead innovative research projects by teaming up with junior faculty. While there will always be some senior faculty who will resist this and become increasingly less productive and ineffective--both with scholarship and teaching, many others will not. What many fail to recognize is that retirement is a state of mind and not determined by age. Some of the most productive and renowned scholars are well beyond the age of retirement. The records of these scholars stand on their own merits. The issue of mandatory retirement has already been abolished in policy, but has not been fully accepted by academics.

CREATING OPPORTUNITIES FOR SUCCESS AND ACHIEVEMENT

Although, for the most part, individual experiences of Black faculty women differ, there appear to be numerous similarities. For example, most Black faculty women experience the pleasures of academic life as well as the harsh realities. For many of these women, the height of their professional success in the academy was based on their ability to manage role sets and adapt to the multitude of responsibilities. For Black, (and most other women scholars), this represents a complex challenge, particularly for women with families. Although many

Black women manage work, family, and community, they may often do it at a cost to their personal lives. In 1986, for example, the Carnegie Foundation found that the primary factor of faculty dissatisfaction was the extent to which responsibilities at work interfered with and limited one's personal life. According to McCombs (1989), "African American women who decide to enter the university do so with the understanding that it will be a new experience, but will also be a challenge to their traditions" (p. 137).

In many cases, successful scholars most often receive support and cooperation from those around them, such as from a spouse, family, relatives, friends, colleagues, church members, and professional associations. Several scholars mentioned the lack of a critical mass and reported experiencing cultural, social, and intellectual isolation, resulting in numerous conflicts within the role set. "From predominantly white institutions, blacks were more likely to encounter barriers to mobility and little support for the emotional aspect of the experience" (Higginbotham, 1981, p. 264). Isolation can often affect both an individual's professional performance and personal well-being, which in turn may force some Black academics to leave.

In Dickens and Dickens (1982) book *The Black Manager*, they described three types of strategies for success: internal, external, and environmental strategies. These strategies, although based on Black professionals in predominately White major corporations, may help to explain some of the means in which Black faculty may create better opportunities for individual success and achievement, particularly at predominately white institutions.

The Dickens' describe seven components of internal strategies as those that help the Black professional better understand how and what drives his or her thoughts and actions. These include: effective style of one's persona; managing anger as a constructive tool; understanding all of the position's responsibilities; resisting power when logic and explanation fail; regularly performing and documenting self evaluations; developing an aggressive action plan to achieve stated goals; and maintaining a positive self identify to combat racism and discrimination, which can sometimes lead to self hate.

In comparison, there are five external strategies that reconcile factors affecting a person. These components include: managing racial attitudes; developing effective relationships with supervisors, colleagues and junior staff; identifying and cultivating resources; reading between the lines to effectively break into informal communications networks; and selectively and intelligently choosing battles and managing conflict.

The final strategy is called environmental and most often deals with the workplace. The four distinct components of environmental strategies include: strategic management and effective negotiation skills; learning to effectively pass and receive important personal and administrative information through the supportive grapevine; empowering oneself whenever possible through position, expertise, influence, or charisma and maintaining that power; and constantly improving oneself and one's skills, and sharing those skills with other Black and women professionals. Dickens' argues that the combination of these three strategies can help to empower Black professionals and improve management and survival strategies.

Since obtaining tenure at any four-year institution can be a tremendous feat to reach, it is important to understand the politics surrounding the process of meeting and reaching publication goals. Whicker, Kronenfeld, and Strickland (1993) suggest four methods of assessing the political aspects of securing tenure. They suggest one: 1) examine the effects of your being granted tenure on the department as a whole—are you seen as a threat or contribution?; 2) determine the effect of you being granted tenure on those already tenured; 3) be supportive of your chair and dean; and 4) determine whether there is a need for your expertise within your institution.

Achieving tenure is not just all politics. Using your common sense is important as well, although this author recognizes how challenging that might be in situations where tempers are high and the credibility of your work is being challenged. There are several things I would recommend young doctorate students and faculty keep mind.

First, when you begin to see the light at the end of that dissertation, you should be pulling out your Chronicle of Higher Education and Black Issues in Higher Education and searching for conferences where you can present your preliminary findings or present you literature review. The helpful critiques of your work, the contacts you make, and the visibility you receive will far outweight the cost of the trip. Hopefully, you can find a conference close to home or in a place where you might share accommodations. You be happy to learn that a lot of ABD's (all but dissertations) come to conferences to network, share research, or just rejuvenate themselves before they get back to that grind.

Second, learn how to say no and always give a sound reason. Some new faculty are afraid to say no, but if you do not protect your time no one else will. You should carry your own weight with committee and advising work, but not to the detriment of your research. Some institutions allow new faculty to take a reduced teaching and/or advising load or give them a graduate assistant to share with a senior faculty member. If any of these are offered, grab them and run fast. Do not accept anything that will distract you from your research. Once your set your research agenda and get into that writing groove, you can start to add things to your plate. Remember that many of those who serve on time-consuming committee may already have their tenure, or may not be seeking tenure for a host of other reasons, so make sure you cover yourself.

Third, learn who your friends are and who your friends aren't. Determine who you can trust and who you should avoid. Your research ideas and strategies should only be discussed with those whom you trust. Remember to listen much more than you talk. When appropriate, resist to comment on important issues until you know where everyone else in the room stands. Remember that people in academe, and particularly at the department level, have very long memories. The moment you come up for promotion or tenure, everything you have ever said or done will be scrutinized.

Fourth, find an academic mentor, within or outside your institution, with whom you feel comfortable with and share common interests. Meet with them and welcome others with similar beliefs. If possible, try brown bag lunch discussions on campus each month among colleagues of similar mind.

Fifth, build a coalition among colleagues in and outside your department and institution. Seek out those whom you admire in your field and get them on the phone and talk to them or write occasionally and let them know what you are doing and ask their advice. At tenure time, these may be the very people who are called upon to give their opinion of the quality and value of your work.

Sixth, make yourself visible in the community and build community support. Join a professional organization or two and become active on their boards. Offer to speak at community functions, give talks at schools, join a community organization or submit articles to the local newspapers on issues of interest.

Seven, think your battles through and choose them very carefully. Be sure to consider who you are up against and what power they yield among others. Determine the relative value of the fight and whether or not winning the battle is more important than losing the war. Also be cognizant of your timing.

Eighth, when you submit publications you should never submit the same manuscript to more then one publication source at a time for obvious reasons. The time it takes from submission to publication can vary from 6 months to two years. Most take between 9 and 18 months, depending upon the publication. This can be discouraging, but what you can do is write two papers using the same research but different focuses and submit them both at the same time to different journals. For example, if your work is on the academic of minority students you could write a piece about the factors that influence academic achievement of Latino students and another on African American students. Or possibly, write two different papers on the same data and same populations using different variables. There are numerous ways to get around this and minimize the time it takes to get published.

And finally, try to quietly succeed and don't toot your own horn, especially to those in your own department. You need to be seen as a team player and not a threat to others. If you are vocal about your successes, not only will you make enemies quickly but you might also find others questioning the merits of your accomplishments and others working diligently to put you back in 'your place.'

Aisenberg and Harrington (1987) make seven recommendations for learning how to play by the political rules in the academy. They include finding out what's going on; getting practice in political skills, such as volunteer work, managing people, running meetings, and effectively presenting; assuming opposition when consensus is unfathomable; being appropriately aggressive and persistent; learning to ask 'what's in it for me' before agreeing to take on more tasks; using contacts to network; and recognizing the battles worth fighting for and it's value for one's career.

It has become apparent that Black faculty women need to do all they can to accept, support, and promote other women and faculty of color. As discussed at length in Chapter Four, developing a critical mass of professional Black and faculty women provides numerous benefits. By surrounding oneself with supportive colleagues, a person is more likely to be protected from some of the external barriers often experienced by Black faculty women.

One of the best methods to help enhance one's professional academic career is to gain name and face recognition through the publication of articles and books, and the presentation of papers, seminars, lectures, and workshops. The visibility of one's presence when presenting a paper at a national conference can greatly increase mobility potential. Each paper presented should become the subject of the next forthcoming article. Important also is actively participating and supporting professional Black or women's national associations to promote one's work and the interests of women and persons of color. In addition, many scholarly and professional journals are often seeking faculty of color to serve on editorial review boards. This not only serves to increase one's visibility, but often guarantees a person at least one article in that journal as well as prestige and the opportunity to increase skills. Also consider seeking grants for research and travel to international conferences.

In conducting my research, I have found that many faculty of color are less likely to pick up the phone to call a colleague they do not know, particularly if that colleague is a white male or established scholar. The reluctance to establish these potentially advantageous relationships can hinder mobility because these are the very people who are asked by college leaders to make recommendations for leadership positions, grants, and other opportunities. Without ties to these knowledge holders, Black faculty and women will continue to lack access to the 'better' positions. Most academics would agree with the saying 'knowledge is power.' As Black women faculty, we must do a better job of empowering ourselves through strategies such as these if we wish to survive and succeed.

In business it is often said that many deals are made on the golf course. In education, many agreements are made at large national and professional conferences. As a professional, I have been offered almost as many job offers, grant opportunities, and consulting contracts at these types of conferences, than I have by soliciting letters to prospective organizations. Unfortunately, the saying, "it's all about who you know" has some merit. This is why networking is critical for all professionals, as is continually building relationships with other people, collaborating with researchers, and forging ties with institutions inside and outside the academy.

VIII. *The Plight of International Faculty Women*

This chapter has been added to the revised 1999 edition of *Black Women in the Academy: The Secrets to Success and Achievement* in an effort to gain greater understanding and appreciation for the struggles and triumphs of faculty women around the world. It is the authors hope that readers will learn more about the history and status of women in the academy, and with this knowledge join the author in helping to eradicate acts of injustice, discrimination, racism, sexism, and ageism that continue to plague the corridors of academic institutions here and abroad.

Educated women were present in early history, but they were the exception rather than the rule. During the Vendic period (1500 to 600 BC) in India, for example, there were women scholars. In ancient Egypt, some women traditionally practiced medicine. In addition, nuns conducted scientific projects in cloisters from 700 to 1400 AD. Also Bologna around 1200 AD, there were women professors of philosophy. Elena Lucrezia Cornaro Piscopia was the first woman to receive her Ph.D. in Padua in 1687.

In the United States, women were first admitted into higher education institutions in 1833 at Oberlin College and the first bachelors degree was awarded to a woman there in 1841. Women took longer to graduate because they were also required to work and complete household tasks while attending school. In contrast, women were allowed to study at Cambridge University in 1869 but they were not allowed to attend university lectures. It was not until 1947 that women at Cambridge University were formally admitted and given equal status as men. At the University of Durham's College of Science in Newcastle women were first admitted in 1871 and in 1878 at the University of London.

In the United States, the enrollment of women in higher education multiplied by almost eight between 1870 and 1900. At the University of Chicago, for example, the percentage of women rose from 24 percent in 1892 to 52 percent in 1902. To manage the rapid changes, the university segregated their classes by sex. The University California decided to deal with the growth of women by creating junior colleges throughout the state. During this same period, women attending the University of Chicago accounted for 56.3 percent of all the Phi Beta Kappa awards. By 1921 in the United States, there were 8,516 assistant professors, associate professors and full professors in colleges and universities across the country, yet only 7 percent, or 627 were women (Kasper, 1989). In 1989, women comprised of 25 percent of faculty in the US, but were unequally distributed among the least prestigious institutions and in the lower ranks.

This section discusses a collection of studies dealing with different aspects of the careers and lives of international academic women from a comparative perspective. Details of their status and experiences from a socio-economic context are included from the following twenty countries, including: Central and South America, Puerto Rico and Cuba; Hawaii; Canada; West Indies (Jamaica, Barbados and Trinidad-Tobago); Japan; China; Korea; Norway; West Germany; Netherlands; Britain; Australia; New Zealand; India; Israel; Turkey; Jordan and; Egypt.

Central and South America, Puerto Rico and Cuba

According to the Census Bureau statistics, Latinos are the second largest growing "underrepresented" population in the United States, but by the year 2020, Latinos are expected to number between 37 and 47 million. A 1993 report from the American Council on Education indicated that in the past ten years alone, the number of Hispanics attending higher education institutions had risen by 84 percent, from 472,000 to 867,000 students. Between 1989 and 1990, Latinos earned only 2 percent (or 783) of the total doctorates awarded in the United States. In 1995, Latinos earned only 496 doctorates in the U.S. (Milem and Astin, 1993). Like African Americans, they tend to be in education, the social sciences, and the humanities. For Latinos, only one in eight doctorate recipients go into college or university teaching (Garza and Cohen, 1987). In 1991, only 2.3 percent of the tenured faculty women were Latina as compared to 88.2 percent for white female faculty (Rodriguez, 1993). As faculty, Latinos in the United States are more often found in community and state colleges and among the lowest ranks.

One reason Latina faculty struggle in the academic community has been because of the lack of mentors. Often, some the few senior Latina faculty are unable to take anyone under their tutelage because they are overwhelmed themselves. Many Latina academics, particularly Chicanas and Mexicanas, have *comadres* and *compadres* (godmothers and godfathers) as their first mentors.

The research interest of many Latina academics lies within their culture. Like African American and other faculty of color, they tend to conduct research in their own communities that later often devalued and considered minor in comparison to other scholarship. Institutions around the country now have departments, such as Chicano studies where many Latina faculty chose to work, but unfortunately some of these programs have been reduced, cutback or eliminated altogether. To overcompensate for research, many Latinas seek committee and community work that other faculty refuse and may often overextend themselves.

Hawaii

In Hawaii in 1894, when Queen Lili'uokalani ruled a sovereign state, white businessmen and sugar growers (*haoles*) illegally and successfully worked to overthrow the government. Soon after, when Hawaii became decolonized, higher education witnessed more and more Hawai'ian students, staff, and faculty. These changes had implications for the language, culture, and history in the curriculum (Tehranian, 1991).

According to the 1990 census, the population of Hawaii reflected 61.8 percent Asian/Pacific Islander (including Japanese, 22.3 percent; Filipino, 15.2 percent, Hawai'ian, 12.4 percent, Chinese, 6.2 percent, Korean, 2.2 percent, and others 3.3 percent); 33.4 percent White; 7.3 percent Hispanic; 2.5 percent Black; and 0.5 percent Native American (U.S. Bureau of the Census, 1992). However, the college and university student enrollment at the time, did not proportionately reflect these same numbers. Furthermore among the tenure-track faculty, nearly 70 percent were White in 1991. Overall, the resident ethnic population of Hawaii was far greater than the ethnic student population and the number of ethnic faculty in Hawai'ian colleges and universities was a fraction of the number of enrolled students. Interesting enough, there are current discussions underway to determine whether Hawai'ians will still be considered Asian/Pacific Islanders or become included as Native Americans. This will be decided before the next census.

The state of Hawaii has one of the highest costs of living in the United States. This is important to acknowledge because it increases the severity of numerous problems, such as low salaries, and lack of adequate resources for research funds, travel monies, secretarial support, office space, graduate assistants, and other resources. When publishing, Hawaiian faculty like other racial and ethnic minorities, have reported having their work devalued and dismissed from the mainstream when they focus on ethnic issues. Socially and professionally they are made to feel unwelcome, unappreciated and unwanted (Reyes and Halcon, 1988).

A 1998 study from Johnsrud and Sadao identified three distinct but related experiences common to various ethnic and racial minority groups. The first was the necessity of being and cultivating biculturalism. This does not mean assimilation. What it does mean is learning how to successfully function in white Anglo-Saxon, Western institutions while at the same time maintaining their own distinct ethnic values, culture, and heritage. A Japanese woman eloquently and succinctly stated:

> I think there's a presumption that because we've reached this level of an academic, we have our Ph.D.'s or whatever, that we've become acculturated. We know how to behave; we've developed a repertoire of social skills that allows up to move fluidly through a variety of social situations. But I think that's not always the case. There's a lot of energy that goes into just contemplating your differences compared to other people's experiences....
>
> There's a cognitive or emotional thing that goes on that doesn't meet the eye. And that requires a lot of energy. It predisposes us to certain kinds of stressors that I don't think white faculty really relate to. There's this presumption that we are all alike despite differences in our skin color—it does much deeper than that. It's inherent in the way we view the world and our upbringing and our own social development. We have to overcompensate in many ways

in order to be able to express ourselves in certain ways and behave in certain ways (Johnsrud and Sadao, 1998).

Biculturalism represents continual problems for many faculty of color, especially with regard to communication and professional styles, research, service and a host of other issues related to tenure. Many see biculturalism as a game that you must play well in order to succeed in a majority institution.   Most successful Latino faculty women contributed their achievement, in part, to their ability to successfully play the game.

The second is the feeling of ethnocentrism on the part of white administrators and faculty who often share an elite mainstream American mentality to maintain the status quo that corresponds with the views of dominant white males. Ethnocentric views describe those who believe one's own group is superior to another. I find this quite disturbing and frightening that colleges and universities whose purpose are to train the minds of others, often hold these beliefs and possibly consciously or unconsciously perpetuate these views.

The third include discriminatory practices against persons of color. It is obvious that many non-majority persons in our culture are treated differently than others. They are often excluded from enjoying some of the same benefits that other people receive, even though they may be equal or more deserving. Discriminatory practices have often been cited with regard to faculty salaries, resources, access to information, and fairness of promotion and tenure practices.

One Hawai'ian faculty woman said:

> I don't think confrontation is profitable. I've really reached the age where I no longer protest for the sheer joy or it, or as a matter of principle. I'm into effectiveness. At this point I am more concerned with what works and what doesn't. I'm much more apt to try to work around the problem, than my bulldozing my way through it. I've sort of gotten past the you-can't-do-this-to-me stage of my life. Well, your doing it to me like this, but maybe I can find another way around.
>
> Again, that's also a cultural thing. In my case it's more related to age, but I know of people from similar ethnic backgrounds who've done this—always avoided head-on confrontation.
>
> There are very, very few women of my ethnic background at this university in this kind of position, either teaching or administrative. You can just count them on the fingers of one hand. And part of it's

due to internal factors.   But part of it is that some of my
contemporaries, when they encounter barriers, chose to go away.
I've known people, for instance, who've been successful—whatever
that means in terms of the academic system—who got to a point
where they were no longer able to deal with the kinds of things they
had to deal with in a course of an ordinary day and said, "This isn't
funny, and I'm not happy here and this doesn't fit into who I am.   I
can earn a living somewhere else, doing something else, and
left."...It's a very common coping strategy with people of my
background. "Forget this, I don't need it" and walk away (Johnsrud
and Sadao, 1998).

The faculty women in the Johnsrud and Sadao study who I have
chosen to quote were highly educated and highly accomplished. The
majority at the institution were tenured. The most surprising aspect of
this study was that these women were not only tenured, but enjoyed a
campus that had three times as many minority faculty members than
most others of its type. This can attest to the fact that a critical mass is
helpful, but should not be a goal in and of itself.

Canada

In Canada, the *Report of the Royal Commission on the Status of
Women in Canada* indicated slightly higher completion rates than men
in several areas. Women, for example, received over 50 percent of all
bachelors' degrees awarded from 1955 to 1981, and the overall
percentage of women earning post-graduate degrees (20 percent of
masters' degrees and 8 percent of doctorates) have continued to
increase. In 1982, 40 percent of all masters' and 25 percent of all
doctoral degrees were awarded to women. Similarly, in 1989, women
earned 45 percent of all masters' and 30 percent of all doctoral
degrees. In 1992, these rates rose even higher to 47.8 percent of
masters' and 33.2 percent of doctorates.   Overall, the number of
women awarded doctoral degrees increased more than four-fold in
1971, while the corresponding percentages of increase for men was
merely 15 percent.
The numbers for academic faculty women are not as encouraging.
Between 1960 and 1980, the proportion of full women professors
increased by only 4.8 percent. At the same time, the proportion of
male professors with doctorates was 41 percent.

The climate for Canadian women is similar to that of their sisters in other parts of the world. Women continue to report they are marginalized, dismissed or ignored, the butt of discriminatory jokes, and otherwise treated unfairly (Lattin, 1983). In 1992, Symons and Page argued that Canadian faculty women were unfairly stereotyped (by gender, age, class, sexual orientation, disability, and religious or cultural affiliation), devalued, excluded and isolated, and revictimized.

The Canadian woman stated:

> The acknowledged inequitable situation of women in universities is a very complex and multi-faceted problem. It has only recently been recognized, that factors such as the 'chilly climate,' demanding family responsibilities, and the subtle lack of recognition of women's scholarship contribute to the...conundrum.

West Indies (Jamaica, Barbados and Trinidad-Tobago)

For Caribbean faculty, teaching still remained the primary work activity although research was required. None reported being overburdened with student advising, but almost half mentioned having more committee work than they would have liked. This can be explained, in part, by the following. Caribbean faculty reported: 1) greater autonomy in their departments and college; 2) having more dependents (children and elderly parents) living at home which required their attention; 3) more opportunities for international travel which precluded them from spending much time on campus; 4) and having more centralized academic departments which handled many administrative and advising functions. These women had higher rates of job satisfaction and were more likely to be tenured, although they reported having greater external barriers than their African American sisters in the states. This may be attributed to the lack of mobility options in the Caribbean and the ability to seek tenure more than once. More than 70 percent of the women surveyed had international teaching or research experience and a third had obtained a graduate degree in another country (Gregory, 1999).

The demands of caring for elderly parents were also concerns for Caribbean women. One Jamaican professor stated:

I think the main conflict I feel is really that of being a daughter. I think my mother brought us up to be very independent, but she is at a time now when she needs a lot of attention. It has also been very traumatic for me and I have also had to come to terms with myself by the fact that I have probably not been spending enough time with her, not making allowances for her or adapting to the changes that are happening in her life. So I think that has been one of the biggest conflicts. How do I deal with my mother and father as aging parents.

Another Jamaican professor expressed the same concern when she said:

Strangely enough, the greatest conflict I have now is taking care of my aging parents. I have increasing work demands because of the stage in my career, and I feel the tremendous pressure of my parents and mother-in-law making demands on me. These demands cannot be delegated to other members of my family because I am the only child here in Jamaica, so I have to face up to them and often I really get torn.

In addition, almost a quarter of these academic women perceived barriers to career advancement, such as personal factors, inability to manage role sets, personal demands of family, and limited upward mobility opportunities within the current institution. These barriers may influence some of these women to seek other opportunities, especially if they are prepared to leave the Caribbean. Although they may have sought more attractive career opportunities elsewhere, most accepted alternative administrative posts or a combination of teaching and administrative positions within the current institution.

Since Caribbean scholars are able to apply for tenure more than once at the same institution, they are less likely to leave after being denied tenure the first time, but are at a tremendous disadvantage. In this study, 25 percent of the Caribbean faculty women had been denied tenure at least once but chose to remain at the institution and try again.

Caribbean faculty women reported receiving greater resources for teaching and research but experienced similar events with regard to the existence of supportive colleagues. As one Indian woman from Trinidad-Tobago stated:

Being very ethnic I was often alone. I never had anyone to talk to
the way that you would with other colleagues. Being Indian I rarely
had anyone that I could share ideas with and whom I had similar
experiences with as a woman.

Virtually no racist practices were cited in the study and the few
discriminatory practices reported were more in regards to gender and
age, than ethnicity.

In contrast others have had more positive experiences. For
example, a professor from Barbados explained:

The best thing about my job now is that I have a certain amount of
control over my activities and what I do. Granted there are certain
deadlines of some things that I have to do, but I have basic control.
The other thing I like about my job is working with young people. I
find that tremendously satisfying. I find that their minds are very
sharp and keen. They are so full of energy and I just love to see that
and to hear their ideas. They renew you and give you fresh light and
they make me feel young as well. I think that that is the greatest
reason I am staying. I know that I am not going to get that from
outside academe. I do like that contact with the students and
sharing ideas with each other. There is something about that that is
special.

A Barbadian professor replied:

What I love most about the academy is the personal freedom that I
have. Although I have constraints here and there for class and
meetings or for students, there is a certain kind of intellectual
freedom as well. I think I like that best. I can write whatever I wish
in certain areas and explore what I like. I like that.

For Caribbean faculty women, this was less of a concern regarding
scholarship because there was a common understanding of which
journals were more competitive and rigorous. However, a few
Caribbean women who published pieces on gender development did
report experiencing difficulty in gaining respect from some of their
male counterparts.

Comparatively, academic women from Jamaica, Barbados and
Trinidad-Tobago did differ in several respects. Demographically,
Jamaica is a little more than twice the size (in square miles) of

Trinidad-Tobago and more than 26 times the size of Barbados. The population of Jamaica is 2.4 million, as compared to 1.25 million in Trinidad-Tobago and only 259,000 in Barbados (United Nations, 1991, 1994). Barbados also has the lowest illiteracy rate in the Caribbean at less than one (.9) percent, as compared to Trinidad-Tobago at 9.7 percent and Jamaica at 4.5 percent. Not surprisingly, every faculty woman from Barbados had household help (100 percent) and spent the least amount of time on household chores (23 hours a week as compared to 26 and 31 hours). Women from Trinidad-Tobago were most likely to have dependents (87.5 percent, as compared to 54 and 64 percent) and most likely to be married (93.8 percent, as compared to 23 and 54 percent).

In terms of professional characteristics, faculty women from Trinidad-Tobago were most likely to be tenured, but least likely to obtain tenure the first time around. The four academic disciplines most represented in the study were Biology, Social Science, Sociology, and Literature. Jamaican faculty women had the highest job satisfaction rate and Trinidad-Tobago had the lowest. In Jamaica, the Mona campus was by far the largest of the three and therefore had greater on-site resources. Trinidad-Tobago is the farthest island in the Caribbean Sea located just off the tip of Caracas, Venezuela and is somewhat isolated. When asked to identify obstacles to professional achievement, faculty women from Jamaica and Trinidad-Tobago both cited research inequities, while Barbados faculty reported academic climate. Barbados is one of the wealthiest (per capita) islands in the Caribbean and is relatively small. When asked which factors they considered most important for individual success and achievement, integrity was most often cited as their first or second choice and professional reputation along with scholarship rounded out the most common second and third choices. Family life was reported fourth. The most common variable of job satisfaction was unanimously a sense of accomplishment, followed by personal autonomy, and support for teaching. In terms of salary, Barbadian faculty women were paid the most and faculty from Trinidad-Tobago were paid nearly 40 percent less. However, faculty women from Barbados were most likely to have tenure and therefore have higher salaries. In addition, the cost of living difference between Barbados and Trinidad-Tobago was as significant as comparing the cost of living between California and Mississippi or between Cairo and Hurghada. The Barbados dollar was also much stronger, although the unemployment rate in Barbados was the highest of the three.

In summary, those Caribbean women who chose to remain in the academy represented a total of over 68 percent of the sample and had three major characteristics. First, they had the highest rate of job satisfaction (.72, as compared to .64 for those who return and .48 for those who leave), achieved the highest academic faculty rank (3.68, 3.20 and 2.84, respectively), and were most likely to hold tenure (.62, .46 and .28, respectively). The mobility rate for Caribbean scholars was not quite as high as for African American scholars. This may possibly be explained in part because Caribbean faculty had the opportunity to go up for tenure more than once, although they often have little choice of academic institutions unless they choose to leave the Caribbean altogether.

Japan

In Japan, the government helped to establish and develop the modern universities and therefore, has continued to exert strong influence on university governance. As a result of the 1991 Standards for the Establishment of Universities Act, numerous changes are currently underway in Japanese universities. These changes will result in reforms of the curriculum, university self-monitoring and self-evaluation, and a host of other initiatives. In Japan, private colleges and universities are centralized much like their counterparts in the United States, but Japanese public universities are decentralized. Therefore in public universities, faculty have input into the hiring of colleagues and promotion and tenure. In most cases, faculty decisions in public universities carry more weight than decisions made by administrators. The Japanese Ministry of Education determines the total budget for each public university and has the power to make appointments, although faculty can make recommendations. This in not the case for Japanese private universities (Clark, 1983).

Academia in Japan continues to be dominated by men, especially in public universities. Fifty percent of full-time Japanese faculty were full professors, and the other half were associate professors. Most full professors were in private institutions. Tenure in Japan was not an issue because faculty members automatically receive tenure once employed, guaranteeing the status, rights, and employment as professors as long as they did not neglect their duties. In Ehara's 1998 study, over 90 percent of Japanese faculty said they felt their job was guaranteed until retirement. This had tremendous financial implications for Japanese institutions because an increasing number of the faculty were young when they joined the academy. More than 30 percent also reported working part-time at another institution.

In Japan, teaching-oriented faculty were in the minority in both public (15.3 percent) and private (38.5 percent) institutions, as compared to more than 60 percent of U.S. faculty in both private and public institutions. Nearly 70 percent of Japanese faculty reported that their administrators supported academic freedom. In addition, nearly 80 percent reported that they can determine course content, almost 90 percent stated they can research any topics of interest, and 80 percent said academic freedom was protected in Japan.

In terms of job satisfaction, Japanese faculty rated the opportunity to pursue one's own ideas the highest, followed by security and assigned courses. The lowest job satisfaction rate involved the way in which institutions were managed.

China

In China in 1987, there were 17,087 faculty in Chinese colleges and universities and of those, 1,570 (or 9.2 percent) were women who worked in the following disciplines: medical science (52 percent); science (13.9 percent); engineering (10.5 percent); art and literature (9.3 percent); agronomy (7.1 percent); economics (2.5 percent); pedagogy (2.4) percent; history (1.3 percent); philosophy (0.6 percent); and law (0.4 percent).

The average age of women professors was 60.9 as compared to 61.7 for men. The youngest woman professor was 37 and the eldest was 89. The average age women faculty women graduated was 24.5 years. Most faculty women work in the cities where most of the colleges and universities are located. Those working in Beijing and the surrounding coastal provinces account for 59.4 percent of the total number of faculty women in China.

Only 5.3 percent of faculty women reported studying abroad. Of those, a third had left China for advanced study abroad in the late 1970s and early 1980s before they received their doctorates. The majority of women professors were appointed after the reforms of the 1970s and 1980s.

Korea

In Korea, private universities that received no governmental support, educated approximately 76 percent of all students and employed 69 percent of all faculty (Ministry of Education, 1990). Ewha Women's University was founded in 1886 by the first woman missionary sent by the United States Methodist Episcopal Church. Prior to 1886, women had been denied access to education in Korea. Although the college was forced out of Seoul in 1950, Ewha returned in 1953 to rebuild. Today, Ewha offers a high quality education and is considered a first-class university by the Ministry of Education. The university offers bachelors, masters, and doctorate degrees, maintains an enrollment of 15,500 students, and has a healthy supply (roughly 50 percent) of faculty women.

Yonsei is the oldest and largest university in Korea serving over 30,000 students in 74 different undergraduate programs and 9 graduate schools. Yonsei has numerous research institutes and houses the largest medical complex in all of Asia. Overall, women at Yonsei represented roughly 10-15 percent of all faculty, although some department had no women faculty (such as the business department) and others represented more than 15 percent.

In a 1984 study of Korean faculty women, Lee Hie Sung reported that women generally perceived the achievement process to be "smooth and uneventful" (p. 226). Many mentioned the support of family and husbands. Furthermore, participants reported no "serious role conflict" (p. 227) in their experiences as professors, wives, and mothers, although time constraints were a common complaint. These results may be explained by the fact that these women were all employed at prestigious women's universities where women were dominant.

Cho Hyoung (1986) argued that there continues to be indirect pressures to maintain male dominance in the professional sector. She mentioned, for example, that the enrollment of women in teachers colleges has been restricted to accommodate the need and concern that woman teachers "feminize" school-boys (p. 168). Even though women comprised of 28 percent of college students in 1989, only 17 percent of professors were women (Ministry of Education, 1990). Faculty and other Korean professional women are still expected to perform the dual roles of a career woman and domestic caretaker (Lee Dong-won, 1986).

In a 1995 study, Johnsrud found that Korean faculty women identified three sets of experiences that include: 1) difficulty in obtaining a faculty position; 2) the tasks and priorities they balance in their professional lives; and 3) the pressure of personal responsibilities that affected performance and a sense of accomplishment. These problems were exacerbated by the high faculty-student ratio of 1:40, and the low faculty turnover. In addition, faculty men knew that once a woman was hired, there was virtually no way to get rid of them (Johnsrud, 1993). It was not uncommon for Korean faculty to teach three or sometimes four courses in a semester. Faculty women especially had a difficult time securing a full-time position because the part-time women in line for a position were well-educated and had quality credentials so competition was steep. Academic women and men worked long hours advising, teaching, administering, researching and writing (Johnsrud, 1993)

In summary, Korean women recognized the challenges in maintaining family, students, and career obligations and Korean academic men expect them to be less productive professionally. They do not feel, for the most part, that they are unfairly treated because of gender.

Norway

In Scandinavian Norway, the ideals of equality and neutrality allegedly guaranteed that benefits are equally distributed among people, however, women were treated differently. Scandinavia presupposes a society where men were responsible for production and women were responsible for reproduction (Skrede, 1988). As a result, the labor market had a dearth of professional women due to family obligation, lack of childcare, and poor pension rights.

In terms of education, Norway did not have as many doctorate-holding faculty, as in the United States. In 1985, only 40 percent of tenured men and 14 percent of tenured women had doctorates (Olsen, 1988). Kyvik (1990) found that academic men were more productive than academic women. Men published an average of 5 articles or their equivalents, as compared to 3.5 for women. Overall, women published roughly 30 percent less than men, although this rate was influenced by faculty status, rank, and age. The difference in the percentage of productivity was smallest in the sciences (20 percent) and associate professor women were just as productive as their male counterparts. According to Cole (1987) and Long (1987), the differences in the productivity of Norwegian academic by gender was associated with personal characteristics, such as age, marital status and age of children, rather than gender.

In the Kyvik study, women had higher entrance grades than men, but men had slightly better examination results. Furthermore, fewer women (63 percent) had regular contact with their colleagues than men (75 percent) with regard to their research. Women (70 percent) also received less funding than men (81 percent) from outside their institutions. Cole (1987) reported that both Norwegian women and men spent about the same amount of hours on teaching and administration per week, but women spent two hours less on research per week. Men in the study were more likely to be married and have larger families. Women, of course, were at a disadvantage because they did not have wives to handle the children and household. Surprisingly, women without children were less productive than women with children, married women were more productive than single women, and married women with children published more books than single women. The higher productivity for married women may be explained by the support married women received from their spouse and family, relatively more stable social lives, the reduced threat of a married faculty colleague who puts family first, and the increased stamina and drive needed to raise children (Gregory, 1995; Luukhonen-Gronow, 1987).

Women faced several barriers in Norway. They were less integrated in their respective institutions, received fewer resources, and spent less time on research. Personally, academic women in Norway (64 percent) indicated discontinuity in their careers, while men's careers were rarely interrupted. This may be the result of inadequate childcare. Because academic women earned good salaries, they could not access public day care. Norway only accommodates roughly 25 percent of the women who need childcare and Norway has been cited (Kaul and Brandth, 1988) to have the worst access to childcare in Western Europe with the exception of Portugal.

West Germany

In West Germany, there are fewer faculty women than most other European countries. Women constitute almost 40 percent of the student population but less than 5 percent of full-time professors and the numbers are declining. These numbers have contributed to the marginal status of faculty women (Kanter, 1977). The only slight increase of faculty women has been in the assistant and associate professor ranks (Schultz, 1990). Many departments do not have any women who are full professors, so very rarely will junior female faculty be mentored by senior faculty women. In fact, thesis advisors in West Germany are called 'doctoral fathers.' Faculty men in West Germany universities are known for their dominance and exclusion of faculty women (Lipman-Blumen, 1976). Although there is clear data indicating that gender discrimination exists among faculty, women deny they have been victims.

Personally, West German women spend a lot of time and energy deciding whether or not to be become involved in a relationship and have children. Some women were already caring for aging parents and that alone was an enormous mental, emotional, and physical strain. For men, having children is not an issue because they were not responsible or obligated for their day-to-day care. Faculty women often reported feeling isolated in their departments and some openly admitted to being a victim of discrimination (Hawkins and Schultz, 1990).

Netherlands

In the Netherlands, governmental statistics have indicated that overall there is an increase in the number of women employed in universities.   But women were more likely to hold part-time, temporary positions. Furthermore, women were much less likely to be hired and promoted than men to permanent posts in universities during times of retrenchment. A 1984 study (Hawkins and Van Balen) revealed that the presence of women in academe had deteriorated rather than improved, with women still concentrated in the lowest ranks and in only a handful of disciplines. For example, in 1988 the number of full women professors in the Netherlands had declined to 2.1 percent, down from 2.7 percent in 1970. Similarly in 1988, associate women professors accounted for 4.6 percent, down from 9.4 percent, while the number of women assistant professors rose from 11.8 in 1970 to 14.7 in 1988 (Hawkins and Van Balen, 1984).

In an attempt to reduce the cost of graduating each student, numerous measures were introduced in the 1980s that put faculty women at a greater disadvantage. First, several small departments (such as modern language) where women tended to excel, were merged or eliminated altogether (roughly 33 percent). Second, academics ranks were redefined. The position of assistant professor (*lektor*) was eliminated. New faculty were appointed at the *lektor* level but with the title of full professor. As a result, assistant professors had to reapply for their own positions. Just a third of the assistant professors were reappointed and women only constituted a few.

Professionally, women in the Netherlands (Hawkins and Schultz, 1990) were found to be just as productive as men and just as likely to hold advanced degrees, although it took women longer to complete their doctoral work. The greatest gender difference was with regard to external funding for research. Women were less likely to apply, and therefore less likely to be granted research funds. Women also were less likely to be appointed to and serve on influential university committees.

Britain

In Britain in the early 1970s, collective bargaining was established for academic and related staff in UK universities. Although there was a little flexibility to allow universities to recruit and retain scarce staff, salary scales for appointments were introduced according to age and progression was based on years of tenure (AUT, 1992). In 1989, performance-related pay we introduced and decentralization of pay bargaining was no longer considered.

In 1990, the *Report of the Hansard Society Commission on Women at the Top* reported that women were under-represented in positions of responsibility and influence in professional labour markets as a whole. Furthermore, they indicated that universities in Britain had one of the lowest proportions of senior women employees in all of the professions (Hansard Society Commission, 1990). In terms of compensation, *Britain's Association of University Teachers* (AUT) Report indicated that in 1989-90, academic women earned 16 percent less then men in comparable positions. In addition, the number of women on short-term contracts was more than a quarter which was more than any other profession in Britain (Aziz, 1990). In 1986 and 1987, more than 60 percent of the women who were recruited, received short-term contracts. The use of short-term contracts exploited those on them because pay increases were rare with contract renewals, positions were not secure and they did not receive health and other benefits. In 1990, a British newspaper (*The Independent*) article estimated that sex bias in the United Kingdom was robbing women workers of about 15 billion (in British pounds) a year.

In Britain, readers and senior lecturers were considered the career grades and were equivalent to the combination of assistant and associate professors. These two positions were usually internal appointment and only a restricted number were allocated for any given year throughout the university. Professorships are sometimes internal appointments but were often nationally advertised. Rarely would you find more than one or two in any one department and they could only be appointed to that rank if the previous position had been vacated.

Overall, the employment of academic women had increased from 10 percent in 1975 to 16 percent in 1992. British academics also indicated low levels of career mobility. Women were found to be disproportionately under-represented in senior positions in the sciences and engineering. For example in 1992, 5 percent of professors were women (3 percent in 1975), 10 percent were readers and senior lecturers (6 percent in 1975), and women lecturers accounted for 30 percent (12 percent in 1975). Both in 1975 and 1992, the highest proportion of women were found in the disciplines of the arts (16 percent) and medicine (21 percent). The smallest numbers of faculty women were located in the disciplines of science (6 percent) and engineering (2 percent) (McNabb and Wass, 1997). Because women were scattered in sparse number across the disciplines, they lacked a critical mass and rarely held positions of influence.

According to Bagilhole (1993), women academics in British universities made up a small minority and were concentrated in the lower ranks. She studied a group of 43 women and found that they suffered from isolation and exclusion from their male colleagues, and were often challenged by their male students. In addition, they had fewer support systems, few role models or mentors, and little access to communication networks. They reported problems with work relationships and experienced hostility from male colleagues and students. These challenges created an environment where women felt pressured to perform better than their male counterparts to avoid being identified with female stereotypes.

In the McNabb and Wass study (1997), women academic were clearly career oriented and had high levels of human capital until their careers were interrupted. Sloane and Theodossiou (1993) and Jones and Makepeace (1995) suggest that period of inactivity for faculty women were associated with child rearing and other domestic activities. Lazear and Rosen (1990) suggested that employers set higher standards for women because they expect them to be absent and have their careers interrupted. They further argued that this has made it difficult for women to obtain promotions. Therefore, the lack of promotions for academic women influenced salary differentials based on gender.

A Cambridge University study (Spurling, 1990) reported that British women academics experience strain caused by conflict between home and work. This was understandable because women were overwhelmingly in part-time, temporary, short-term of low-level positions. Furthermore, they often needed to attend late meetings and had little access to childcare and were further discriminated against by age restrictions on certain positions and funding. In Acker's 1992 article, she mentions her post-it pad from the United States that is entitled 'the careers woman's checklist for success,' which reads: "Look like a lady, act like a man, and work like a dog."

Bagilhole (1993) argues that British faculty women lack confidence in their ability to be successful in the academy. She states:

> The majority have become convinced that the concept of a woman is a paradox. They have become convinced that they do not really belong. This can lead them to react by putting considerable pressure on themselves to perform better than their male colleagues and to avoid being identified with other women. This means that the women who do succeed as 'honorary men,' are in no position to support other women, and the process continues (p. 446).

Australia

In Australia, there are 19 universities in its states and territories. They range from the large institutions, like Queensland with 2,632 academics, to smaller institutions like Deakin in Victoria with 284 academics. All universities have some women at the rank of senior lecturer or above except Griffith, Flinders, Murdoch, and Tasmania which have no women professors. Macquarie University had the greatest number of senior academic women (17.1 percent), while Tasmania had the least (3.6 percent). However, those institutions with the highest numbers of senior women faculty also had the highest numbers of junior women faculty.

After the enormous growth experienced in Australian universities during the 1960s, 70s, and 80s, the expansion among academic faculty has ceased. In fact, the low-rate (fewer than 4 percent in 1983) at which senior appointments become vacant through resignation, retirement, or death, severely limits career advancement for current faculty and career prospects of graduating doctoral students. Therefore, fewer graduates are likely to choose the academic profession. Women were particularly disadvantaged because many who entered the system during the expansion period were finding that there were no opportunities for career advancement. Furthermore, women were most represented in the humanities, education, and social and behavioral sciences disciplines where competition was even greater. With the average age of retirement at 65 and no early retirement incentives, few positions are expected to become available (Over, 1985).

In June 1995, the Sydney Morning Herald (Australia) printed an article by a prominent academic, Dame Leonie Kramer. She contended that "women go limp when things get tough..." The study involved seven women in senior management positions in Australian universities. As a whole, they had not followed traditional career paths and had all been derailed at various times because of family commitments. Mentoring had been very important for them, whether it had been a woman or man. And all of them had found creative ways to play out agendas in environments that were uncomfortable and constraining. Finally, all of the women had a clear since of purpose and were resolute in their determination to bring about changes in their respective institutions, through clearly articulated policies and practices.

Between 1989 and 1992, women accounted for 22 percent of lecturers, 6 percent of senior lecturers, and only 3 percent of professors among full-time faculty in Australia. In addition, women were paid salaries on average 16.1 percent less than men of comparable rank (AUT, 1992, Halsey, 1992) even thought they were just as likely than men to have a Ph.D.

In Australia, career advancement was highly correlated with research publication (Over, 1993). The Over study found that men and women published roughly the same amount of research, but men were most likely to publish a book than women. Personally, women were on average older than men when they completed their post doctoral degree and gained their first tenure position. Also, women were less likely to have overseas academic qualifications, more likely to be employed in the departments where they had trained, and most likely to have family responsibilities and commitments conflict with their professional lives. Finally, faculty women were less confident about career advancement at their present institutions.

In a 1993 study (Romanin and Over), Australian academic women were found to spend more time outside of the workforce than men due to childcare responsibilities. In addition, they frequently moved as result of a spouse's job, and were most likely to have recently held a non-tenured position. Women also reported that they experienced unfavorable treatment for appointments, promotion, tenure and study leave.

Numerous studies (Baldwin, 1985; Bramley and Ward, 1972; Davies, 1982) have examined women's participation in academic employment and found that the growth rate for women is slow and they tended to be in the lowest ranks because of: 1) selection and promotion procedures; 2) low levels of turnover; 3) the reluctance of women to apply for positions; 4) conflicts between academic employment and domestic responsibilities; and 5) gender-based differences in academic merit.

Overall, Australian academic women are less likely to enjoy tenure and the job security it provided, superannuation, study leave, and maternity leave. Only 1 in 16 academic were full-time faculty women and women were still concentrated among the lowest ranks. Allen (1990) argued that there has been almost no change in the rank of women academic over the last decade.

New Zealand

In New Zealand universities, women accounted for 22 percent of the full-time faculty in 1991. Academic patterns indicated that they were primarily located in the lower ranks. For example, women only comprised 4 percent of professors, 7 percent of associate professors, and 49 percent of all assistant lecturers (Ministry of Education, 1992).

A 1996 study (Vasil) of 655 academic faculty from the six major universities in New Zealand revealed numerous gender differences. Academic men were found to be more productive than academic women, and had significantly stronger self-efficacy perceptions than females in the area of self-promotion skills (developing strategies to promote oneself, negotiating/applying for promotions, and evaluating a colleague for promotion). Academic women were found to be least confident in areas that involved "playing the system." For example, men occupied the overwhelming majority of senior positions so they were the ones who, for the most part, determined promotion and tenure decisions.

India

In India, the teacher has traditionally been a position of great social eminence second only to one's parents. A teacher is the 'guru' or 'learned one' in Indian society. The teaching profession is considered to be the most venerated and respectable career.

The history of education for women in India dates back to the Vedic period of 1500 to 600 BC. Women were teachers, philosophers, and poets (Altekar, 1962). Once a woman sought education she could become a student for life and devote all her time to study and meditation, which was called *Brahmvadinis*. If they chose to end their education to marry, they were called *Sadyovadhus*. During the post-Vedic period, from around 500 BC to 500 AD, the caste system marked the deterioration in the status of women. The code of *Manu* (or *Manusmriti*) described the rights and obligations of men and women. According to *Manu*, females were to be subordinate to males and females were denied their right to study scriptures, become educated, and to remain unmarried. *Manu* clearly stated that the father had authority over the daughter during childhood, her husband in youth, and her son when she was elderly (Liddle and Joshi, 1986.)

When Buddhism was introduced, it assigned an honoured place to women in society. However, the impact on the status and education of women was limited because only the nuns (or *Upasikas*) had access to education, culture and social service. Some of these nuns did, however, achieve distinction as scholars, poets, thinkers and writers (Kuppuswamy, 1986).

Once Buddhism faded and Muslim rule was instituted, women suffered even worse. The Hindu social order and principles of ascribed caste became much more rigid, such as very early marriages, the dowry system, *sati* (the sacrifice of a wife together with her dead husband on his funeral pyre), *purdah* (observance of segregation of women from men), and *kulinism* (kulin Brahman practice where men could take several wives to increase the wealth of his *kul* [clan] and status) which were most prevalent among high-caste Hindus and upper-class Muslims (Sharma, 1981). The exceptions were low-caste rural women and noble women. Low-caste rural women who were uneducated, had the freedom to divorce and remarry, and travel and work in agriculture together with men (Kuppuswamy, 1986). Women of nobility had much greater social freedom and a few became eminent women scholars, administrators and rulers (Sharma, 1981). The status of women continued to decline until the late 1700s (Altekar, 1962).

In the mid 1700s during British rule, Indian women were still unequal to men and the British were reluctant to institute policies toward women's rights out of respect for traditional social, and religious cultural values, and norms. Schools were segregated by gender, tuition was extremely high, and transportation had to be provided because of distance. Compounded walls were built around the girl's schools to protect them from the view of outsiders. Traditionally, marriage of young girls among Hindus and Muslims resulted in many illiterate girls who were forced out of school. This is one reason there were very few women teachers (Gill, 1990). It was not until the 19th century during British rule when social reforms emphasized liberal views towards women. During this time, *sati* and the marriage of children under the age of 12 was made illegal. It was not until 1870 that training colleges for women were established and with the recommendations of the Education Commission in 1882, India began to see women teachers in girl's schools.

Unlike the Western experience, Indian women freely entered higher education in 1877 and Calcutta University was the first to permit women to sit for the entrance and BA examinations. Bombay University began admitting women in 1883, followed by London University in 1878. Oxford and Cambridge did not begin to admit women until after World War I (Government of India, 1975). Even though these women had access, the purpose of a woman's education was seen as a vehicle for making her more capable of fulfilling her traditional roles. The few thousand or so women who were educated during this period were from mostly middle and upper-class urban families and were typically Christian, Anglo-Indian, Parsi, or upper-caste Hindu.

In 1981, female literacy rose from 7.8 percent in 1951, to 24.9 percent. But today, three-quarters of all Indian women and half of all Indian men are illiterate. Even today, those women in India with a college education are few. In 1971, the government of India reported that only 0.3 percent of women had graduated from a college or university. The enrollment of women increased from 23 percent in 1974 to 29 percent in 1985 (Government of India, 1985).

In 1985, the University Grants Commission stipulated that at least 30 percent of research fellowships be awarded to women candidates. The distribution of enrollments in India by discipline in 1985 was: 48 percent education, 39 percent in arts, 29 percent science, 27 percent medicine, 18 percent commerce, and 7 percent law, 5 percent engineering and technology, 5 percent veterinary sciences, and 4 percent agriculture (University Grants Commission, 1985). In 1980, faculty women represented 22 percent of all faculty in general education colleges, 14 percent in professional educational colleges, and 10 percent in research institutions (Association of Indian Universities, 1987).

In India, the highest rank is professor, followed by associate professor, reader or associate lecturer, assistant professor and lecturer. Most women are college lecturers and very few are professors or readers. Most universities stipulate that lecturers who do not complete a Ph.D. of Masters of Philosophy within 8 years of appointment cannot be considered for future salary increases. Upward mobility is not common in the academic profession and most college lecturers actually retire at the same professional status as when they began their careers. This trend has resulted in many young, bright educators seeking positions outside of academe and low self-esteem and apathy among lectures currently in the position (Bali, 1986 and Nayar, 1988).

The attitude of faculty women about the existence of gender discrimination has been mixed. Many denied inequities existed at all (5 percent), while others perceived themselves directly responsible (15 percent). Twenty percent felt discrimination began once they were recruited and 90 percent believed they were denied equal wages because of gender. Over seventy-five percent felt they had to be much better qualified than their male counterparts in the same position (Gill, 1990).

In summary, Indian women have significantly improved their status, however gender equality has not yet been achieved. Gill argues, "Women academics live in two worlds: the one in which they are a privileged social elite, the other where they are less equal" (p. 192).

Israel

In Israel, the academic labor market is segregated by gender. Women only account for 12 percent of faculty and the profession is still seen as inappropriate for women (Toren, 1990). Faculty women in Israel are primarily in the following disciplines: 31.3 percent in education, 18.3 percent in humanities, 16 percent in social work, 15.2 percent in law and criminology, and 11.3 percent in sociology. The disciplines with the least number of faculty women were architecture 3.4 percent and the natural sciences at 8.4 percent.

In Israel, there does not tend to be any gender differences with regard to working conditions. All faculty have a Ph.D or equivalent, salaries are primarily based on rank and seniority, teaching loads are the same, and most emphasize research.

In a study of full professors in Israel, gender was not considered to be a factor in the academic careers of faculty women (Torren, 1990). A majority of the 33 women interviewed reported they did not perceive themselves as being discriminated against based on gender. Furthermore, they viewed their success as a result of personal ability and effort. Women averaged roughly four years longer to progress to full professor as a result of personal decisions regarding family and scholarship.

Turkey

In Turkey prior to 1923, most of the Turks adhered to the strict Islamic religious code.   Women were subordinate to men and polygamy was encouraged.   In the mid-1920s, the state of the Turkish Republic enacted a series of reforms in an effort to give women equal status with men.   The reforms encouraged higher education for women and career orientation.   Since household help was reasonably cheap and most families were extended, women could pursue careers (Kandiyoti, 1982).

In Turkey, 32 percent of all academics were women and part of a elite group (Acar, 1989).   According to Kandiyoti, other members of this elite group of women included attorneys (20 percent) and physicians (30 percent).

In a 1983 study, Acar found that faculty women from Turkey appeared to have no doubt about pursuing an academic career as opposed to not working or being a housewife.   They were highly career-motivated and ambitious.   Although most were married, they had chosen partners with similar views and some planned the births of their children during summer breaks so it would not interfere with their position.   However, as professional demands escalated for both faculty women and their partners, so did the role conflict for women between responsibilities of career and family.   To cope, many women choose to compartmentalize or integrate their family and career responsibilities, but most took on more than they could effectively manage (Erkut, 1982).   The women were determined to succeed because they viewed their education as an investment and felt guilty if they were to waste it by deciding to leave academe.

Jordan

In Jordan, the traditional Muslim Arab heritage encouraged education. More recently, it has encouraged political equality that has allowed women to find high-status careers in the public and private sectors. Many men, on the other hand, have left Jordan seeking white-collar positions elsewhere (Zaghal, 1984).

Acar's 1983 study indicated that Jordanian academic women had little initial interest of obtaining a faculty position.   In fact most said they would have really enjoyed doing something else other than teach. Many chose academic careers because they would be able to travel abroad, live in a campus town, or to continue their education. One unmarried Jordan lecturer who had returned home after obtaining her Master's degree in the states said:

> I am now planning to go abroad to get my Ph.D., but I am awaiting for a family decision. A while ago, I got a contract for a job (in another Arab country) but my family said 'no way.' It actually offered good money and I would have liked to try it. But I could not. You see, it is OK to go abroad to study but not to work (Acar, p. 133)

Jordanian academic women indicated that their careers were not their first priority. Families often supported women in obtaining an education but not always a job (Barhoum, 1983). A woman's responsibility inside the home was still considered more important than her career by women and men alike. Because household obligations were given top priority and did not conflict with career responsibilities, Jordanian women reported experiencing very little role conflict and discontinuity in their role perceptions (Acar, 1983).

In summary, Jordanian faculty women viewed their roles as mothers and wives to be more important than their careers and therefore, were professionally passive, rather than competitive or ambitious. As a result, they were not a threat to their male counterparts or to traditional Jordan gender roles.

Egypt

In the past four decades, women of the Third World have achieved significant gains in level of education, but these gains have improved very slowly over time. In Egypt, women still face substantial educational disadvantages and very few women are in the tertiary levels of education. Some of the disadvantages include the need for women to tend to the household, the opportunity costs of a girls education and a woman's employment.

Many studies indicate that the higher the income of the family, the greater the desire of parents for their daughters' education. In addition, the higher the education level of the parents, the greater their tendency to favor education for their daughters. In rural and poor families, the education of girls was seen as worthy of consideration only up to marriageable levels. In traditional societies, cultural practices such as bride's dowry, affected the education of women. The amount of dowry demanded by the bridegroom depended on his educational and occupational background, so the higher these were, the more dowry parents must pay. Poor parents, therefore, preferred to have uneducated daughters because they tended to marry less educated men who commanded a smaller dowry

A study of 1,700 husbands and wives in rural and urban Egypt areas found that the two most consistent factors affecting a students enrollment were the educational aspirations of the father and those of the mother (Cochrane, Mehra and Osheba, 1985). Women's career choices were significantly affected by social and cultural norms. In many Third World countries, certain professions must be formally defined as "female" before women may join them. The Ministry of Education had encouraged access by women to such professions as nursing and teaching (Meleis, El-Sanabary & Beeson, 1979).

Several reasons have been given to help explain the condition of women's education and achievement in the Third World. Cultural norms and the division of labor within the home tend to function to the detriment of girls and women. The level of a woman's education constitutes a key indicator of their condition in society. Although education does not assure women access to employment, without it their chances of attaining formal employment and well-numerated occupations are extremely limited. Those women in the higher socioeconomic classes, however, experience less restriction in gaining access to academia, but were limited to a certain number of fields of study. Furthermore, their experiences once they enter the academic environment tended to reinforce rather than challenge the division of labor by gender (Stromquist, 1989).

In conclusion, faculty women around the world, with the exception of a few privileged elite, are still disproportionately in the lower ranks and primarily in traditional disciplines. In the face of tremendous challenges, academic women are discovering new and creative ways to cope, while maintaining quality in their professional and personal lives. They are also working towards achieving equality in education and employment. It is through education that women can gain better knowledge of how to organize their lives and acquire attitudes that may challenge the prevailing social and gender order.

IX. *Where Do We Go From Here?*

RECOMMENDATIONS TO POLICYMAKERS

Daily academic life for many Black women scholars, as well as for other minority and international women scholars, is very different than that of White faculty men. Differences range from their language to their daily experiences in academic life. Some women and minority faculty have reported that the quality of work-life experiences are inferior to that of their majority peers. For example, minority scholars have often reported the need to continuously prove their capabilities. Black faculty also experience numerous barriers, such as the lack of access to resources, tokenism, exclusion from important groups, and disproportionate service demands interfering with tenure and promotion. Black faculty women also have continuously cited extraordinary time demands placed upon them because of their relatively small numbers. Unfortunately, Black faculty women also have fewer institutional support systems. Menges and Exum (1983) have contended that working in the academy requires not only securing positions, but surviving promotion and tenure as well.

Racial and sexual discrimination has also been a reality that many academic women face. In 1985, Moore and Wagstaff found that over 95 percent of all Black faculty reported discriminatory activity by persons within their institutions. Among Black academic administrators, Hoskins (1978) found that the primary reason Black administrators reported leaving predominantly White institutions was because of limited opportunities for promotion, as well as perceived racial discrimination. McCombs (1989) has argued that "for blacks, the challenge is to enter and remain within the university and perform all responsibilities without losing integrity. The central problems of isolation, alienation, promotion, and tenure play an important role in determining who will remain" (p. 141).

Unfortunately, many academic departments around the country fail to provide adequate support to women and minority faculty, which is reflected in the number, salary, and rank of minority and faculty women. Departments can provide support in numerous ways and many are not as costly as one would expect. Several examples include encouraging service activities with system-wide visibility and compensation for service overload; integrating ethnic and gender related materials into the curriculum and pedagogy; accepting differences in teaching styles, curriculum, and research foci; and encouraging collaborative projects by providing resources and funding. Since research indicates that a greater value is placed on publication, institutions should provide faculty rewards, encourage faculty to discuss articles in progress, and support cross-fertilization to avoid isolated research projects (Swoboda, 1990).

It is evident that we still have much work to do to encourage the permanence of minority and international women scholars. Regardless of talent, a faculty member cannot reasonably function in an inhospitable academic environment. In order to attract and retain successful Black scholars, the quality of life at the institution and within the department should be appropriately evaluated. First, new faculty should be given clear guidelines, both oral and written regarding the expectations and requirements for tenure and promotion. Examples illustrating the level and quality of scholarly work should be readily available. Since women and minority faculty tend to be at greatest risk for disproportionately high service demands, departments should protect against service overload and offset as needed. Second, new faculty should be given supportive mentors of both genders inside and outside the department. Colleges may want to consider giving senior faculty service credit or other rewards for mentorships. Third, regular performance reviews should include input from mentors, and persons (minority and majority) who are familiar with the faculty member's research. Fourth, accountability should be allocated on the part of department chairs, deans, and vice chancellors to ensure active participation in the recruitment, support, and retention of faculty members. Fifth, departments should consider providing supportive arrangements for faculty with families with regard to time and tenure. Sixth, institutions should reassess how teaching, research, and service are defined and create new standards for research and pedagogy. And finally, the frequent concern of isolation must be addressed for Black faculty women, as well as other women and minorities. Colleges should offer faculty greater opportunity to become involved in their academic departments and institutions, as well as working with other Black, minority, and women colleagues (Swoboda, 1990).

NEW DIRECTIONS FOR FUTURE RESEARCH

In light of the previous discussion, the research possibilities are robust. First, findings in this study indicate a need to improve upon the research design by adding additional variables most likely to be associated with the career mobility of Black, minority and international faculty women. The study might also consider the inclusion of both voluntary and involuntary leavers to determine whether or not involuntary movement can account for a greater degree of variance.

Second, as mentioned earlier, the family structures of most Black families are very different from the nuclear families most scholars have previously researched. Black families often include extended families, such as grandparents, aunts, uncles and other relatives, friends, neighbors, community folk, and church members. Future research needs to recognize extended families in the context of the Black culture. For example, when examining support systems for Black families, it is important, but difficult, to capture all of the complex familial relationships involved in operationalizing the variables, such as family and support systems. In this study, significant others and elderly parents living in the household were considered part of the family unit. Future research needs to go further in defining these complex variables, ultimately providing more information on the roles of extended families and support systems.

Third, a longitudinal study that examines the dynamics of each career move within and outside the academy needs to be made. Necessary variables would include: the time the decision was made; the immediate family circumstance at the time of the decision; the current and future salary; and the comparable alternative salary in the academic and nonacademic marketplace. The timing of respondents' answers were also important. For example, if the questions are asked at the time in which events occur, a respondent's memory will be more sound, whereas asking respondents their salaries in a position they held several years prior, may not provide accurate responses.

Job satisfaction can also cause a similar problem. By collecting better data in a more timely manner, responses will likely be more accurate. Longitudinal studies could provide a wealth of data about the major correlates of academic mobility, and may possibly uncover a number of influences not revealed here. In light of the few numbers of Black men doctorate recipients, a study which compared these finds with a similar group of Black faculty men would contribute greatly to this untapped area of research. A better description of these career experiences could give additional data to offer possible alternative explanations that influence the propensity to leave.

Fourth, this study suggests that there is a positive relationship between job satisfaction and the decision to remain in, return to, or voluntarily leave the academy. To determine the significant factors associated with a high job satisfaction rate among academic women (remainers and returners), the author conducted a T-test on the following 12 variables: tenure status, institutional type, academic employment offers, nonacademic employment offers, annual salary, intent to leave in two years, marital status, number of dependents, other barrier, lack of support at home, never married, and age. Of these 12 variables, only nonacademic employment offers and age were statistically significant. Academics who reported a high job satisfaction rate were least likely to receive nonacademic employment offers, and most likely to be older in age. In comparison, those academics with an average or low job satisfaction rate tended to receive twice as many nonacademic employment offers and be, on average, three years older than those who reported a high or very high job satisfaction rate. Therefore, job satisfaction should be explored further to determine what can be done to improve the job satisfaction level of these academic women, thus increasing the rate of retention.

Fifth, the tremendous gap that presently exists in this area of research concerning mobility patterns of Black women, minority and international faculty needs to close. Scholars need to examine the successes of institutions, and the failures of others, in terms of successful retention efforts. By understanding what works in some environments and what doesn't in others, we can develop better tools to create a more precise model for why some faculty women leave, and what can be done to enhance permanence and academic success.

A sixth area of importance includes new directions for theory and research. It is important for the academy to create a better environment for faculty and make the teaching field more attractive to new Black doctorate recipients who have a host of other favorable opportunities elsewhere from which to choose. Higher education institutions could greatly benefit from the growing presence of young Black scholars in the academy.

Seventh, the findings in this study are intended to provide new data to help increase the awareness of academic mobility as well as illustrate what factors appear to increase the opportunities for success and achievement for Black and other faculty women. It is the author's hope that the results of this study will stimulate scholars, educators, and administrators to seek out additional knowledge. Also, additional resources will be required to help examine the issues as to why an increasing number of Black and international faculty women are leaving the academy. It is vital to discover how retention rates can be strengthened, thereby ensuring that these women scholars are not denied the tools necessary to succeed and are well represented among the faculty ranks. If we continue to lose Black and other women scholars, the future of the academy and ultimately the future success of Black and minority students are likely to suffer.

*A*ppendix

Study Methodology

RESEARCH DESIGN

The study upon which this book is based was a quasi-experimental design employed to assess the primary factors of career mobility and to determine patterns of success and achievement among Black faculty women. All respondents in this study were Black women who were present or past full-time teaching faculty at a four-year or two-year American college or university.

In order to secure adequate data to apply the proper statistical procedure and ensure the study examined what it purported to, several internal and external factors were controlled for in the analyses to eliminate any confounding effects of the variables, as well as any possible threats which would jeopardize internal and external validity--possibly questioning it's generalization across populations. While the Institutional Cycle Design typically controls for the main internal effects of history, testing, and instrumentation (Campbell and Stanley, 1963), the internal threat of maturation appeared more likely due to the disparity in age among respondents. The design further failed to control for maturation and selection, which were the two major internal validity threats identified for this type of design. The Institutional Cycle Design warned against the interaction of selection and it's corresponding independent variable, although Campbell and Stanley (1963) did not identify any clear external factors which would typically jeopardize the external validity of this type of design.

Threats to Internal Validity

Campbell and Stanley (1963) identify two primary threats to internal validity in the Institutional Cycle Design. Maturation was the first threat to internal validity resulting from this type of study design. Since the subjects in this study ranged in age, failing to control for maturity could pose a serious limitation. A 58 year-old Black woman professor would most likely have more significant differences than a 32 year-old Black woman professor. Older faculty might tend to be more conservative, less upwardly mobile, and less likely to report concerns than younger faculty. Several methods could be employed to control for maturation, such as a test/retest reliability measure. In this study, the effect of maturation was controlled for by age. In other words, in the descriptive and inferential analyses, group differences were statistically analyzed on the basis of age, as well as other important attributes, to ensure validity and comparability of the sample.

   The second concern to internal validity was the possible bias in the selection of the sample. This threat can exist if the likelihood of the propensity of a Black woman professor to remain in, return to, or voluntarily leave for alternate employment, could be attributed to the specific selection differences that distinguish professors in the study. If this occurred, the study might not be examining what it purported to examine in the analysis, thereby severely limiting the   internal validity. Although the respondents in this study were selected from a 100 percent sample of members and associates of the Association of Black Women in Higher Education (ABWHE), there were no means to ensure that the respondents were equally susceptible to the propensity to remain in, return to, or voluntarily leave. In this study, the sample was self-selected into the organization with a range of varying characteristics, such as age and experience. Furthermore, these self-selected ABWHE members were again self-selected to participate in this study. The evidence of participation in a study on the career mobility of Black women professors, may have been the impetus for Black professors in this sample to respond who were most mobile and more inclined to leave. Furthermore, because the survey instrument was entitled "Academic Survey," some members who did not respond and had left the academy may have incorrectly assumed that the survey was only meant for those currently in academia. On the other hand, those respondents choosing to participate may have had less of a propensity to leave than the rest of the population of Black women Ph.D.'s. According to Earl Babbie (1990), "a sample will be representative of the population from which it is selected if all members of the population have an equal chance of being selected in the sample" (p. 71), although the degree of representation is affected by the sample size and the characteristics of the larger population. Babbie further argues that an equivalent group is not an ideal substitute for random selection.

The third potential internal threat to validity in this study may be personal history, because of the variation of historical and other events experienced by respondents providing possible alternative explanations for their decision to remain in, return to, or voluntarily leave the academy. The dual ascribed status of being Black and a woman presented a number of potentially significant issues which could be attributed to history. First, the historical periods of the 1940s, 1950s, 1960s, 1970s, and 1980s brought major changes into the gates of higher education. Significantly greater numbers of Black students sought higher education in institutions other than community colleges and Historically Black Colleges and Universities (HBCU), justifying greater numbers of Black minority faculty. After being denied access for well over a century, the Civil Rights movement gave many Blacks a greater passion and drive to seek faculty positions in the more prestigious institutions.

Affirmative Action programs, coupled with heavy minority faculty recruitment in the 1970s, provided numerous opportunities for many Blacks. For example, a Black woman professor who experienced teaching before or during the Civil Rights struggle may have, as a result of this experience, very different views than a young faculty member who did not experience the same struggle and entered the academy in the mid 1970s, when faculty positions were not difficult to acquire. Second, as a Black woman who may typically have been more likely to be married with a greater number of dependents (both children and elderly parents) than her White female counterpart, these numerous responsibilities could potentially have affected choice patterns and career mobility. A married Black woman professor whose husband was the principal wage earner may have chosen to leave her position if her husband was transferred out-of-state. Or she may have chosen to teach part-time and raise her children. On the other hand, a Black woman may have been unable to take advantage of promotion and advancement opportunities because of responsibilities to her family, which are traditionally of greatest value and priority. A younger Black woman who had not experienced the responsibilities of marriage, children, or dependent parents, may have been more voluntarily mobile and, therefore, had a greater propensity to seek alternate full-time employment.

Threats to External Validity

The Institutional Cycle Design does not typically pose any major threats to external validity. However, Campbell and Stanley (1963) warn against generalizing the effects of the independent variables found in this particular study of Black women professors in the Association of Black Women in Higher Education (ABWHE) to the universe of Black women professors. In other words, the effects of the independent variables might be specific to the ABWHE respondents under study, rather than to the population of Black women Ph.D.'s at large.

Although the 384 members of ABWHE were a relatively homogeneous group who shared a common set of professional, academic, social, and cultural characteristics, the respondents in the survey may have differed from other professional academic women in a number of ways.

First, the study was limited to all members and associates of ABWHE who are or were full-time faculty at a two or four-year American college or university. This small sample self-selected themselves as members of ABWHE, and as participants in this study. Although this group of 336 represented 78.9 percent of ABWHE membership, the characteristics and corresponding findings may not be generalizable to the 8,771 Black faculty women population reported in 1985.

Second, the characteristics of Black women academicians who choose to join a professional women's organization such as ABWHE, may be significantly different than those who do not. For example, ABWHE members may join professional organizations for social and professional reasons, and, likewise, benefit to a greater degree by developing networks which can help enhance career mobility. Since several university and community college presidents, senior administrators, deans, faculty, and the like are members of ABWHE, the small size of the organization may allow for greater professional support and networking not available in larger professional organizations. Those who do not participate in small professional organizations such as ABWHE may find other professional organizations as a means to network, or may choose not to participate in professional organizations due to time constraints and other factors. This suggests that if professional networking is a primary factor in the acquisition of possible employment opportunities, membership in ABWHE or a similar small professional women's organization may have a greater influence on the career mobility of its members than other larger professional organizations or the absence of participating thereof.

Third, since the establishment of ABWHE in 1978, the number of members have steadily grown, while the characteristics of ABWHE have changed very little. The current membership was initially composed of roughly 55 percent academic administrators and 45 percent faculty. In the first two years after its founding, however, membership grew modestly to 87 members in 1980. In 1982, membership had grown to 140 and steadily rose to a peak of 350 in 1988. And in 1989, membership fell to just below 400 members and associates, and remains relatively stable with slight increases each year. In 1994, the ABWHE membership totaled 384.

DESCRIPTION OF THE VARIABLES

Wherever possible, the variables n this study were defined in the same or similar fashion as other research to allow for a greater degree of comparison. The first section defines the categorical dependent variable (the decision to remain in, return to, or voluntarily leave), followed by the independent variables (salary, tenure status, institutional type, intention to leave, marital status, number of dependents, support systems, and external barriers), and other variable attributes (age, never married, when marriage occurred, education of spouse, employment of spouse, current employment status, job satisfaction, academic faculty rank, recent employment offers, type of community, discretionary activities, hours of domestic activities, and hours at work) to help delineate the study.

Categorical Dependent Variable

The decision to leave is an on-going, dynamic process resulting from a series of life-cycle stages and changing values placed on an academic career. This study focused only on those Black women who held a full-time academic faculty position at a two or four-year American college or university at any time in their professional career history. In this context, the categorical dependent variable (the decision to remain in, return to, or voluntarily leave) was operationally defined in the following manner and classified into one of three categories: the "remainers," the "returners," and the "voluntary leavers."

The first category included those who: (1) were currently employed in a two-year or four-year American college or university; and (2) had remained in academic employment throughout their professional career and had never held a nonacademic position since graduate training. Current employment in a two or four-year American college or university was identified by the respondent selecting the appropriate response in the questionnaire, which asked respondents to select one of 17 choices that best described their principal employment during January, 1993. Those who never held a nonacademic position since receiving graduate training and remained in academic employment were identified by asking respondents to indicate the approximate number of full-time professional positions held among 17 delineated categories. Respondents who currently held academic positions and remained in the academy, without ever working in the nonacademic sector since graduate training, were deemed "remainers" and were coded as "1."

A second category included those who: (1) were currently employed in a two or four-year American college or university; and (2) had worked outside of the academy in at least one nonacademic position since graduate training. Current employment in a two or four-year institution was again identified by the respondent selecting the appropriate response which identified one among 17 choices which best described their principal employment during January, 1993. Those who worked outside of the academy in at least one nonacademic position since graduate training were identified by asking respondents to indicate the approximate number of full-time professional positions held among 17 given categories. This group potentially included: 1) those who worked outside of the academy for a number of years, and then, once rejoined, remained in the academy; and 2) those who joined the academy, left for nonacademic employment, and then returned to accept a position in a two or four-year American college or university. Respondents in this category were deemed "returners," and were coded as "2."

The third category included those who: (1) were currently employed outside of the academy; and (2) had previously held at least one full-time faculty position in a two or four-year American college or university, but voluntarily or involuntarily left for a position outside academia. Current employment outside of the academy was identified by the respondent selecting the most appropriate response out of 17 choices which best described their principal employment during January, 1993. Those who currently worked outside of the academy in at least one nonacademic position since graduate training were identified by respondents indicating the approximate number of full-time professional positions held among 17 given categories. Voluntary movement was operationally defined within the constraints of tenure status for those employed at a four-year American college or university. For example, if faculty members were tenured in a four-year American college or university before they left the academy, movement was automatically considered voluntary. If the faculty members were nontenured at the time they left, the movement was only considered voluntary if: (1) respondents were not denied tenure; and (2) respondents did not perceive themselves as having little prospect of obtaining tenure. Voluntary movement was identified by respondents selecting one of the following two sets of responses: (1) response "1" (yes) which asked respondents to indicate if they had ever held tenure at a four-year American college or university; (2) response "0" (no) which asked respondents if they had ever been denied tenure from a four-year American college or university; or (3) response "0" (no) which asked respondents to indicate if they ever left a faculty position because they felt they had little prospect of obtaining tenure. Respondents currently working outside of the academy who were either (1) tenured; (2) nontenured and not denied tenure; or (3) nontenured and not perceived as being unable to achieve tenure, which were deemed as "voluntary leavers."

Independent Variables

With the dependent variable defined as the decision to remain in, return to, or voluntarily leave a full-time faculty position at a two or four-year American college or university, the set of predictors or independent economic and psychosocial variables are as follows.

Salary data was determined by asking respondents to indicate annual salary, before taxes, associated with their principal professional employment. The mean was obtained by averaging the salaries, which were calculated on a 12-month work year.

Current tenure status was identified for respondents currently working in the academy by a discrete variable indicating a response of "1" if tenured and "0" if nontenured or if tenure was not applicable.

Institutional type was also identified for respondents currently working in the academy by a discrete variable indicating a response of "4" for a four-year American college or university, or "2" for a two-year college or university. In the case of conflicting or missing data, a visual inspection of the respondents' principal employer were used to resolve the conflict.

The intention to leave for those who were currently employed in the academy was indicated by using a three-point Likert scale to identify the respondents likelihood to leave their current position within two years. Respondents indicating they were "Very Likely" or "Possibly" inclined to leave within two years were coded as "1" and deemed to have the "Intention to Leave." Responses of "Not Likely" in those three groups were coded as "0."

Two discrete variables were coded and represented as "1" for those who were "Married" at the time of the study, or "0" for those who were "Not Married" at the time of the study.

The number of dependents were identified by a continuous variable indicating the combined number of; (1) children between the ages of 0 and 17 living with the respondent; and (2) custodial (elderly dependent) parents living in the household. The total number of children and elderly dependents living in the household were classified as the "Number of Dependents."

The primary method employed to indicate support systems was an ordinal scale composed of 12 factors asking respondents to choose four. Each of the four factors chosen were given separate individual variable names and coded as binomial variables. Respondents who selected any of the 12 variables as one of the top four were coded as

"1" if supportive. The 12 individual binomial variables representing support were spouse, parents, relatives, friends, church, minority mentor, majority mentor, supervisor, professional minority network/association, professional academic network/association, colleague, or other.

External barriers were indicated by employing a three-point Likert scale of 15 factors in the questionnaire defined as a "Major Problem" and coded as "1," "Minor Problem" and coded as "2," or "Not a Problem" and coded as "3." Each barrier was assigned an independent variable name. The 15 individual binomial variables representing external barriers were support at home, spouses job mobility, spouses negative views toward career, qualifications challenged, salary differentials, tenure and promotion policies, committee appointment, academic climate, teaching inequities, research inequities, service obligations within institution, service obligations outside institution, discrimination/racism, family factors, and other. Respondents indicating a factor was a "Major Problem" or "Minor Problem" were coded as "1" and deemed an "external barrier." Not a problem and non-responses were coded as "0."

Other Variable Attributes

In addition to the eight independent variables discussed above, several other variable attributes possibly relating to the mobility decisions of Black women professors were prepped for analysis. Since previous studies indicated that Black women professors tended to be older and married (Brown, 1988; Zumeta, 1984), and by the nature of their profession classified as mobile (Brown, 1967), it was important to identify and account for 13 additional factors to determine to what extent, if any, these variables may be associated with the decision to remain in, return to, or voluntarily leave the academy. The 13 additional factors included: (1) age; (2) when marriage occurred; (3) never married; (4) education of spouse; (5) employment of spouse; (6) current employment status; (7) job satisfaction; (8) academic faculty rank; (9) recent employment offers; (10) type of community; (11) discretionary activities; (12) hours of domestic activities; and (13) hours of work responsibilities.

The continuous variable "age" was determined by subtracting the year of birth from the 1994 calendar year. Respondents who had not yet reached their birth date in the 1994 calendar year, were represented inaccurately as being a year older.

The date indicating when the respondent was first married was classified into three variables: "0" before graduate school, "1" during graduate school, "2" after graduate school, or "9" not applicable. If the first marriage occurred during graduate school, the variable was coded as "1," or "0" otherwise. If the first marriage occurred after graduate school, the variable was coded as "1," or "0" otherwise. Due to the method of coding, the referent group for these two variables were those persons who were married "before graduate school." Non-responses were coded as "9" and excluded from the analysis.

Two discrete variables were coded and represented as "1" for those who were "Never Married" at the time of the study. Non-responses were excluded from the analysis.

The highest education level achieved by a spouse for married respondents were classified into three variables: "0" indicating at most a high school diploma; "1" indicating at most a baccalaureate degree; or "2" indicating at most a graduate or professional degree. If the spouse's highest education achieved was at most a baccalaureate degree, the variable was coded as "1," or "0" otherwise. If the spouse's highest education achieved was at most a graduate or professional degree, the variable was coded as "1," or "0" otherwise. Due to the method of coding, the referent group for these two variables were those spouses who had obtained at most a high school diploma. Non-responses were excluded from the analysis.

For respondents who were currently married, the spouse's employment was indicated first by it's status, and second by the number of hours worked per week. Employment status was indicated as "1" if employed full-time, and "0" if otherwise. Non-responses from unmarried respondents (indicated in numerous other items) were assumed not applicable and excluded from the analysis.

The respondent's employment status was indicated by a "1" if employed full-time or "0" if not employed full-time. Non-responses were assumed to be not employed full-time and were coded as "0."

"Job Satisfaction" was determined for full-time employed respondents using a simple five-point Likert scale, indicating non-missing responses as "1" for Very High, "2" High, "3" Average, "4" Low, or "5" Very Low, to determine the rate of job satisfaction with regard to the respondents' principal employment. Respondents indicating job satisfaction as "Very High" or "High" were coded as "1" and deemed as having a high job satisfaction. Respondents indicating job satisfaction as being "Average," "Low," or "Very Low" were coded as "0" and were deemed as having an "average or low job satisfaction.". Non-responses were excluded from the analysis.

Faculty rank was indicated by a set of discrete variables employed to identify the position(s) held as "0" for Professor, "1" for Associate Professor, or "2" for Assistant Professor. If the position of Associate Professor was held, the variable was coded as "1," or "0" otherwise. If the position of Assistant Professor was held, the variable was coded as "1," or "0" otherwise. Due to the method of coding, the referent group for these two variables were those persons who held the position of Professor. Respondents who selected choices other than 1, 2, or 3, were identified as holding faculty or administrative positions without rank, and non-responses were coded as "0."

"Recent employment offers" were captured by two separate continuous variables classifying the types of institutions or organizations making inquires or offers as "1" if academic, or "0" if nonacademic. The number of individual employment offers or inquiries made in each of the two categories were simply added separately to get the total for each category

Three discrete variables were created to determine which one best described the community where the respondent lived. The three choices were identified as follows: "0" for Small Town, "1" for Large Central City, or "2" for Suburbs. If the type of community was a Large Central City, the variable was coded as "1," or "0" otherwise. If the type of community was the Suburbs, the variable was coded as "1," or "0" otherwise. Due to the method of coding, the referent group for these two variables were those respondents who lived in a Small Town.

To determine discretionary activities, a set of eight variables on a three-point Likert scale were ranked as a participatory discretionary activity on a scale of "1" for Regular Basis, "2" for Occasionally, or "3" for Never. The eight variables representing discretionary activities were family, religious, social, professional association, volunteer, educational, neighborhood, and political. Respondents who classified any of the eight activities as participating in on a "Regular Basis" or "Occasionally" were coded as "1" and deemed a Discretionary Activity. Respondents selecting "Never" were coded as "0." Non-responses were assumed not applicable, and were excluded from the analysis.

To determine the number of hours spent on domestic household activities--representing a total of eight discrete variables--the numbers were simply added to obtain the total hours spent on domestic activities. To determine the total number of hours spent on work activities, the number of hours spent on professional work time were added to obtain the total number of hours.

STUDY DESIGN

Sample Description

This study was undertaken in the winter of 1994, and was based on a 100 percent sample of the 384 members and associates (persons who had not paid 1993-94 dues, but were on the membership or mailing list) of the Association of Black Women in Higher Education (ABWHE) to survey career mobility patterns of Black women professors from two and four-year American colleges and universities. A random sample was not selected due to the relatively small number of the ABWHE membership.

On Tuesday, January 4, 1994, the first survey instrument was distributed to the 384 members and associates of ABWHE. One week after the first mailing on Tuesday, January 11, a reminder postcard was mailed to each of the 384 members. A total of 63 responses were received before the second follow-up letter of January 18--two weeks later. Between the second follow-up of January 18 and the third follow-up of February 1, 110 responses were received. Finally, between the distribution of the third mail follow-up and the final day of the survey period some six weeks later on March 15, a total of 163 responses were received.

Of the 384 instruments distributed, 336 were returned, yielding an overall response rate of 79 percent. Of the 336 responses, 107 were ineligible; 87 respondents were Black women but never had held a full-time faculty position at a two or four-year American college of university; 12 were not Black women but held a full-time faculty position at a two or four-year American college of university; and eight were not Black women and had never held a full-time faculty position at a two or four-year American college of university. Most of those who had never taught full-time were administrators, and many had held adjunct or part-time faculty positions. Twenty-five instruments were returned unopened with no forwarding address, and three were returned marked deceased. Also, 16 postcard responses were received indicating their choice not to participate. And four instruments were returned but not processed, because they were received after the pre-established survey period for the data collection. Consequently, 182 usable instruments (47 percent of the total sample) were analyzed. Throughout the data-collection period, whenever possible through the limited phone list of ABWHE members and associates, the researcher made follow-up telephone calls to those who had not responded.

To test the reliability of the survey instrument, two methods were used. First, 30 respondents were randomly selected to receive duplicate surveys for completion in approximately 21 days after the first instrument was received. The purpose of the Test-Retest method was to determine to what extent the survey instrument would yield the same results if applied twice. Of these 30 instruments, 13 were received and compared in a correlation analysis. The results of the correlation on the nine descriptive variables ranged from a low of .928 to a high of 1.0. Second, the data from each survey instrument was printed out by data-name in an Excel spreadsheet and cross-checked using a two-person team reading the data from the instrument while confirming the corresponding data on the Excel spreadsheet.

Data Collection

Prior to the distribution of the survey instrument for this study, the questionnaire was pretested in a modest pilot study on 18 academicians of diverse characteristics ranging in age, gender, ethnicity, employment status, discipline, and experience to: (1) complete the entire survey to the best of their ability so the researcher could determine if the instrument was consistently measuring what it was intended to measure; and (2) offer feedback to help minimize errors, vagueness, and interpretable bias. As a result, 11 major revisions were made to improve the instrument before going to print.

A green, 58-question, four-page, double-sided questionnaire was distributed. The survey instrument was mailed to all 384 members of ABWHE, whose leaders provided the mailing list with additions and deletions. Few telephone numbers, however, were available on most members since the most recent membership directory was for 1990-

1992. Therefore, there were no means to verify the accuracy of most addresses, nor identify past or present full-time faculty. Hence, a 100 percent sample was employed rather than a stratified random sample which would have potentially minimized eligible responses since less than half the membership were current faculty members.

Each ABWHE member was sent a survey instrument which included a cover letter, letter of support from the president of ABWHE, questionnaire, and self-addressed stamped return envelope. In addition, a postcard reminder was sent one week after the initial distribution of the survey instrument.

Each of the three cover letters concisely explained: (1) what the study was about; (2) the usefulness of the study; (3) the value and importance of ABWHE member responses; (4) adherence to confidentiality; (5) availability of study results; (6) sponsorship from the ABWHE president; (7) thanks and appreciation for their responses; (8) researchers original signature in blue ink; (9) the researcher's telephone number in the event of questions regarding the study; and (10) an explanation of the identification number system recommended by Dillman (1978). The cover letter and envelope were printed on the University of Pennsylvania, Graduate School of Education stationary generously and graciously provided by George Keller, Senior Fellow and Chair of the Higher Education Division in the Graduate School of Education at Penn. At the bottom of each envelope, the researcher stamped "First Class" in bright red ink to illustrate importance and obtain the highest mail priority. This is important because mail stamped first class is forwarded automatically for up to one year if the respondent has moved. Furthermore, if the instrument is returned by the postal service, it will include helpful messages on the status of the intended recipient, such as "left no forwarding address," "address expired," "refused," or "deceased." Each envelope and postcard also carried a preprinted address label for each respondent, as well as a preprinted return label of the researcher.

A one-page letter of support was kindly provided by Delores Smalls, the president of ABWHE. The letter re-emphasized the importance of the study, its benefits to the organization, and its possible implications for Black women Ph.D.'s, and higher education in general. Babbie (1990) indicated that the existence of a sponsor appears to increase response rates.

The questionnaire was professionally printed on green paper with black ink. Babbie (1990) stated that "authors... report that the color of the questionnaire can affect response rates (green does better than white)" (p. 182). Each cycle of survey instruments was also color coded to distinguish which cycle produced the stated response. For example, the identification numbers located on the top right-hand corner of the first page in the questionnaire mailed on January 4 were written in black ink; January 18 blue ink; and February 1 red ink. The January 11 postcard reminder was not color-coded because it was unique and had the respondents full address on the opposite side of the postcard. All questionnaires were logged by the date they were received and tallied, both on the top left-hand corner of each questionnaire and in a separate log. For example, if in the first survey, identification number 174 was received on January 8, it was logged as: (1) "1/8" to indicate the date received; (2) "174" to indicate the corresponding identification number; and (3) "1" to indicate the order the survey was received. Each survey received thereafter was also logged by the date received, the identification number, and the order received (1, 2, 3, 4, etc.).

A post-card reminder was distributed to all 384 members, seven days after the original mailing. The purpose of the postcard was to thank those who had already responded, and to remind those who had not. If members had not responded, they were asked to indicate why and return the postcard by simply flipping it over, stapling the bottom corner, and placing it in the mail. The opposite side of each postcard was self-addressed and stamped to enhance its prompt return to the researcher. On the bottom left corner of the postcard, was printed "Please return if undeliverable" in the event an address was incorrect. Of the 384 distributed postcard reminders, 180 were returned. The majority of respondents did not return the post-cards until several weeks later. Of the 180 returned postcards, 97 reported returning the questionnaire, 34 indicated they had completed and would return the questionnaire that day, 26 were undeliverable, 16 indicated they chose not to participate, and 7 said they had not received the questionnaire but were willing to participate and were promptly re-sent the survey instruments after confirming the addresses.

Postcard Responses

Last week, a survey on the career mobility of Black women was mailed
to you.   Because it has been sent to only a small but representative
sample, it is extremely important that yours also be included in the
study if results are to be accurately represented.   If you have already
completed and returned the survey, please accept my sincere thanks.
If not, please indicate with a check the reason(s) why below, fold and
staple all three sides in the middle, and mail it back to me today.

  7   Did not receive but willing to participate.   Please mail a
duplicate.

 97   Already completed and returned questionnaire.

 34   Completed and will return questionnaire today.

 16   Have received but choose not to participate because:

        ____ Survey instrument is too complex or difficult.

        _3_ Survey is intrusive; does not benefit me as an individual.

        ____ Survey takes too much time to complete.

        ____ I am too busy to complete a 10-15 minute survey.

        _1_ Survey will not benefit current situation of black women.

        _2_ I am tired of being surveyed by social scientists.

        _10_ I am not interested in participating because:

 2   I do not answer mail surveys.

 3   I am not interested in participating because it asks too many
personal questions.

 1   the questions about my specific date of birth, marital history
and   family background are too personal for my comfort.

 3   the survey takes longer than 15 minutes.

 1 the survey will not affect ABWHE as an organization.

LIMITATIONS

The study design, data collection, statistical analysis, and methodology
have several limitations which must be recognized.

    First, the economic and psychosocial model this study examined
did not receive adequate support.   This lack of support for the model
may have had more to do with the measurement of the instrument,
rather than with the actual content of the data.   In this study, for
example, salary differentials could not be determined because the

instrument failed to: 1) report the salary of each respondent at the time they left the academy; 2) the new salary of the alternate position; and 3) the immediate family circumstance.

Second, the design of the study had some common problems associated with many study designs. The data was collected from a 100 percent sample of the Association of Black Women in Higher Education. The commonly-preferred random sample was not conducted due to the small sample size. Also, since the members of ABWHE self-selected themselves into the organization and as participants in this study, results may have been confounded by what may be systematic differences in the membership population of the association. In addition, since the size and composition of ABWHE was composed of mostly women in the fields of education and academic administrators, the study was not generalizable to the greater population of 8,771 Black women doctorates. However, since ABWHE had maintained a relatively stable composition in the past six years, the results of the study would be generalizable to comparable associations or organizations composed of Black women educators in higher education.

Third, the descriptive statistics compared with the Brown study (1988) could not be accurately ascertained because the Brown study was over a nine-year period, as compared to an averaged 20-year time frame in this study. In addition, standard errors were not available, therefore it was not possible to determine if the differences in percentages were statistically significant. Furthermore, the Brown study focused exclusively on nontenured faculty, and excluded those in education and the professions.

Fourth, to allow for a greater number of analyzed cases in the statistical analysis, non-responses for continuous variables were given the mean value. This method of coding may not be as accurate as a smaller, more conclusive value.

Fifth, by defining "returners" as those who currently work in a two or four-year institution, and have held at least one job outside academia, the group may have potentially included: 1) those who began in the academy, left and later returned; as well as those who 2) worked outside of the academy for a number of years and then joined the academy for the first time and remained. This second group had the potential to be roughly classified in the "remainers" category and may have reduced the accuracy of the model. Also, by defining the "leavers" as those who voluntarily left the academy, the analysis failed to include those who involuntarily left. Although the population of those who involuntarily left in this particular study proved to be insignificant (two respondents), the argument could have been made that perhaps a more important issue is why Black faculty leave involuntarily, which was omitted from this study.

Finally, environmental factors that may have been beyond the scope of most measures (i.e. family, support systems, external barriers related to family) are often difficult to capture in a survey instrument. For example, the family structures of most Black families are unlike most others and include extended families, such as grandparents, aunts and uncles and other relatives, friends, neighbors, community folk, church members, and others. Most research defines the family structure in terms of the nuclear family and fails to recognize extended families which are inherent for most Black families. Regardless of the difficulty in measurement, every attempt should be made to discount the possible indirect effects of these complex variables.

*B*ibliography

Abramson, J. 1975. *The Invisible Woman: Discrimination in the Academic Profession*. San Francisco: Jossey-Bass.

Acar, F. 1989. *Women's Participation in Academic Science Careers: Turkey in 1989*. Paper presented at OECD and Turkish Employment Organization, Istanbul, Nov.

Acker, S. 1992. New Perspectives on an Old Problem: The Position of Women Academics in British Higher Education, *Higher Education* 24: 57-75.

Adams, H. 1976. *The Academic Tribes*. Liveright, New York.

Adelman, C. *Women at Thirtysomething: Paradoxes of Attainment*. Washington, D.C.: Office of Research, U.S. Department of Education, 1991.

Ahern, N. and E. Scott. 1981. *Career Outcomes in a Matched Sample of Men and Women Doctorates*. Washington, D.C.: National Academy Press.

Ahmeduzzaman, M. and J Roopnarine. 1992. Sociodemographic Factors, Functioning Style, Social Support, and Fathers' Involvement with Preschoolers in African American Families. *Journal of Marriage and the Family* 54(Aug): 699-707.

Aisenberg, N. and M. Harrington, 1988. *Women of Academe: Outsiders in the Sacred Grove*. Amherst: University of Massachusetts Press.

Akbar, N. 1985. Our Destiny: Authors in a Science Revolution. In H. McAdoo and J. McAdoo (eds.) *Black Children*, p. 17-32. Beverly Hills, CA.: Sage.

Aldridge, D. Dec. 1989. African American Women in the Economic Marketplace: A Continuing Struggle. *Journal of Black Studies* 20(2): 129-154.

Allen, F.   1990.   *Women Academics in Australian Universities.* Australian Government Publishing Service, Canberra.

Allen, H.   1988.   *The Career Mobility of Black College Faculty: A Study of Relations Between Ascription, Professionalism, and the Determinants of Mobility in the Academic Marketplace.* Unpublished dissertation, University of Chicago.

Altekar, A.   1962.   *The Position of Indian Women in Hindu Civilization,* Motilal: Banarsidas.

Amatea, E. and E. Cross.   1981.   Competing Worlds, Competing Standards: Personal Control for the Professional Career Woman, Wife, and Mother. *Journal of the National Association of Women Deans, Administrators, and Counselors* 44: 3-10.

Amatea, E. and M. Fong.   1991.   The Impact of Role Stressors and Personal Resources on the Stress Experience of Professional Women. *Psychology of Women Quarterly* 15: 419-430.

American Association of University Professors.   1977.   Academic Freedom and Tenure, 1940 Statement of Principles and Interpretive Comments. *AAUP Redbook.* Washington, D.C.

_____.   1988.   Academic Women and Salary Differentials. *Academe* (Jul/Aug): 33-36..

_____.   1988.   The Annual Report on the Economic Status of the Profession, issues annual. *Academe* (Jul/Aug).

American Council on Education.   1987.   *One-Third A Nation: A Report on the Commission on Minority Participation in Education and American Life.*   Washington, D.C.: Education Commission of the States.

_____.   1988.   *Minorities in Higher Education, Seventh Annual Status Report 1988.*   Washington, D.C.: U.S. Equal Employment Opportunity Commission.

_____.   1993.   *Minorities in Higher Education.*   Washington, D.C.: Office of Minority Concerns, 11th Annual Report.

Andersen, C., D. Carter, and A. Malizio.   1989.   *1989-90 Fact Book on Higher Education.*   New York: ACE/Macmillan.

Andrulis, D., I. Iscoe, M. Sikes, and T. Friedman.   1975.   Black Professionals in Predominantly White Institutions of Higher Education: An Examination of Some Demographic and Mobility Characteristics. *Journal of Negro Education* 44 (Winter): 6-11.

Apter, T.   1993.   *Working Women Don't Have Wives.*   St. Martin Press.

Aquirre, A. 1992. An Interpretive Analysis of Chicano Faculty in Academe. *Social Science Journal*, 29: 124-140.

Archbold, P.. 1983. Impact of Parent-Caring on Women. *Family Relations* 32:39-46.

Arnold, H. and D. Feldman. 1982. A Multivariate Analysis of the Determinants of Job Turnover. *Journal of Applied Psychology* 67(3):350-360.

Association of Indian Universities. 1987. *Educational Statistics at a Glance*. New Delhi: AIU.

Association of University Teachers (AUT). 1992. *Sex Discrimination in Universities: Report of an Academic Pay* Audit Carried Out by the AUT Research Department, AUT: London.

Astin, A. 1982. *Minorities in American Higher Education*. San Francisco: Jossey-Bass.

Astin, H. 1969. *The Woman Doctorate in America: Origins, Career, and Family*. Russell Sage Foundation.

_____. 1973. Career Profiles of Women Doctorates. In *Academic Women on the Move*, Alice S. Rossi and Ann Calderwood, pp. 139-162. Russell Sage Foundation: New York.

Astin, H. and A. Bayer 1973. Sex Discrimination in Academe. In *Academic Women on the Move*, Alice S. Rossi and Ann Calderwood, pp. 333-358. Russell Sage Foundation: New York.

Astin, H. and M. Snyder. 1982. A Decade of Response. *Change* 14: 260-31, 59.

Ault, D., G. Rutman, and T. Stevenson. 1979. Mobility in the Labor Market for Academic Economists. *American Economic Review* 69(2):148-153.

Austin, A. and Z. Gamson. 1983. *Academic Workplace: New Demands, Heightened Tensions*. ASHE-ERIC Higher Education Report No. 10. Washington, D.C.: Association for the Study of Higher Education.

Azibo, D. 1992. Understanding the Proper and Improper Usage of the Comparative Research Framework. In *African American Psychology: Theory, Research, and Practice*, (eds.) Kathleen H. Burlew et. al., 18-27.

Aziz, A. 1990. Women in UK Universities – the Road to Causalization? In *Storming the Tower: Women in the Academic World*, Lie, S and V. O'Leary, (Ed.). London: Kogan Page

Babbie, E. 1990. *Survey Research Methods*. Wadsworth Publishing.

____. 1992. *The Practice of Social Research.* Wadsworth Publishing.

Bagilhole, B. 1993. Survivors in a Male Preserve: A Study of British Women Academics' Experiences and Perceptions of Discrimination in a UK University, *Higher Education* 26: 431-447.

Bailyn, L. 1975. Family Constraints on Women's Work. In *Women and Success,* (ed.) Ruth B. Knundsin. New York: William Morrow.

Baldwin, G. 1985. *Women at Monash University,* Monash University Press.

Baldwin, R. and R. Blackburn. 1981. The Academic Career as a Developmental Process: Implications for Higher Education. *Journal of Higher Education* 52(6): 598-614.

Bali, A. 1986. College Teachers: Challenges and Responses. New Delhi.

Ball, R. 1983. Marital Status, Household Structure, and Life Satisfaction of Black Women. *Social Problems,* 30(4): 400-409.

Ball, R. and L. Robbins. 1986. Marital Status and Life Satisfaction Among Black Americans. *Journal of Marriage and the Family,* 48 (May): 389-394.

Balswick, J. and C. Avertt. 1977. Differences in Expressiveness: Gender Interpersonal Orientation and Perceived Parental Expressiveness as Contributing Factors. *Journal of Marriage and Family* 39: 121-128.

Banks, W. 1984. Afro-American Scholars in the University: Roles and Conflicts. *American Behavioral Scientist* 27(3):325-338.

Baran, P. 1965. *The Commitment of the Intellectual.* Monthly Review Press. (March), 1-11.

Barbezat, D. 1988. Gender Differences in the Academic Reward Structure. In *Academic Labor Markets and Careers* (eds.) David W. Breneman and Theodore I. K. Yuon, 138-164. New York: Falmer Press.

Barhoum, M. 1983. Attitudes of University Students Toward Women's Work: the Case of Jordan. *International Journal of Middle Eastern Studies,* V. 15.

Baron, J. and W. Bielby. 1980. Bringing the Firms Back In: Stratification, Segmentation, and the Organization of Work. *American Sociological Review* 45: 737-765.

Barresi, C. and G. Menon. 1990. Diversity in Black Family Caregiving. In *Black Aged: Understanding Diversity and Service Needs*, (eds.) Zev Harel, Edward A. McKinney, and Michael Williams. National Council on the Aging.

Bartel, A. 1979. The Migration Decision: What Role Does Job Mobility Play? *The American Economic Review* (December): 775-786.

Baruch, G., L. Biener, and R. Barnett. 1987. Women and Gender in Research on Work and Family Stress. *American Psychologist* 42: 131-136.

Bayer, A. 1973. *Teaching Faculty in Academe, 1972-1973*. Washington, D.C.: American Council on Education.

Bayer, A. and H. Astin. 1968. Sex Differences in Academic Rank and Salary Among Science Doctorates in Teaching. *Journal of Human Resources* 3:191-201.

____. 1975. Sex Differences in the Academic Reward System. *Science* 188: 796-802.

Becker, G. 1957. *The Economics of Discrimination*. University of Chicago Press.

Beckham, B. 1987/1988. Strangers in a Strange Land: The Experiences of Blacks on White Campuses. *Educational Record* (Fall/Winter): 74-78.

Behymer, C.E. 1974. *Institutional and Personal Correlates of Faculty Research Productivity*. Ph.D. dissertation, University of Michigan.

Bell, D. 1994. *Confronting Authority: Reflections of an Ardent Protester*. Boston, Ma: Beacon Press.

Bell, D. 1989. The Effects of Affirmative Action on Male-Female Relationships Among African Americans. *Sex Roles* 21(1/2): 13-24.

Bell, R. 1970. The Relative Importance of Mother and Wife Roles Among Lower Class Women. In Charles C. Willie (ed.), *The Family Life of Black People*. Columbus, OH.: Charles E. Merrill Publishing.

Bell-Scott, P. 1984. *Black Women's Higher Education: Our Legacy*. Sage: A Scholarly Journal on Black Women, (Spring) p. 8-11.

Benokraitis, N. and J. Feagin. 1978. *Affirmative Action and Equal Opportunity*. Boulder, CO.: Westview Press.

Bentley, R.J. 1990. *Faculty Research Performance Over Time and Its Relationship to Sources of Grant Support.* Ph.D. dissertation, University of Michigan.

Benton, S. 1986. Women Administrators in the 1980's: A New Breed. In *Strategies and Attitudes: Women in Educational Administration,* (ed.) P. A. Farrant. Washington, D.C.: National Association of Women Deans, Administrators, and Counselors.

Bergmann, B. 1985. Comparable Worth for Professors. *Academe* (July/Aug) 71(4): 8-10.

Bernard, J. 1964. *Academic Women.* University Park, PA: Pennsylvania State University Press.

_____. 1966. *Marriage and Family Among Negros.* Englewood Cliffs, NJ.: Prentice-Hall Publishing.

_____. 1987. *The Female World from a Global Perspective.* Bloomington: Indiana University Press.

Berry, M. and J. Blassingame. 1982. *Long Memory: The Black Experience in America.* New York: Oxford University Press.

Bibb, R. and W Firm. 1977. The Effects of Industrial, Occupational, and Sex Stratification on Wages in Blue-Collar Markets. *Social Forces* 55: 974-996.

Biernat, M. and C. Wortman. 1991. Sharing of Home Responsibilities Between Professionally Employed Women and Their Husbands. *Journal of Personality and Social Psychology* 60: 844-860.

Biklen, S. and M. Brannigan (eds.) 1980. *Women and Educational Leadership.* Lexington MA.: D.C. Heath & Co.

Billingsley, A. 1968. *Black Families in White America.* Englewood Cliffs, NJ.: Prentice-Hall.

_____. 1972. *Children of the Storm: Black Children and American Child Welfare.* New York: Harcourt Brace Jovanovich.

_____. 1982. Building Strong Faculties in Black Colleges. *Journal of Negro Education* 51: 4-15.

_____. 1992. *Climbing Jacobs Ladder: The Future of African American Families.* New York: Simon and Schuster.

Billingsley, A. and C. Caldwell. 1991. The Church, the Family, and the School in the African American Community. *Journal of Negro Education,* 60(3): 427-439.

Blackburn, R. and C. Aurand. 1972. *Mobility Studies On Academic Men: Some Methodological Concerns and Substantive Findings.* ERIC Document Reproduction Service No., ED 065 092.

Blackburn, R, C. Behymer, and D. Hall. 1978. Research Note: Correlates of Faculty Publications. *Sociology of Education*, 51: 132-41.

Blackburn, R., J. Bieber, J. Lawrence, and L. Trautvetter. 1993. Faculty at Work: Focus on Research, Scholarship, and Service. Research in Higher Education, 32: 385-413.

Blackburn, R. and R. Havighurst. 1979. Career Patterns of U.S. Male Academic Social Scientists. *Higher Education* 8: 553-572.

Black Issues in Higher Education. August 1, 1987. Miami of Ohio Successful in Faculty Recruiting, 4:10.

Blackwell, J. 1981. *Mainstreaming Outsiders: The Production of Black Professionals.* New York: General Hall.

_____. 1983. *Networking and Mentoring: A Study of Cross-Generational Experiences of Black Graduate and Professional Schools.* Atlanta, GA: Southern Education Foundation.

_____. 1985. *The Black Community: Diversity and Unity*, 2d ed. New York: Harper & Row.

_____. 1988. Faculty Issues: The Impact on Minorities. *Review of Higher Education* 11(4): 417-438.

_____. 1989. Mentoring: An Action Strategy for Increasing Minority Faculty. *Academe* (Sept/Oct): 8-14.

Blalock, H. 1982. *Race and Ethnic Relations.* Englecliffs, NJ: Prentice-Hall.

Blum, D. 1988. Black Woman Scholar at Emory U. Loses 3-Year Battle to Overturn Tenure. *Chronicle of Higher Education* 22 June, A15.

_____. 1991. Environment Still Hostile to Women in Academe, New Evidence Indicates. *Chronicle of Higher Education*, 9 October 1991, A-20.

Bok, D. 1982. Access to the University and the Problems of Racial Inequity. In *Beyond the Ivory Tower*, Cambridge, MA: Harvard University Press.

Bowen, H. and J. Schuster. 1985. Outlook for the Academic Profession. *Academe*, (Sept/Oct): 9-15.

_____. 1986. *American Professor's: A National Resource Imperiled.* Cary, NC: Oxford University Press.

Bowen, W. and J. Sosa. 1989. *Prospects for Faculty in the Arts and Sciences: A Study of Factors Affecting Supply and Demand.* Ewing, NJ: Princeton University Press.

Boyd, J. 1992. *In the Company of My Sisters: Black Women and Self Esteem.* New York: Dutton Books.

Bramley, G. and M. Ward. 1972. *The Role of Women in the Australian National University*, Australian National University Press, Canberra.

Brayfield, A. and W. Crockett. 1955. Employee Attitudes and Employee Performance. *Psychological Bulletin* 52: 396-402.

Brazziel, W. 1987/1988. Road Blocks to Graduate School: Black Americans Not Achieving Parity. *Educational Record* (Fall/Winter.): 108-115.

Breneman, D. and T. Youn. 1989. *Academic Labor Markets and Careers.* PA.: Falmer Press.

Brewington, D. and J. Comerford. 1974. *A Look at the Kin Family Network of Black and White Families.* Unpublished masters research paper. Washington, D.C.: Howard University, School of Social Work.

Brody, E., M. Kleban, P. Johnsen, C. Hoffman, and C. Schoonover. 1987. Work Status and Parent Care: A Comparison of Four Groups of Women. *Gerontologist* 27: 201-208.

Brown, D. 1967. *The Mobile Professors.* Washington, D.C.: American Council on Education.

Brown, R., S. Bond, J. Gerne, L. Krager, B. Krantz, M. Lukin, and D. Prentice. 1986. Stress on Campus. *Research in Higher Education* 24: 97-112.

Brown, R. and C. Speth. Spring 1988. Professorial Responses to Stress: A Self-Assessment Scale. *Review of Higher Education* 11(3): 285-296.

Brown, S.. 1988. *Increasing Minority Faculty: An Elusive Goal..* Princeton, NJ.: Educational Testing Service.

Bryant, J. 1970. *Survey of Black American Doctorates.* New York: Ford Foundation, Special Projects in Education.

Bunker, B., J. Zubek, V. Vanderslice, and R. Rice. 1992. Quality of Life in Dual-Career Families: Commuting Versus Single-Residence Couples. *Journal of Marriage and the Family* 54 (May): 399-407.

Burke, D. 1986. *Change in the Academic Marketplace: A Study of Faculty Mobility in the 1980s.* Unpublished doctoral dissertation, University of North Carolina at Chapel Hill.

_____. 1988. *A New Academic Marketplace.* Westport, CT.: Greenwood Press.

Burke, R. 1987. The Present and Future Status of Stress Research. In *Job Stress: From Theory to Suggestion*, (ed.) J. Ivancevich and D. C. Ganster. New York: Haworth Press.

Burrell, L. 1980. Is There a Future for Black Students on Predominantly White Campuses? *Integrated Education* 18: 23-27.

Busch, J. 1985. Mentoring in Graduate Schools of Education. *American Educational Research Journal* 292 (Summer): 257-265.

Cameron, S. 1978. *Women Faculty in Academia: Sponsorship, Informal Networks, and Scholarly Success.* Unpublished dissertation, University of Michigan.

Campbell, D. and J. Stanley. 1963. *Experimental and Quasi-Experimental Designs for Research.* Boston, MA.: Houghton Mufflin Company.

Caplow, T. and R. McGee. 1958. *The Academic Marketplace.* New York: Basic Books.

Carey, P. 1990. Beyond Superwoman: On Being A Successful Black Woman Administrator. *Initiatives* 53(1): 15-20.

Carnegie Foundation for the Advancement of Teaching. 1978. *Making Affirmative Action Work in Higher Education: An Analysis of Institutional and Federal Policies with Recommendations.* San Francisco, CA.: Jossey-Bass.

_____. 1986. The Satisfied Faculty. *Change*, (Mar/Apr): 31-34.

_____ 1989. *The Condition of the Professoriate: Attitudes and Trends, 1989.* Princeton, NJ.: Princeton University Press.

Carroll, C. 1973. Three's a Crowd: The Dilemma of the Black Woman in Higher Education. In *Academic Women on the Move*, Alice S. Rossi and Ann Calderwood, 173-186. New York: Russell Sage Foundation.

Carter, D., C. Peterson, and D. Shavlik. 1987/1988. Double Jeopardy: Women of Color in Higher Education. *Educational Record* 68, 69 (Fall/Winter): 98-103.

Cartter, A. 1959. *Theory of Wages and Employment.* Richard Irwin Publishing.

_____. 1976. *Ph.D.'s and the Academic Labor Market.* Carnegie Foundation for the Advancement of Teaching.

Centra, J. and N Kendall. 1974. *Women and Men and the Doctorate.* Princeton, NJ.: Educational Testing Service.

Chamberlain, M. 1988. Faculty Women: Preparation, Participation, and Progress. In M. Chamberlain (Ed.), *Women in Academe: Progress and Prospects* (pp. 255-273). New York: Russell Sage Foundation.

Chamberlain, M. (ed.) 1991. *Women in Academe: Progress and Prospects.* New York: Russell Sage Foundation.

Chatters, L., R. Taylor, and J. Jackson. 1986. Aged Black Choices for an Informal Helper Network. *Journal of Gerontology* 41: 94-100.

Cho, H. 1986. Labor Force Participation of Women in Korea. In Chung Sei-wha (Ed.) *Challenges for Women: Women's Studies in Korea.* Seoul, Korea, Ewha Women's University Press, 150-172.

Clark, B. 1983. The Higher Education System: Academic Organization in Cross-National Perspective. Berkeley and Los Angeles: University of California Press, p. 108.

Clark, S. and M. Corcoran. 1986. Perspectives on the American Socialization of Women Faculty: A Case of Accumulative Disadvantage. *Journal of Higher Education* 57:20-43.

Clark, S., M. Corcoran, and D. Lewis. 1986. The Case for an Institutional Perspective on Faculty Development. *Journal of Higher Education* 57: 176-195.

Colbeck, C. 1998. Merging in a Seamless Blend: How Faculty Integrate Teaching and Research. *Journal of Higher Education,* 69(6): 646-664.

Cole, J. 1987. *Fair Science: Women in the Scientific Community.* New York: Columbia University Press.

Cole, J. and S. Cole. 1973. *Social Stratification In Science.* Chicago, IL: The University of Chicago Press.

Cole, J. and H. Zuckerman. 1984. The Productivity Puzzle: Persistence and Change in Patterns of Publications on Men and Women Scientists. In P. Maehr and M. W. Steinkamp (eds.) *Advances in Motivation and Achievement,* 217-256. Greenwich, CT.: JAI Press.

Coleman-Burns, P. 1989. African American Women - Education For What? *Sex Roles* 21(1/2): 145-160.

Cooke, R. and D. Rousseau. 1984. Stress and Strain from Family Roles and Work-Role Expectations. *Journal of Applied Psychology* 69: 252-260.

Cornelius, L., S. Moore, and M. Gray. 1997. The ABC's of Tenure: What all African American Faculty Should Know. *Western Journal of Black Studies,* 21(3): 150-156.

Cose, E. 1993. *The Rage of a Privileged Class.* New York: Harper Collins Publishers.

Coser, R. and G. Rokoff. 1982. Women in the Occupational World: Social Disruption and Conflict. In *Women and Work: Problems and Perspectives* (ed.) Rachel Kahn-Hut et. al. New York: Oxford University Press.

Cotton, J. and J. Tuttle. 1986. Employee Turnover: A Meta-Analysis and Review with Implications for Research. *Academy of Management Review* 11 (Jan): 55-70.

Cox, S. (ed.) 1976. *Female Psychology.* Chicago, IL.: Science Research Associates.

Crane, D. 1970. The Academic Marketplace Revisited: A Study of Faculty Mobility Using the Cartter Ratings. *American Journal of Sociology* 75: 953-964.

Crawford, M. 1982. In Pursuit of the Well-Rounded Life: Women Scholars and the Family. In *Handbook for Women Scholars: Strategies for Success,* (ed.) M. L. Spencer, M. Kehoe, and K. Speece. San Francisco: Center for Women Scholars.

Creswell, J. 1985. *Faculty Research Performance: Lessons from the Sciences and Social Sciences.* ASHE-ERIC Higher Education Report No. 4 Washington, D.C.: Association for the Study of Higher Education.

Crocker, J. and K. McGraw. 1984. What's Good For the Goose Is Not Good For the Gander: Solo Status as an Obstacle to Occupational Achievement for Males and Females. *American Behavioral Scientist* 27(3): 357-369.

Crosby, F. 1982. *Relative Deprivation and Working Women.* New York.: Oxford University Press.

Curry-Williams, M. 1985. *Factors That Influence 'Other Race' Faculty Decisions to Accept, Remain In, or Consider Leaving Faculty Positions at Four Southeastern Public Universities.* Unpublished dissertation, Virginia Polytechnic Institute and State University.

Daloz, L 1986. *Effective Teaching and Mentoring: Realizing the Transformational Power of Adult Learning Experiences.* San Francisco: Jossey-Bass.

Davies, B. 1982. Discrimination, Affirmative Action, and Women Academics: A Case Study of the University of New England, *Vestes,* 25: 15-22.

Davis, L. 1985. Black and White Social Work Faculty: Perceptions of Respect, Satisfaction, and Job Permanence. *Journal of Sociology and Social Welfare* 12: 79-94.

DeFour, D. 1990. Some Thoughts On Ethnic Minority Mentoring. *Mentoring International* 4: 14-17.

DeFour, D. and B. Hirsch. 1990. The Adaptation of Black Graduate Students: A Social Network Approach. *American Journal of Community Psychology* 18: 487-503.

DeJoie, C.. 1977. The Black Woman in Alienation in White America. *Negro Educational Review* 28:4-12.

DeSole, G., and L. Hoffmann. 1981. *Rocking the Boat: Academic Women and Academic Processes.* New York: Modern Language Association of America.

Dex, S.. 1987. *Women's Occupational Mobility.* New York: Martin's Press.

Dey, E., J. Korn, and L. Sax. 1996. Betrayed by the Academy: The Sexual Harassment of Women College Faculty. *Journal of Higher Education,* 67:149-173.

Diaz, S. 1975. *A Study of Personal, Perceptional, and Motivational Factors Influential in Predicting the Aspiration Level of Women and Men Toward the Administrative Roles in Education.* Unpublished dissertation, Boston University.

Dickens, C. 1997. Feminists at Work: Collaborative Relationships Among Women Faculty. *Review of Higher Education,* 21(1) 79-101.

Dickens, F. and J. Dickens. 1982. *The Black Manager.* New York: AMACOM.

Dillman, D. 1978. *Mail and Telephone Surveys: The Total Design Method.* New York: Wiley.

Dodgson, J. 1986. Do Women in Education Need Mentors? *Education Canada* (Spring): 28-33.

Douglass, P. 1979. *Black Working Women: Factors Affecting Labor Market Experience.* Wellesley, MA.: Wellesley College Center for Research on Women Working Papers.

Dublin, T. 1979. *Women at Work: The Transformation of Work and Community.* New York: Columbia University Press.

DuBois, W.E.B. 1898. The Study of the Negro Problem. *Annuals,* 1: 1-23.

____. 1903. *The Souls of Black Folk.* Chicago, IL.: A.C. McClury.

____. 1908. *The Negro American Family.* Atlanta, GA.: Atlanta University Press.

Eckert, R. 1971. Academic Women Revisited. *Liberal Education* 57(Dec): 479-487.

Eckert, R. and J. Stecklein. 1961. *Job Motivation and Satisfaction of College Teachers: A Study of Faculty Members in Minnesota Colleges.* Washington, D.C.: Government Printing Office.

Edson, S. 1988. *Pushing the Limits: The Female Administrative Aspirant.* State University of New York Press.

Ehara, T. 1998. Faculty Perceptions of University Government in Japan and the United States. *Comparative Education Review,* 42(1): 61-73.

Ehrenberg, R., H. Kasper and D. Rees. 1991. Faculty Turnover at American Colleges and Universities: Analyses of AAUP Data. *Economics of Education Review* 10(2): 99-110.

Eichenbaum, L. and S. Orbach. 1987. *Between Women.* Viking Penguin, Inc.

Elam, J. 1989. *Blacks in Higher Education: Overcoming the Odds.* Lanham, MD.: University Press of America.

Elmore, C. and R. Blackburn. 1983. Black and White Faculty in White Research Universities. *Journal of Higher Education* 54(1): 1-15.

Epps, E. 1989. Academic Culture and the Minority Professor. *Academe* 75(Sep/Oct): 23-26.

Epstein, C. 1970. *A Woman's Place: Options and Limits in Professional Careers.* Berkeley, CA.: University of California Press.

____. 1973. Positive Effects of the Multiple Negative: Explaining the Success of Black Professional Women. *American Journal of Sociology* 78(4): 912-935.

Erickson, K. and N. Pitner. 1980. The Mentor Concept is Alive and Well. *NASSP Bulletin* (December): 8-13.

Erkut, S. 1982. Dualism in Values Toward Education of Turkish Women. In *Sex Roles, Family, and Community in Turkey,* C. Kagitcibasi (Ed.). Bloomington, IN: Indiana University Turkish Studies, 121-32.

Etaugh, Ce. 1984. Women Faculty and Administrators in Higher Education: Changes in Their Status Since 1972. *Journal of the National Association of Women Deans, Administrators, and Counselors* 48: 21-25.

Etaugh, C. and H. Kasley. 1981. Evaluating Competence: Effects of Sex, Marital Status, and Parental Status. *Psychology of Women Quarterly* 6(2): 196-203.

Ethington, C., J. Smart, and M. Zeltmann. 1989. Institutional and Departmental Satisfaction of Women Faculty. *Research in Higher Education* 30: 261-271.

Evans, S. 1989. *Born for Liberty: A History of Women in America.* New York: The Free Press.

Exum, W. 1983. Climbing the Crystal Stairs: Values, Affirmative Action, and Minority Faculty. *Social Problems* 30 (April): 383-399.

Exum, W., R. Menges, B. Watkins, and P. Berglund. 1984. Making It At The Top: Women and Minority Faculty in the Academic Labor Market. *American Behavioral Scientist* 27(3) 301-324.

Featherman, D. and R. Hauser. 1976. Sexual Inequities and Socioeconomic Achievement in the US, 1962-1973. *American Sociological Review* 41: 462-483.

Federico, J., P. Federico, and G. Lundquist. 1976. Predicting Women's Turnover as a Function of Extent of Met Salary Expectations and Biodemographic Data. *Personnel Psychology* 29: 559-566.

Feldman, S. 1973. Impediment or Stimulant: Marital Status and Graduate Education. *American Journal of Sociology* 78 (Jan): 982-994.

Felmlee, D. 1980. *Women's Job Transitions: A Dynamic Analysis of Job Mobility and Job Leaving.* Unpublished dissertation, University of Wisconsin-Madison.

_____. 1982. Women's Job Mobility Processes Within and Between Employers. *American Sociological Review* 47 (February): 142-151.

Fichter, J. 1964. *Graduates of Predominantly Negro Colleges: Class of 1964.* Public Health Services Publication, No. 1571. Washington, D.C.: Government Printing Office.

Fields, C. March 5, 1998. A Scant Presence: Black and Latino Faculty at Research Institutions. *Black Issues in Higher Education* 15(1): 28-33.

Fikes, R. 1978. Control of Information: Black Scholars and the Academic Press. *Western Journal of Black Studies* 2(3): 219-221.

Finkel, S., S. Olswang, and N. She. 1994. Childbirth, Tenure, and Promotion for Women Faculty. *Review of Higher Education* 17(3): 259-270.

Finkelstein, M. 1984. *The American Academic Profession*: A Synthesis of Social Scientific Inquiry Since World War II. Columbus, OH.: Ohio State University Press.

____. 1987. Women and Minority Faculty. In ASHE-ERIC Reader *Faculty and Faculty Issues in Colleges and Universities*, (ed.) M. Finkelstein. Lexington, MA.: Ginn Press.

Finkin, M. 1996. *The Case for Tenure*. Ithaca: Cornell University Press.

Finnegan, D. 1993. Segmentation in the Academic Labor Market: Hiring Cohorts in Comprehensive Universities. *Journal of Higher Education* 64(6): 621-656.

Fishbein, M. 1967. Attitude and the Prediction of Behavior. In M. Fishbein (ed.) *Readings in Attitude Theory and Measurement*. New York: Wiley.

Fleming, J., G. Gill, and D. Swinton. 1978. *The Case for Affirmative Action for Blacks in Higher Education*. Washington, DC.: Howard University Press.

Flowers, V. and C. Hughes. 1973. Why Employees Stay. *Harvard Business Review* (July/Aug), 49-60.

Fogarty, M., R Rapoport, and R. Rapoport. 1971. *Sex, Career, and Family*. Newbury Park, CA.: Sage Publications.

Fox, M. 1974. 1985. "Publication, Performance, and Reward in Science and Scholarship." *In Higher Education: Handbook of Theory and Research*, vol. 1. Edited by J. Smart, 255-82. New York: Agathon Press.

Freeman, B. 1977. Women Faculty in the American University: Up The Down Staircase. *Higher Education* 6: 165-188.

Frierson, H. 1990. The Situation of Black Educational Researchers: Continuation of a Crisis. *Educational Researcher* 19: 12-17.

Fulton, O. and M. Trow. 1974. Research Activity in American Higher Education. *Sociology of Science*, 47:29-73.

Gappa, J and B. Uehling. 1979. *Women in Academe*. Washington, D.C.: American Association for Higher Education.

Garcia, S. 1989. My Sisters Keeper: Negative Effects of Social Welfare and Affirmative Action Programs on Black Women. *Sex Roles* 21(1/2): 25-43.

Garza, H and E. Cohen. 1988. *Minority Researchers and Minority Education: A Position Paper,* AERA Standing Committee on the Role and Status of Minorities in Educational Research and Development.

Gavin, J. and R. Ewen. 1974. Racial Differences in Job Attitudes and Performance: Some Theoretical Considerations and Empirical Findings. *Personnel Psychology* 27: 455-452.

Gerystl, J. 1971. Leisure, Taste, and Occupational Milieu. In C. Anderson and J. Murray (eds.) *The Professor.* Cambridge, MA: Schenkman.

Getzels, J. and E. Guba. 1954. Role, Role Conflict and Effectiveness. *American Sociological Review,* 19: 164-175.

Gilkes, C. 1983. Going Up for the Oppressed: The Career Mobility of the Black Women Community Workers. *Journal of Social Issues* 39(3): 115-139.

Gill, V. 1990. In Two Worlds: Women Academics in India. In *Storming the Tower: Women in the Academic World,* Lie, S and V. O'Leary, (Ed.). London: Kogan Page

Glowinkowski, S. and C. Cooper. 1987. Managers and Professionals in Business/Industrial Settings: The Research Evidence. In *Job Stress: From Theory to Suggestion* (ed.) J. Ivancevich and D. C. Ganster. Binghamton, New York: Haworth Press.

Gmelch, W., N. Lovrich, and Phyllis K., Wilke. 1984. Sources of Stress in Academe. *Research in Higher Education* 20(4): 477-490.

Gmelch, W., P. Wilke, and N. Lovrich. 1986. Dimensions of Stress Among University Faculty: Factor Analytic Results from a National Survey. *Research in Higher Education* 24(3): 266-286.

Gordon, M. 1974. *Higher Education and the Labor Market.* Carnegie Foundation for the Advancement of Teaching.

Government of India. 1975. *Towards Equity.* Report of the Committee on the Status of Women in India. New Delhi.

Graham, P. 1973. Status Transitions of Women Students, Faculty, and Administrators. In *Academic Women on the Move,* Alice S. Rossi and Ann Calderwood, 163-172. New York: Russell Sage Foundation.

Graham, S. 1992. Most of the Subjects Were White and Middle Class: Trends in Published Research on African Americans in Selected APA Journals, 1970-1989. *American Psychologist* 47: 629-639.

Graves, S. 1990. A Case of Double Jeopardy? Black Women in Higher Education. *Initiatives* 53(1): 3-8.

Gray, M. 1985. The Halls of Ivy and the Halls of Justice: Resisting Sex Discrimination Against Faculty Women. *Academe* (Sep/Oct): 33-41.

Green, M. (ed.) 1989. *Minorities on Campus: A Handbook for Enhancing Diversity.* Washington, D.C. American Council on Education.

Greenhaus, J. and J. Gavin. 1972. The Relationship Between Expectations and Job Behavior for White and Black Employees. *Personnel Psychology* 25: 449-455.

Gregory, S. 1994a. Revisiting Affirmative Action. *Planning for Higher Education* 23(1): 49-50.

_____. 1994b. Why African American Faculty Women Leave the Academy: Barriers and Opportunities for Retention. *Association of Black Nursing Faculty Journal* (Fall), 5(6): 24-36.

_____. 1994c. *African American Women Professors: Identifying Obstacles, Opportunities, and Career Paths.* Paper presented in June at the 7th Annual National Conference On Race and Ethnicity in American Higher Education, Atlanta, GA.

_____. 1995. *Economic and Psychosocial Factors Which Influence Career Mobility Among African American Women Professors.* Published dissertation. University of Pennsylvania, Philadelphia, PA.

_____ and H. Horton. 1994. Educational Opportunity Programs for Students of Color in Graduate and Professional Schools. *The Trotter Review*, William Monroe Trotter Institute. University of Massachussetts at Boston, 8(2): 16-19.

Gustafson, S. and D. Magnusson. 1991. *Female Life Careers: A Pattern Approach.* New Jersey: Lawrence Erlbaum Associate Publishers.

Guy-Sheftall, B. and P. Bell-Scott. 1989. Finding a Way: Black Women Students in the Academy. In *Educating the Majority: Women Challenge Traditions in Higher Education.* (eds.) Carol Pearson, Donna Shavlik, and Judy Touchton. American Council on Education. New York: Macmillan Publishing.

Haiqing, W. 1989. *The Current Status of Women Professors in China.* Women's Studies, No. 3, May, p. 15.

Halaby, C. 1979. Sexual Inequity in the Workplace: An Employer Specific Analysis of Pay Differences. *Social Science Research* 8:79-104.

Hale, J. 1980. The Black Woman and Child Rearing. In *The Black Woman*, (ed.) La Frances Rodgers-Rose, 79-88. Newbury Park, CA.: Sage Publications.

Halsey, A. 1992. *The Decline of Donnish Dominion: The British Academic Profession of the Twentieth Century*, Claredon Press, Oxford.

Hammond, L. 1988. *Mediators of Stress and Role Satisfaction in Multiple-Role Women.* Paper presented in April/May at the Annual Meeting of the Western Psychological Association, Burlingame, CA.

Hamovitch, W. and R. Morganstern. 1977. Children and the Productivity of Academic Women. *Journal of Higher Education* 48(6) 633-645.

Hansard Society Commission. 1990. *The Report of the Hansard Society Commission on Women at the Top.* The Hansard Society, London.

Hansen, W. 1985. Salary Differences Across Disciplines. *Academe* 71(4): 6-6.

Harley, S. and R. Penn. 1978. *The Afro-American Woman: Struggles and Images.* Port Washington, N.Y.: Kennikat Press.

Harrigan, B. 1977. *Games Mother Never Taught You.* New York: Warner.

Harrison, A. 1989. Black Working Women: Introduction to a Lifetime Perspective. In R.L. Jones (ed.) *Black Adult Development and Aging.* Berkeley, CA.: Cobb and Henry Publishing,

Harry, J. and N. Goldner. 1972. Null Relationship Between Teaching and Research. *Sociology of Education* 45: 47-60.

Harvard, P. 1986. *Successful Behaviors of Black Women Administrators in Higher Education: Implications for Leadership.* Paper presented in April at American Educational Research Association Meeting, San Francisco, CA.

Harvey, J. 1972. *Minorities and Advanced Degrees.* Eric Clearinghouse on Higher Education. Washington, DC.: George Washington University.

Harvey, W. and D. Scott-Jones. 1985. We Can't Find Any: The Elusiveness of Black Faculty Members in American Higher Education. *Issues in Education* 3 (Summer): 68-76.

Havens, E 1973. Women, Work, and Wedlock: A Note on Female Marital Patterns in the U.S. *American Journal of Sociology* 78: 975-981.

Hawkins, A and D. Schultz. Women: The Academic Proletariat in West Germany and the Netherlands. In *Storming the Tower: Women in the Academic World*, Lie, S and V. O'Leary, (Ed.). London: Kogan Page.

Hawkins, A and Van Balen. 1984. De positit van vrouwen in het wetenschappelijk onderwijs van 1970-1980. (The Position of Women in Universities 1970-1980). Universiteit en Hogeschool, 30(3): 194-209.

Hendderson, J. 1991. *SPSS/PC+ Made Simple*. Belmont, CA.: Wadsworth Publishing.

Hennig, M. and A. Jardim. 1977. *The Managerial Women*. New York: Doubleday.

Hensel, N. 1990. Maternity, Promotion and Tenure: Are They Compatible? In *Women in Higher Education: Changes and Challenges*, (ed.) L.B. Welch. New York: Preager.

_____ 1991. *Realizing Gender Equality in Higher Education: The Need To Integrate Work/Family Issues*. ASHE-ERIC Higher Education Report No. 2, Washington, D.C.

Heppner, P. and D. Gonzales. 1987. Men Counseling Men. In M. Scher, M. Stevens, G. Goode, and G. B. Eichenfield (eds.) *Handbook of Counseling and Psychotherapy with Men*, 30-38.

Herzberg, F. 1972. *Work and the Nature of Man* . New York: World Publishing.

Herzberg, F., B. Mausner, R. Peterson, and D. Capwell. 1957. *Job Attitudes: A Review of Research and Opinion*. Pittsburgh, PA.: Psychological Service of Pittsburgh.

Herzberg, F., B. Mausner, and B. Snyderman. 1959. *The Motivation to Work*. New York: John Wiley & Sons.

Hess, J., C. Ottinger, and J. Lippincott. 1990. A Decade of Change: The Status of U.S. Women Doctorates, 1978-1988. *Research Briefs* 1(6): 1-8.

Hexter, H. 1990. Faculty Salaries in Perspective. *Research Briefs* 1(1): 1-7.

Higginbottham, E. 1981. Is Marriage a Priority? Class Differences in Marital Options of Educated Black Women, 259-267 in Peter Stein (ed.), *Single Life*. New York: St. Martin's Publishing

Hileman, S. 1990. The 'Female Determined Relationship': Personal and Professional Needs of Academic Women in Commuter Marriages. In *Women in Higher Education*, (ed.) L.B. Welch. New York: Preager.

Hill, M.. 1984. Faculty Sex Composition and Job Satisfaction of Academic Women. *International Journal of Women's Studies* 1 (March/April): 179-189.

Hill, R. 1972. *The Strength of Black Families.* New York: National Urban League.

Hill, R., with A. Billingsley, et al. 1993. *Research on the African American Family: A Holistic Perspective.* Westport, CT.: Greenwood Publishing.

Hines, E. and J. Higham. 1996. *Faculty Workload and States Policy.* Paper presented at the annual meeting of the Association for the Study of Higher Education, Memphis, TN.

Hines, G. 1973. Achievement Motivation, Occupations, and Labor Turnover in New Zealand. *Journal of Applied Psychology* 58: 313-317.

Hochschild, A. 1974. Making It: Marginality and Obstacles to Minority Consciousness. In B. Kundsin, *Women and Success*. New York: William Morrow.

_____. 1975. Inside the Clockwork of Women's Careers. In Florence Howe (ed.),*Women and the Power to Change*. New York: McGraw-Hill, 47-80.

Hoffman, R. 1984. An Assessment of the Teaching, Research, and Service Function of a College Faculty. *Journal of Research and Development in Education* 17 (Winter): 49-54.

Hollon, C. and G. Gemmill. 1976. A Comparison of Female and Male Professors Participation in Decision Making, Job-Related Tension, Job Involvement, and Job Satisfaction. *Education Administration Quarterly* 12 (Winter): 80-93.

hooks, b. 1989. *Talking Back: Thinking Feminist, Thinking Black.* Boston, MA.: South End Press.

Hornig, L. 1980. Untenured and Tenuous: The Status of Women Faculty. *Annals of the American Academy of Political and Social Science* 448: 115-125.

Hoskins, R. 1978. *Black Administrators in Higher Education: Conditions and Perspectives.* New York: Praeger Publishing, Inc.

Howard-Vital, M. 1989. African American Women in Higher Education: Struggling To Gain Identity. *Journal of Black Studies* 20 (December): 180-191.

Huber, J. 1973. From Sugar and Spice to Professor. In *Academic Women on the Move*, Alice S. Rossi and Ann Calderwood, pp. 125-138. New York: Russell Sage Foundation.

Hudson-Weems, C. 1989. The Tripartite Plight of African American Women as Reflected in the Novels of Hurston and Walker. *Journal of Black Studies* 20 (December): 192-207.

Hulin, C. and P. Smith. 1964. Sex Differences in Job Satisfaction. *Journal of Applied Psychology* 48: 88-92.

Hunt, J. and L. Hunt. 1982. Dilemmas and Contradictions of Status: The Case of the Dual Career Family. In *Women and Work: Problems and Perspectives* (ed.) Rachel Kahn-Hut et. al. New York: Oxford University Press.

Hurlbert, J., and R. Rosenfeld. 1992. Getting a Good Job: Rank and Institutional Prestige in Academic Psychologists' Careers. *Sociology of Education* 65: 188-207.

Hutcheson, P. 1998. Tenure: Traditions, Policies, and Practices. *Review of Higher Education*, 21(3): 303-313.

Independent Newspaper. April 16, 1990, p. 17.

Ivancevich, J. and J. Donnelly. 1968. Job Satisfaction Research: A Manageable Guide for Practitioners: *Personnel Journal* 47(March): 172-177.

Jackson, B. 1990. Black Women as Role Models: Where Can We Find Them? *Initiatives* 53(1): 37-45.

Jackson, J. 1991. *Life in Black America.* Newbury Park, CA.: Sage Publications, Inc.

Jackson, J. 1971. But Where Are The Men? *Black Scholar* (Dec): 30-41.

Jackson, K 1991. Factors Associated with Alienation Among Black Faculty. *Research in Race and Ethnic Relations* 6: 123-144.

Jaynes, G. and R. Williams. 1989. *A Common Destiny: Blacks and American Society.* Washington, DC.: National Research Council, National Academy of Sciences.

Jeffers, C. 1967. *Living Poor.* Ann Arbor, MI.: Ann Arbor Publications.

Johnson, G. and F. Stafford. 1979. Pecuniary Rewards of Men and Women Faculty. In *Academic Rewards in Higher Education.* Darrell R. Lewis and William E. Becker, Jr. (eds.) Cambridge, MA.: Ballinger Publications Co., 231-243.

Johnsrud, L. 1995. Korean Academic Women: Multiple Roles, Multiple Challenges. *Higher Education* 30: 17-35.

Johnsrud, L and K. Sadao. 1998. The Common Experience of "Otherness:" Ethnic and Racial Minority Faculty. *The Review of Higher Education,* 21(4): 315-342.

Jones, B. 1983. The Economic Status of Black Women. In *The State of Black America.* New York: National Urban League.

Jones, D. and G. Makepeace. 1995. Equal Worth, Equal Opportunities: Pay and Promotion in an Internal Labour Market, *Economic Journal,* 6:401-410.

Jones, L. 1979. *Black Students Enrolled in White Colleges and Universities: Their Attitudes and Perceptions.* Atlanta, GA.: Southern Regional Board of Education.

Jones, M. 1992. *Learning To Lead: A Study of the Developmental Paths of African-American Women College Presidents.* Unpublished dissertation. Washington, D.C.: George Washington University.

_____. 1994. *Black Women in Academia: Empirical Investigations.* Paper presented at Black Women in the Academy: Defending Our Name, 1894-1994 Conference, Boston, MA.

Jones, Reginald (ed.). 1991. *Black Psychology.* Berkeley, CA.: Cobb and Henry Publishing.

Justus, J., S. Freitag, and L. Parker. 1987. *The University of California in the Twenty-First Century: Successful Approaches to Faculty Diversity.* Los Angeles: University of California.

Kandel, D., M. Davies, and V. Ravies. 1985. The Stressfulness of Daily Social Roles for Women: Marital, Occupational, and Household Roles. *Journal of Health and Social Behavior* 26: 64-78.

Kandiyoti, D. 1982. Urban Change and Women's Roles in Turkey: An Overview and Evaluation. In *Sex Roles, Family, and Community in Turkey,* C. Kagitcibasi (Ed.). Bloomington, IN: Indiana University Turkish Studies.

Kanter, R. 1977. *The Men and Women of the Corporation.* New York: Basic Books.

_____. 1983. *The Change Masters.* New York: Simon and Schuster.

Kasper, H. 1989. High Education Goals: Low Salary Increases: the Annual Report on the Economic Status of the Profession, 1988-89, *Academe*, Bulletin of the American Association of University Professors.

Kaufman, D. 1978. Associational Ties in Academe: Some Male and Female Differences. *Sex Roles*, 4(1): 9-21.

Kaul, H. and B. Brandth. 1988. Lov og Liv: Ensammenlikning av omsorgspermisjoner I Norden, IFIM SINTEF. Gruppen, Nor, p. 9.

Kauper, M. 1991. *Factors Which Influence the Career Decisions of Minority Faculty at a Predominantly White Liberal Arts Institution: A Case Study.* Unpublished dissertation, Indiana University.

Kershaw, T. 1992. The Effects of Educational Tracking on the Social Mobility of African Americans. *Journal of Black Studies* 23(1): 152-169.

Kornhauser, W. 1962. *Scientists in Industry.* Berkeley, CA.: University of California Press.

Kuppuswamy, B. 1986. *Social Change in India.* New Delhi: Ministry of Social and Women's Welfare.

Kyvic, S. 1990. Motherhood and Scientific Productivity. *Social Studies of Science*, 20(1): 149-60.

Ladd, E. 1979. The Work Experience of American College Professors: Some Data and an Argument. In *Faculty Career Development.* Current Issues in Higher Education No. 2. American Association for Higher Education, Washington, D.C.

Ladd, E. and S. Lipset. 1976. *Survey of the Social, Political, and Educational Perspectives of American College and University Faculty.* Final Report. Storrs, CT: University of Connecticut.

Ladner, J. 1071. *Tomorrow's Tomorrow: The Black Woman.* Garden City, N.Y.: Anchor Books.

Landino, R. and S. Owens. 1988. Self-Efficacy in University Faculty. *Journal of Vocational Behavior* 33: 1-14.

Landy, F. 1989. *Psychology of Work Behavior.* Belmont, CA.: Brooks-Cole Publishing.

Lattin, P. 1983. Academic Women, Affirmative Action, and Mid-America in the Eighties. *Women Studies International Forum*, 6(2):224.

Lazear, E. and S. Rosen. 1990. Male-Female Wage Differentials in Job Ladders, *Journal of Labor Economics*, 8:S106-123.

Lee, Dong-won. 1986. The Changes in the Korean Family and Women. In Chung Sei-wha (Ed.), *Challenges for Women: Women's Studies in Korea*: Korea Women's Institute, 24-53.

Lee, Hie-sung. 1984. A Case Study on Achievement Motivation of Women Professors in a Women's University. *Women's Studies Review*, 1. Ewha Women's University: Korea Women's Institute, 24-53.

Leggon, C. 1980. Black Female Professionals: Dilemmas and Contradictions of Status. In *The Black Woman*, (ed.) La Frances Rodgers-Rose, 161-174. Newbury Park, CA.: Sage Publications.

Leon, C. 1988. Good-Bye, Mr. Chips. *American Demographics* (Oct): 33-35.

Levinson, D. 1978. *The Seasons of a Man's Life*. New York: Knopf.

Levinson, W., S. Tolle, and C. Lewis. 1989. Women in Academic Medicine: Combining Career and Family. *New England Journal of Medicine* 321:1511-1517.

Lewis, E. 1989. Role Strain in African-American Women: The Efficacy of Support Networks. *Journal of Black Studies* 20(2): 155-169.

Liddle, J. and R. Joshi. 1986. *Daughters of Independence*, London: Zed Books.

Lie, S. 1992. The Juggling Act: Work and Family in Norway. In *Storming the Tower: Women in the Academic World*, Lie, S and V. O'Leary, (Ed.). London: Kogan Page.

Likert, R. 1961. *New Patterns of Management*. New York.: McGraw-Hill.

Lipman-Blumen, J. 1976. Towards a Homosocial Theory of Sex Roles. An Explanation of the Sex-Segregation of Social Institutions. *Signs* 3:15-32.

Lincoln, Y. and E. Guba. 1980. The Distinction Between Merit and Worth. In *Evaluation, Educational Evaluation, and Policy Analysis* 4: 61-71.

Linnell, R. 1982. *Dollars and Scholars: An Inquiry into the Impact of Faculty Income Upon the Function and Future of the Academy*. University of Southern California Press.

Lipset, S. 1963. *Political Man: The Social Bases of Politics*. Garden City: Anchor Books.

Lipset, S. and E. Ladd, Jr. 1975. Professor's Religious and Ethnic Backgrounds. *Chronicle of Higher Education*, 22 Sep, 11:2.

Lloyd, S. et al. 1982. *Support Networks of Dual-Career Couples.* Washington, DC.: National Council on Family Relations.

Locke, E. 1969. What Is Job Satisfaction? *Organizational Behavior and Human Performance* 4: 309-336.

Locke, E. 1976. The Nature and Courses of Job Satisfaction. In M. Dunnette, *Handbook of Industrial Organizational Psychology.* Chicago, IL.: Rand-McNally.

Locke, E., W. Fitzpatrick, and F. White. 1983. Job Satisfaction and Role Clarity Among University and College Faculty. *Review of Higher Education* 6 (Summer): 343-365.

Logan, C. 1990. *Job Satisfaction of African-American Faculty at Predominantly African-American and Predominantly White Four-Year, State-Assisted Institutions in the South.* Unpublished dissertation, Bowling Green State University, Ohio.

London, M. 1983. Toward a Theory of Career Motivation. *Academy of Management Review* 8(4): 620-630.

Long, J. 1978. Productivity and Academic Position in the Scientific Career. *American Sociological Review* 43 (December): 889-908.

Long, J. 1987. Problems and Prospects for Research on Sex Differences in the Scientific Career. In *Women: Their Under-representation and Career Differentials in Science and Engineering, Proceeding of a Workshop,* S. Dix (Ed.). Washington, DC: National Academy Press.

Long, J., P. Allison, and R. McGinnis. 1979. Entrance into the Academic Career. *American Sociological Review* (44): 816-830.

____. 1993. Rank Advancement in Academic Careers: Sex Differences and the Effects of Productivity. *American Sociological Review* 58 (October): 703-722.

Long, J. Scott, and Robert McGinnis. 1981. Organizational Context and Scientific Productivity. *American Sociological Review* (46): 422-442.

____. 1985. The Effects of the Mentor on the Academic Career. *Sociometrics* 7: 255-280.

Lubwig, M. 1996. Framing the Public Policy Debate on Faculty: What is the Role of Research? In J. Braxton (Ed.), Faculty Teaching and Research: Is There a Conflict? *New Directions for Institutional Research,* No. 90: 67-78. San Francisco: Jossey Bass.

Luukkonen-Gronow, T. 1987. University Career Opportunitites fro Women in Finland in the 1980s. *Acta Sociologica,* 30: 193-206.

Lykes, M. Brinton. 1983. Discrimination: Coping in the Lives of Black Women: Analyses of Oral History Data. *Journal of Social Issues* 39(3): 79-100.

Malcolm, Shirley M., Paula Q. Hall, and Janet W. Brown. 1976. *The Double Bind: The Price of Being a Minority Woman in Science.* Washington, D.C.: American Association for the Advancement of Science.

Malson, Michelene R. 1983. Black Women's Sex Roles: The Social Context of a New Ideology. *Journal of Social Issues* 39(3): 101-113.

Mangione, T. 1973. Turnover: Some Psychological and Demographic Correlates. In R. P. Quinn and T. W. Mangione (eds.). *The 1969-70 Survey of Working Conditions.* Ann Arbor: University of Michigan, Survey Research Center.

March, J. and H. Simon. 1958. *Organizations.* New York: Wiley & Sons.

Marsh, R. and H. Mannari 1977. Organizational Commitment and Turnover: A Prediction Study. *Administrative Science Quarterly* 22: 57-75.

Marshall, H. 1964. *The Mobility of College Faculties.* New York.: Pageant Press.

Marshall, M.. and C. Jones. 1990. Childbearing Sequence and the Career Development of Women Administrators in Higher Education. *Journal of College Student Development* 31: 531-537.

Marwell, G., R. Rosenfeld, and S. Spelerman. 1979. Geographic Constraints on Women's Careers in Academia. *Science* 205: 1225-1231.

Matier, M. 1986. *Factors Influencing "Star" Faculty Attrition at Institutions of Higher Education: An Analysis of the University of Oregon's Faculty on the College of Arts and Sciences, 1976/1977-1984/1985.* Published dissertation, University of Oregon.

____. 1988. *Factors Influencing Faculty Migration.* Paper presented at the annual forum of the Association for Institutional Research, Phoenix, AZ.

____. 1990. Retaining Faculty: A Tale of Two Campuses. *Research in Higher Education* 31(1): 39-60.

Maxfield, B. 1981. *Employment of Minority Ph.D.'s: Changes Over Time.* Washington, D.C. : National Academy Press.

Mayfield, B. and W. Nash. 1976. Career Attitudes of Female Professors. *Psychological Reports* 39: 631-634.

McAdoo, H. 1980. Black Mothers and the Extended Family Support Network. In *The Black Woman*, (ed.) La Frances Rodgers-Rose, 125-144. Newbury Park, CA.: Sage Publications.

McCain, B., C. O'Reilly, and J. Pfeffer. 1983. The Effects of Departmental Demography on Turnover: The Case of a University. *Academy of Management Journal* 26(4) 626:641.

McCombs, H. 1989. The Dynamics and Impact of Affirmative Action Processes on Higher Education, the Curriculum, and Black Women. *Sex Roles* 21(1/2): 127-143.

McCray, C. 1980. The Black Woman and Family Roles. In *The Black Woman*, (ed.) La Frances Rodgers-Rose, 67-78. Newbury Park, CA.: Sage Publications.

McGee, G. and R. Ford. 1958. *The Academic Marketplace.* New York: Basic Books.

____. 1987. Faculty Research Productivity and Intention to Change Positions. *Review of Higher Education* 11(1): 1-16.

McGee, R. 1971. *Academic Janus.* San Francisco, CA.: Jossey-Bass.

McKay, N. 1989. The Black Woman Professor-White University. *Women's Studies Journal International* 6: 143-147.

McKenna, J. and A. Sikula. 1981. On the Move Through the Groves of Academe: Mobility Among Business Professors. *Business Horizons* 26 (Nov-Dec): 70-75.

McKinney, K. 1990. Sexual Harassment of University Faculty by Colleagues and Students. *Sex Roles*, 23:421-438.

McNabb, R. and V. Wass. 1997. Male-Female Salary Differentials in British Universities. *Oxford Economic Papers*, 49(3): 328-344).

Melillo, D. 1981. *Role Model and Mentor Influences on the Career Development of Academic Women.* Published dissertation, U. S. International University.

Menges, R. and W. Exum. 1983. Barriers to the Progress of Women and Minority Faculty. *Journal of Higher Education* 54(2): 123-144.

Merriam, S. 1983. Mentors and Protégés: A Critical Review of the Literature. *Adult Education Quarterly* (Spring): 161-173.

Merriam, S., T. Thomas, and C. Zeph. 1987. Mentoring in Higher Education: What We Know Now. *Review of Higher Education* 11(2) Winter: 199-210.

Merton, R. 1957. The Role Set: Problems in Sociological Theory. *British Journal of Sociology* 8: 106-120.

_____. 1968. *Social Theory and Social Structure*. New York: Free Press.

_____. 1972. Insiders and Outsiders: A Chapter in the Sociology of Knowledge. *American Journal of Sociology* 78(1): 9-48.

_____. 1973. *The Sociology of Science*. Chicago, IL.: University of Chicago Press.

_____. 1988. The Matthew Effect in Science II. *Isis* 79:606-623.

Milem, J. and H. Astin. 1993. The Changing Composition of the Faculty: What Does it Realy Mean for Diversity? *Change*, March/April: 21-28.

Mincer, J. and S. Polachek. 1974. Family Investments in Human Capital: Earnings of Women. *Journal of Political Economy* 82: S76-S109.

Ministry of Education. 1992. *Educational Statistics of New Zealand 1992*. Wellington, New Zealand: Ministry of Education.

Ministry of Education. 1990. *Education in Korea: 1989-1990*. Republic of Korea: Ministry of Education.

Mitchell, J. 1983. Visible, Vulnerable, and Viable: Emerging Perspectives of a Minority Professor. In *Teaching Minority Students* (ed.) James H. Cones III, et. al. San Francisco, CA.: Jossey-Bass.

Mobley, W. 1977. Intermediate Linkages in the Relationship Between Job Satisfaction and Employee Turnover. *Journal of Applied Psychology* 62(2): 237-240.

Mobley, W., R. Griffeth, H. Hand, and B. Meglino. 1979. Review and Conceptual Analysis of the Employee Turnover Process. *Psychological Bulletin* 86: 493-522.

Mobley, W., S. Horner, and A. Hollingsworth. 1978. An Evaluation of Precursors of Hospital Employee Turnover. *Journal of Applied Psychology* 63(76): 408-414.

Moch, M. 1980. Racial Differences in Job Satisfaction: Testing Four Common Explanations. *Journal of Applied Psychology* 65(3): 299-307.

Mommsen, K. 1973. Professionalism and the Racial Context of Career Patterns Among Black American Doctorates: A Note on the "Brain Drain" Hypothesis. *Journal of Negro Education* 42 (Spring): 191-204.

_____. 1974a. Black Doctorates in American Higher Education: A Cohort Analysis. *Journal of Social and Behavioral Sciences*, (Spring): 101-117.

_____. 1974b. Black Ph.D.'s in the Academic Marketplace: Supply, Demand, and Price. *Journal of Higher Education* 45(4): 253-267.

Montero-Sieburth, M. 1996. Beyond Affirmative Action: An Inquiry Into the Experiences of Latinas in Academe. *New England Journal of Public Policy: A Journal of the John W. McCormack Institute of Public Affairs*, University of Massachusetts at Boston, 11(2): 65-96.

Moore, D. and A. Salembine. 1980. The Dynamics of the Mentor-Protégé Relationship in Developing Women as Academic Leaders. *Journal of Education Equity and Leadership* 2:51-64.

Moore, K. and M. Sagaria. 1993. The Situation of Women in Research Universities in the United States: Within the Inner Circles of Academic Power. In J. Glazer, E. Bensimon, and B. Townsend (Eds.) *Women in Higher Education: A Feminist Perspective* (pp. 227-240). Needham Heights, MA.: Ginn Press.

Moore, K. and L. Wagstaff. 1974. *Black Educators in White Colleges.* San Francisco, CA.: Jossey-Bass.

Moore, M. 1981. Mainstreaming Black Women in American Higher Education. *Journal of the Society of Ethnic and Special Studies* 5 (Spring/Summer): 61-68.

Moore, W. 1987/1988. Black Faculty in White Colleges: A Dream Deferred. *Educational Record* (Fall/Winter): 117-121.

Morlock, L. 1973. Discipline Variation in the Status of Academic Women. In *Academic Women on the Move*, Alice S. Rossi and Ann Calderwood, 199-238. New York: Russell Sage Foundation.

Morse, N. 1953. *Satisfaction in White-Collar Jobs.* Ann Arbor, MI.: University of Michigan, Institute for Social Research.

Moses, Y. 1989. Black Women in Academe: Issues and Strategies. *Project on the Status of Education of Women.* Association of American Colleges, Washington, D.C.

Mowday, R. and T. McDade. 1979. *Linking Behavioral and Attitudinal Commitment: A Longitudinal Analysis of Job Choice and Job Attitudes.* Paper presented in August at 39th Annual Meeting of the Academy of Management, Atlanta, GA.

Muchinsky, P. and M. Tuttle. 1979. Employee Turnover: An Empirical and Methodological Assessment. *Journal of Vocational Behavior* 14: 43-77.

Murray, S. and D. Harrison. 1981. Black Women and the Future. *Psychology of Women Quarterly* 6(1): 113-122.

Murrell, A., I. Frieze, and J. Frost. 1991. Aspiring To Careers in Male and Female-Dominated Professions: A Study of Black and White College Women. *Psychology of Women Quarterly* 15:103-126.

Mutran, E. 1985. Intergenerational Family Support Among Blacks and Whites: Response to Culture or Socioeconomic Differences. *Journal of Gerontology* 40: 382-389.

Myers, L. 1980. On Marital Relations: Perceptions of Black Women. In *The Black Woman*, (ed.) La Frances Rodgers-Rose, 161-174. Newbury Park, CA.: Sage Publications.

Naisbitt, J. and P. Aburdene. 1990. *Megatrends 2000: Ten New Directions for the 1990s.* New York: William Morrow & Co.

Nakamura, M., A. Nakamura, and D. Cullen. 1979. Job Opportunities, and Offered Wage, and the Labor Supply of Married Women. *American Economic Review*, 69(5): 787-805.

National Research Council. 1985. *Summary Report 1986: Doctorate Recipients from U.S. Universities.* Washington, D.C.: National Academy Press.

_____. 1991. *Summary Report 1990: Doctorate Recipients from U.S. Universities.* Washington, D.C.: National Academy Press.

National Science Foundation. 1990. *Women and Minorities in Science and Engineering.* Washington, D.C.: National Science Foundation.

National Urban League. 1988. *The State of Black America, 1982-1988.* New York: National Urban League.

Nayar, U. 1988. *Women Teachers in South Asia.* Delhi: Chanaka.

Near, J. 1984. Relationships Between Job Satisfaction and Life Satisfaction: Test of a Causal Model. *Social Indicators Research* 15: 351-367.

Near, J. and P. Sorcinelli. 1986. Work and Life Away From Work: Predictors of Faculty Satisfaction. *Research in Higher Education* 25(4): 377-395.

Newman, J. 1974. Predicting Absenteeism and Turnover: A Field Comparison of Fishbein's Model and Traditional Job Attitude Measurements. *Journal of Applied Psychology* 59: 610-615.

Nicholson, E. and R. Miljis. 1972. *Job Satisfaction and Turnover Among Liberal Art's College Professors.* Personnel Journal (Nov): 51: 840-845.

Nieves-Aquires, S. 1991. *Hispanic Women: Making Their Presence on Campus Less Tenuous.* Association of American Colleges: Washington, D.C.

Noble, J. 1956. *The Negro Women's College Education.* New York: Stratford.

Nobles, W. 1974. African Root and American Fruit: The Black Family. *Journal of Social and Behavioral Scientists* (Spring):52-64.

_____. 1975. Africanity in Black Families. *The Black Scholar.* (June): 54-68.

Olsen, T. 1988. *Doktorgrader I Norge: En kvantitativ oversikt,* NAVF Notat, Sept.

O'Reilly, C. and K. Roberts. 1973. Job Satisfaction Among Whites and Non-Whites: A Cross Cultural Approach. *Journal of Applied Psychology* 57(3): 295-302.

Ortiz, F. 1982. *Career Patterns in Education.* New York: Praeger Publishers.

Ottinger, C. and R. Sikula. 1993. Women in Higher Education: Where Do We Stand? *Research Briefs* 4, No. 2. Publication of the Division of Policy Analysis and Research, American Council on Education, Washington, D.C.

Outcalt, D. 1980. *Report of the Teaching Faculty on Teaching Evaluation.* Santa Barbara, CA.: University of California.

Over, R. 1993. Correlates of Career Advancement in Australian Universities. *Higher Education* 26(3): 313-330.

Over, R. 1985. Career Prospects for Academics in Australian Universities, *Higher Education,* 14: 497-512.

Papanek, H. 1973. Men, Women, and Work: Reflections on the Two-Person Career. *American Journal of Sociology* 78(4): 852-871.

Pearson, W. 1985. *Black Scientists, White Society, and Colorless Science.* New York: Associated Faculty Press.

Pepitone-Rockwell, F. 1980. *Dual-Career Couples.* Newbury Park, CA.: Sage Publications.

Perkins, L. 1983. The Impact of the "Culture of True Motherhood" on the Education of Black Women. *Journal of Social Issues* 39(1): 17-28.

Perry-Jenkins, M., B. Seery, and A. Crouter. 1992. Linkages Between Women's Provider-Role Attitudes, Psychological Well-Being, and Family Relationships. *Psychology of Women Quarterly* 16: 311-329.

Peterson, E. 1992. *African American Women: A Study of Will and Success.* McFarland & Company, Inc. Publishers.

Peterson, S. 1990. Challenges for Black Women Faculty. *Initiatives* 53(1): 33-36.

Pfeffer J. and J. Lawler. 1980. Effects of Job Alternatives, Extrinsic Rewards, and Behavioral Commitment on Attitude Toward the Organization: A Field Test of the Insufficient Justification Paradigm. *Administrative Science Quarterly* 25 (March): 38-56.

Ph.D.'s for Women Up, More Leave Academe. 1990. *Higher Education and National Affairs,* 10 Sep, 39:4.

Picknney, A. 1984. *The Myth of Black Progress.* New York: Cambridge University Press.

Polachek, S. 1981. Occupational Self-Selection: A Human Capital Approach to Sex Differences in Occupational Structure. *Review of Economics and Statistics* 63: 60-69.

Porter, L. and R. Steers. 1973. Organizational Work and Personal Factors in Employee Turnover and Absenteeism. *Psychological Bulletin* 80(2): 151-176.

Porter, L., R. Steers, R. Mowday, and P. Boulian. 1974. Organizational Commitment, Job Satisfaction, and Turnover Among Psychiatric Techniques. *Journal of Applied Psychology* 59: 603-609.

Price, J. and C. Mueller. 1986. *Handbook of Organizational Measurement.* Marchfield, MA.: Pitman.

Project on the Status and Education of Women. 1986. Survey Documents Faculty Dissatisfaction. *On Campus With Women* 16: 1-2.

Pruitt, A. 1982. *Black Employees in Traditional White Institutions in the 'Adams' States, 1975-1977.* New York: American Education Research Association.

Queralt, M. 1982. *The Role of Mentor in the Career Development of University Faculty Members and Academic Administrators.* Paper presented at the Annual Meeting of the National Association of Women Deans, Administrators, and Counselors, 3 April, Indianapolis, IN.

Rafky, D. 1972. The Black Scholar in the Academic Marketplace. *Teachers College Record* 74(2): 225-260.

Ransom, M. 1990. Gender Segregation By Field in Higher Education. *Research in Higher Education* 31(5): 477-491.

Rapoport, R. and R. Rapoport. 1965. Work and Family in Contemporary Society. *American Sociological Review 30*: 380-394.

Rathaur, M. 1990. *Unmarried Working Women, Marriage, and Career*. Radiant Publishers.

Reifman, A., M. Biernat, and E. Lang. 1991. Stress, Social Support, and Health of Married Professional Women with Small Children. *Psychology of Women Quarterly* 15: 431-445.

Reskin, B. and P. Phipps. 1988. Women in Male-Dominated Professional and Managerial Occupations. In *Working Women*, (ed.) A.H. Stromberg and S. Harkess. Mountain View, CA: Mayfield Publishing Co.

Reyes, M. and J. Halcon. 1988. Racism in Academia: The Old Wolf Revisited. *Harvard Educational Review*, 58:229-314.

Rhodes, S. and M. Doering. 1983. An Integrated Model of Career Change. *Academy of Management Review* 8(4): 631-639.

Riger, S, J. Stokes, S. Raja and M. Sullivan. 1997. Measuring Perceptions of the Work Environment for Female Faculty. *Review of Higher Education*, 21(1): 63-78.

Robinson, L. 1973. Institutional Variation in the Status of Academic Women. In *Academic Women on the Move*, Alice S. Rossi and Ann Calderwood, 199-238. New York: Russell Sage Foundation.

Robinson, R. 1991. *Through Their Eyes: Reflections of Pennsylvania Female School Administrators Regarding Career Paths, Mentoring, and External Barriers*. Unpublished dissertation, Temple University, Philadelphia, PA.

Roche, G. 1979. Much Ado About Mentors. *Harvard Business Review*, (Jan/Feb) 15.

Rodgers-Rose, L 1980. *The Black Woman*. Newbury Park, CA.: Sage Publications.

Rodriguez, R. 1993. Latina Feminists Carving an Institutional Niche in Academe. *Black Issues in Higher Education*, March, 28.

Rohter, L. 1987. Women Gain Degrees But Not Tenure. *New York Times*, January 4.

Rosenbaum, J. 1979. Organizational Career Mobility: Promotion Chances in a Corporation During Periods of Growth and Contraction. *American Journal of Sociology* 85: 21-49.

Rosenfeld, R. 1978. Women's Employment Patterns and Occupational Achievements. *Social Science Research* 7: 61-80.

_____. 1981. Race and Sexual Differences in Career Dynamics. *American Sociological Review* 45: 583-609.

Rosenfeld, R. and J. Jones. 1986. Institutional Mobility Among Academics: The Case of Psychologists. *Sociology of Education* 59 (Oct): 212-226.

_____. 1987. Patterns and Effects of Geographic Mobility for Academic Women and Men. *Journal of Higher Education* 58(5) 493-515.

Rossi, A. and A. Calderwood. 1973. *Academic Women on the Move.* New York: Russell Sage Foundation.

Ruble, T., R. Cohen, and D. Ruble. 1984. Sex Stereotypes: Occupational Barriers for Women. *American Behavioral Scientist* 27(3): 339-356.

Ruffins, P. Oct. 16, 1997. The Shelter of Tenure is Eroding and for Faculty of Color gaining Membership May be Tougher than Ever. *Black Issues in Higher Education*, 14(17): 19-26.

Rutledge, E. 1980. Marital Interaction Goals of Black Women: Strengths and Effects. In *The Black Woman*, (ed.) La Frances Rodgers-Rose, 145-160. Newbury Park, CA.: Sage Publications.

Sagaria, M. 1988. Administrative Mobility and Gender: Patterns and Processes in Higher Education. *Journal of Higher Education* 59(3): 305-328.

Salancik, G. and J. Pfeffer. 1977. An Examination of Need-Satisfaction Models of Job Attitudes. *Administrative Science Quarterly* 22: 427-456.

Sandefur, Gary. 1981. Organizational Boundaries and Upward Job Shifts. *Social Science Research* 10: 67-82.

Sandefur, G. and M. Tienda. 1988. *Divided Opportunities: Minorities, Poverty, and Social Policy.* New York: Plenum Press.

Sanders, K. and G. Mellow. 1990. Permanent Diversity: The Deferred Vision of Higher Education. *Initiatives* 53(1): 9-14.

Sandler, B. and R. Hall. 1986. *The Campus Climate Revisited: Chilly For Women Faculty, Administrators, and Graduate Students* Project on the Status and Education of Women, Washington, D.C.

Sawyer, D. 1981. Institutional Stratification and Career Mobility in Academic Markets. *Sociology of Education* 54: 85-97.

Schmuck, P. 1975. Deterrants to Women's Careers in School Management. *Sex Roles* 1: 339-353.

Schoen, L. and S. Winocur. 1988. An Investigation of the Self-Efficacy of Male and Female Academics. *Journal of Vocational Behavior* 32: 307-320.

Schultz, D. 1990. *Das Geschlecht Lauft immer mit...* Die Arbeitswelt von Professorinnen und Professoren.

Schuster, J. Dec. 1986. The Faculty Dilemma: A Short Course. *Phi Delta Kappan* 68: 275-282.

____. 1990. Faculty Issues in the 1990s: New Realities, New Opportunities. In *An Agenda for the New Decade*, (ed.) L. W. Jones and F. A. Nowotny, New Directions for Higher Education, No. 70. San Francisco, CA.: Jossey-Bass.

Scott, J. 1992. Competition Versus Collegiality: Academe's Dilemma for the 1990s. *Journal of Higher Education* 63(6): 684-698.

Sears, H. and N. Galambos. 1992. Women's Work Conditions and Marital Adjustment in Two-Earner Couples: A Structural Model. *Journal of Marriage and the Family* 54: 789-797.

Seeborg, I. 1990. Division of Labor in Two-Career Faculty Households. In *Women in Higher Education: Changes and Challenges*, (ed.) L.B. Welch. New York: Preager.

Sekaran, U. 1986. *Dual-Career Families: Contemporary Organizational and Counseling Issues*. San Francisco: Jossey-Bass.

Shapiro, E. et. al. 1978. Moving Up: Role Models, Mentors, and the Patron System. *Sloan Management Review* 19(3): 51-56.

Shapiro, H. 1983. The Priviledge and the Responsibility: Some Reflections on the Nature, Function, and Future of Academic Tenure. *Academe* (Nov/Dec): 1a-7a.

Shapiro, J. 1987. Women in Education: At Risk or Prepared? *Educational Forum* 52(2) 167-183.

Sharma, R. 1981. *Nationalism, Social Reform and Indian Women*. New Delhi: Janaki Prskashan.

Sherman, S., R. Ward, and M. LaGory. 1988. Women as Caregivers of the Elderly: Instrumental and Expressive Support. *Social Work* 33: 164-168.

Silbermann, C 1964. *Crisis in Black and White*. New York: Random House.

Silver, J., R. Dennis, and C. Spikes. 1988. *Black Faculty in Traditional White Institutions in Selected Adams States: Characteristics, Experiences, and Perceptions*. Atlanta, GA.: Southern Education Foundation.

Simeone, A. 1987. *Academic Women: Working Towards Equity.* Granby, MA.: Bergin and Garvey Publishing.

Simon, R., S. Clark, and K. Galway. 1964. The Woman Ph.D.: A Recent Profile. *Social Problems* 221-236.

Skrede, K. 1988. *Likestillingsforskning I velferdsstats perspecpektiv – innfallsvinkler og forskningsoppgaver,* Seminar om lokestilling og kvinneforskning I et velferdaatatsperspektiv, Sondvolden, April 13-15. Arrangor: Norges rad for anvendt samfunnsforskning.

Sloane, P. and I. Thsodossiou. 1993. Gender and Job Tenure Effects on Earnings. *Oxford Bulletin of Economics and Statistics,* 55:421-37.

Smart, J. 1990. A Causal Model of Faculty Turnover Intentions. *Research in Higher Education* 31(5): 405-424.

_____ 1991. Gender Equity in Academic Rank and Salary. *Review of Higher Education* 14(4): 511-526.

Smith, E. 1990. Black Faculty and Affirmative Action at Predominantly White Institutions. *Western Journal of Black Studies* 14: 9-16.

_____. 1991. A Comparative Study of Occupational Stress From a Sample of Black and White U.S. College and University Faculty. *Research in Race and Ethnic Relations* 6: 145-163.

_____. 1992. *A Comparative Study of Occupational Stress in African American and White University Faculty.* New York: Edwin Mellen Press.

Smith, E. and T. Zorn. 1981. *Educational Equity.* American Educational Research Association Conference, Los Angeles, CA.

Smith, J., D. Simpson-Kirkland, J. Zimmeren, E. Goldenstein, and K. Prichard. 1986. The Five Most Important Problems Confronting Black Students Today. *Negro Educational Review* 37 (April): 52-61.

Smith, P., L. Kendall, and C. Hulin. 1969. *The Measurement of Satisfaction in Work and Retirement.* Chicago, IL.: Rand-McNally.

Smith, P., O. Smith, and J. Rollo. 1974. Factor Structure for Black and Whites of Job Description Index and its Discrimination of Job Satisfaction. *Journal of Applied Psychology* 59(1): 99-111.

Snyder, T. 1987. *Digest of Educational Statistics.* Washington, D.C.: Department of Education.

Sojka, G. 1985. Balancing Academic Performance and Market Conditions: An Administrators View. *Academe* (July/August), 11-16.

Solmon, L. 1978. Turnover of Senior Faculty in Departments of Social and Physical Science and Engineering. *Research in Higher Education* 8: 343-355.

Solmon, L., L. Kent, N. Ochsner, and M. Hurwicz. 1981. *Underemployed Ph.D.'s*. Lexington, MA.: Lexington Books.

Soloman, B. 1985. *In the Company of Educated Women: A History of Women and Higher Education in America.* New Haven, CT.: Yale University Press.

Sorcinelli, M. and J. Near. 1989. Relations Between Work and Life Away From Work Among University Faculty. *Journal of Higher Education* 60 (Jan/Feb): 59-81.

Sorensen, A. 1975. The Structure of Intragenerational Mobility. *American Sociological Review* 40: 456-471.

____. 1977. The Structure of Inequality and the Processes of Attainment. *American Sociological Review* 42: 965-978.

Sorensen, A. and N. Tuma. 1981. Labor Market Structures and Job Mobility. In D. Treiman and R. Robinson (eds.), *Research in Social Stratification and Mobility: An Annual Compilation of Research*, 67-94. Greenwich, Conn.: JAI Press.

Sorensen, A. 1983. Women's Employment Patterns After Marriage. *Journal of Marriage and the Family* (May): 311-321.

Spilerman, S. 1977. Careers, Labor Market Structures, and Socioeconomic Achievement. *American Journal of Sociology* 83: 551-593.

Spurling, A. 1990. *Report of the Women in Higher Education Research Project.* Cambridge, England, Kings College.

Stack, S. 1974. *All Our Kin: Strategies for Survival in a Black Community.* New York: Harper and Row.

Staples, R. 1971. *The Black Family.* Belmont, CA.: Wadworth.

____. 1973. *The Black Woman in America: Sex, Marriage, and the Family.* Chicago, IL.: Nelson-Hall Publishers.

____. 1981. Race and Marital Status: An Overview. In H.P. McAdoo (ed.), *Black Families.* Newbury Park, CA.: Sage Publications.

____. 1986. *The Black Family: Essays and Studies.* (3rd ed.) Belmont, CA.: Wadsworth.

Staples, R. and L. Johnson. 1993. *Families at the Crossroads: Challenges and Prospects.* San Francisco, CA.: Jossey-Bass Publishers.

Stapleton, D. 1988. Cohort Size and the Academic Labor Market. *Journal of Human Resources* 24(2): 221-252.

Stark, J., M. Lowther, and B. Hagerty. 1986. Faculty Role and Role Preferences in Ten Fields of Professional Study. *Research in Higher Education* 25(1): 3-24.

Stecklein, J. and R. Lathrop. 1960. *Faculty Attraction and Retention: Factors Affecting Faculty Mobility at the University of Minnesota.* Minneapolis: Bureau of Institutional Research, University of Minnesota.

Steele, C. 1992. Race and School of Black Americans. *The Atlantic Monthly* (April): 68-78.

Steele, S. 1990. *The Content of Our Character: A New Vision of Race in America.* New York: St. Martin's Press.

Steers, R. 1977. Antecedents and Outcomes of Organizational Commitment. *Administrative Science Quarterly* 22: 46-56.

Steers, R. and R. Mowday. 1981. Employee Turnover and Post-Decision Accommodation Processes. *Research in Organizational Behavior 3:235-281.*

Steitz, N. 1982. *Faculty Research Involvement: Organizational and Ststus Predictors at a Major University.* Ph.D. dissertation, University of Michigan.

Steward, R. 1987. *Work Satisfaction and the Black Female Professional: A Pilot Study.* Lawrence, KS.: University of Kansas.

Stokes, J., S. Riger and M. Sullivan. 1995. Measuring Perceptions of the Working Environment for Women in Corporate Settings. *Psychology of Women Quarterly,* 19: 533-526.

Sudarkasa, N. 1987. Affirmative Action or Affirmative of the Status Quo? Black Faculty and Administrators in Higher Education. *American Association of Higher Education* 39(6): 3-6.

Suinn, R. and J. Witt. 1982. Survey on Ethnic Minority Faculty Recruitment and Retention. *American Psychology* 37(11): 1239-1247.

Swaboda, M. 1990. *Retaining and Promoting Women and Minority Faculty Members: Problems and Possibilities.* University of Wisconsin System, Office of Equal Opportunity Programs and Policy Studies, Madison, WI.

Swaboda, M. and S. Millar. 1986. Networking-Mentoring: Career Strategy of Women in Academic Administration. *Journal of the National Association of Women Deans, Administrators, and Counselors* 49: 8-13.

Swann, R. and E. Witty. 1980. Black Women Administrators at Traditionally Black Colleges and Universities: Attitudes, Perceptions, and Potentials. *Western Journal of Black Studies* 4 (Winter): 261-270.

Symons, T and J. Page. 1984. *Some Questions of Balance: Human Resources, Higher Education and Canadian Studies.* Ottawa, CA: Association of Universities and Colleges of Canada.

Szafran, R. 1984. *Universities and Women Faculty: Why Some Organizations Discriminate More Than Others.* New York: Praeger.

Tack, M. and C. Patitu. 1992. *Faculty Job Satisfaction: Women and Minorities in Peril.* Report 4, ASHE-ERIC Higher Education Reports, George Washington University.

Taylor, D. and G Smitherman-Donaldson. 1989. And Ain't I a Woman? African American Women and Affirmative Action. *Sex Roles* 21(1/2): 1-12.

Taylor, M. 1978. *Fact Book on Theological Education, 1977-78.* Association of Theological Schools in the United States and Canada.

Taylor, M., E. Locke, C. Lee, and M. Gist. 1984. Type A Behavior and Faculty Research Productivity: What Are the Mechanics? *Organizational Behavior and Human Performance* 34 (Dec): 402-418.

Taylor, R. 1985. The Extended Family as a Source of Support to Elderly Blacks. *Gerontologist* 25: 488-495.

____. 1988. Correlates of Religious Non-Involvement Among Black Americans. *Review of Religious Research* 30(2): 126-139.

Taylor, R. and L. Chatters. 1986. Patterns of Informal Support to Elderly Blacks Adults: Family, Friends, and Church Members. *Social Work* 31: 432-438.

Taylor, S. 1993. *In the Spirit: The Inspirational Writings of Susan L. Taylor.* New York: Amistad Press.

Tehranian, M. (ed.) 1991. *Restructuring for Ethnic Peace: A Public Debate at the University of Hawaii.* Honolulu: Spark M. Matsunaga Institute for Peace.

Theodore, A. (ed.) 1971. *The Professional Woman.* Cambridge, MA: Schenkman.

Thoits, P. 1983. Multiple Identities and Psychological Well Being. *American Sociological Review* 48 (April): 174-187.

Thomas, G. 1981. *Black Students in Higher Education.* Westport, CT.: Greenwood Press.

Thompson, C and E. Dey. 1998. Pushed to the Margins: Sources of Stress for African American College and University Faculty. *Journal of Higher Education,* 69(3): 324-45.

Thompson, I. and A. Roberts (eds.) 1985. *The Road Retaken: Women Reenter the Academy.* Modern Language Association of America, New York.

Thoreson, R., C. Kardash, D. Leuthold, and K. Morrow. 1990. Gender Differences in the Academic Career. *Research in Higher Education* 31(2): 193-209.

Tien, F. and R. Blackburn. 1996. Faculty Rank System, Research Motivation, and Faculty Research Productivity. *Journal of Higher Education* 67(1): 2-22.

Tierney, W. and E. Bensimon. 1996. *Promotion and Tenure: Community and Socialization in Academe.* Albany: State University of New York Press.

Tobin, M. 1981. *The Black Female Ph.D.: Education and Career Development.* Lanham, MD.: University Press of America.

Tokarczyk, M. and E. Fay. 1993. *Working Class Women in the Academy: Laborers in the Knowledge Factory.* University of Massachusetts Press, Amherst.

Tolbert, P 1986. Organizations and Inequity: Sources of Earnings Differences Between Male and Female Faculty. *Sociology of Education* 59 (October):227-235.

Treiman, D. and K. Terrell. 1975. Sex and the Process of Status Attainment: A Comparison of Working Women and Men. *American Sociological Review* 40: 174-200.

Trent, W. et. al. 1984. Making It To the Top: Women and Minority Faculty in the Academic Labor Market. *American Behavioral Scientist* 27 (Jan./Feb.): 301-324.

Tuckman, H., J Gapinski, and R. Hagemann. 1977. Faculty Skills and the Salary Structure in Academe: A Market Perspective. *American Economic Review* 67(4) 692-702.

Tuma, N. 1976. Rewards, Resources, and the Rate of Mobility: A Nonstationary Multivariate *Stochastic* Model. *American Sociological Review* 41 (April): 338-360.

United Nations. 1994. Statistical Yearbook for Latin America and the Caribbean, New York.

_____. 1991. The World's Women: 1970-1990 Trends and Statistics. Series K, No. 8, New York.

United States Bureau of the Census. 1991. *Statistical Abstract of the United States, 1991.* Washington, D.C.: US Department of Commerce/US Government Printing Office.

United States Department of Commerce. 1980. *Current Population Reports*, P-20, No. 132. Washington, D.C.: Government Printing Office.

United States Department of Commerce, Bureau of the Census. 1979. *The Social and Economic Status of the Black Population in the United States: An Historical View , 1790-1978.* Washington, D.C.: Government Printing Office.

____. 1986. *Estimates of the Population of the United States by Age, Sex, and Race: 1980-1985.* Washington, D.C.: Government Printing Office.

United States Department of Education. 1982. *The Condition of Education.* National Center for Education Statistics, Washington, D.C.: Government Printing Office.

____. 1992. *Digest of Educational Statistics, 1992.* National Center for Education Statistics, Office of Educational Research and Improvement. Washington, D.C.: Government Printing Office.

United States Department of Labor. 1991. *Black Women in the Labor Force.* Facts on Working Women No. 90-4. Washington, D.C.: Women's Bureau.

University Grants Commission. 1985. *Report for the Year, 1984-85.* New Delhi.

Valverde, L. 1980. *Promotion Socialization: The Informal Process in Large Urban Districts and Its Adverse Effects on Non-Whites and Women.* Presented in April at the American Educational Research Association, Boston, MA.

____. 1981. Development of Ethnic Researchers and the Education of White Researchers. *Educational Researcher* (Oct.): 16-20

Vasil, L. 1996. Social Process Skills and Career Achievement Among Male and Female Academics, *Journal of Higher Education*, 67(1): 103-114.

Verbrugge, L. March 1983. Multiple Roles and Physical Health of Women and Men. *Journal of Health and Social Behavior* 24: 16-30.

Villadsen, A. and M. Tack. 1981. Combining Home and Career Responsibilities: The Methods Used by Women Executives in Higher Education. *Journal of the National Association of Women Deans, Administrators, and Counselors* 45: 20-25.

Vroom, V. 1964. *Work and Motivation*. New York: John Wiley and Sons.

Wade-Gayles, G. 1993. *Pushed Back To Strength: A Black Women's Journey Home*. Boston, MA.: Beacon Press.

Walker, G. 1973. *Effective and Ineffective Images: As Perceived by the Male Afro-American University Professor.* Published dissertation, University of Pittsburgh.

Walker, M. 1971. *Jubilee*. New York: Houghton Mifflin.

Wallston, B., et. al. 1978. I Will Follow Him: Myth, Reality, or Forced Choice-Job Seeking Experiences of Dual-Career Couples. *Psychology of Women Quarterly* 3(1): 9-21.

Warren-Moss, A. 1987. *The Impact of Occupational Security on Marital Relations and Family Role Preferences and Participation of Black Academicians.* Unpublished dissertation. New York: St. John's University.

Washington, V. and W. Harvey. 1989. *Affirmative Rhetoric, Negative Action: African-American and Hispanic Faculty at Predominantly White Institutions.* ASHE-ERIC Higher Education Report No. 2. Washington, D.C.

Weaver, C. 1974. Negro-White Differences in Job Satisfaction. *Business Horizons* 17: 67-71.

Weiler, W. 1985. Why Do Faculty Members Leave a University? *Research in Higher Education* 23(3): 270-278.

Weis, L. 1985. Progress But No Parity: Women in Higher Education. *Academe* (Nov/Dec): 29-33.

West, C. 1993. Race Matters. New York: Vintage Books.

West, C. 1993/1994. The Dilemma of the Black Intellectual. *Journal of Blacks in Higher Education* (Winter): 59-67.

Whicker, M., J, Kronenfeld, and R. Strickland. 1993. *Getting Tenure*. Newbury Park, CA: Sage Publications.

Wilkerson, M. 1984. Lifting as We Climb: Networks for Minority Women. *New Directions for Higher Education* 45: 16-20.

_____. 1985-86. A Report on the Educational Status of Black Women During the United Nations Decade for Women, 1976-1985. *Review of the Political Economy* 14 (Fall/Winter): 83-96.

Williams, L. 1986. Chief Academic Officers at Black Colleges and Universities: A Comparison by Gender. *Journal of Negro Education* 55(Fall): 443-452.

_____. 1990. The Challenges Before Black Women in Higher Education. *Initiatives* 53(1): 1-2.

Williams, M. 1974. *Community in a Black Pentecostal Church*. Pittsburgh, PA.: University of Pittsburgh Press.

Willie, C. 1970. *The Family Life of Black People*. Charles E. Merrill Publishing.

_____. 1974. The Black Family and Social Class. *American Journal of Orthopsychiatry* 44(1): 50-60.

_____. 1978. The Black Family and Social Class. In R. Staples (ed.), *The Black Family: Essays and Studies*: 236-243. Belmont, CA.: Wadsworth.

_____. 1981. *The Ivory and Ebony Towers*. Washington, DC.: Heath and Company Publishers.

_____. 1986. *Five Black Scholars*. Lanham, MA.: University Press of America.

Willie, C., A. Garibaldi, and W. Reed. 1991. *The Education of African Americans*, Vol. 3. Boston, MA.: University of Massachusetts Press.

Willie, C., M. Grady, and H. Richard. 1991. *African Americans and the Doctoral Experience: Implications for Policy*. New York: Teachers College Press.

Wilson, C. 1976. Affirmative Action Defended: Exploding the Myths of a Slandered Policy. *The Black Scholar* (May/June): 19-24.

Wilson, L. 1942. *The Academic Man*. New York: Oxford University Press.

Wilson, R. 1982. *Race and Equity in Higher Education*. Washington, D.C.: American Council on Education.

_____. 1987. Recruitment and Retention of Minority Faculty and Staff. *American Association Higher Education Bulletin* 39(6): 11-14.

_____. 1989. Women of Color in Academic Administration. *Sex Roles* 21(1/2): 85-97.

Wilson, R. and D. Carter. 1988. *Minorities in Higher Education: Seventh Annual Status Report*. Washington, D.C.: American Council on Education.

Wilson, R. and S. Melendez. 1985. Down The Up Staircase. *Educational Record* 66 (Fall): 46-50.

____. 1986. *Minorities in Higher Education: Fifth Annual Status Report*, Washington, D.C.: American Council on Education.

Winfield, F. 1987. Workplace Solutions for Women Under Eldercare Pressure. *Personnel* 64: 31-39.

Winkler, L. 1982. *Job Satisfaction of University Faculty in the U.S.* Unpublished dissertation, University of Nebraska.

Witt, S. 1990. *The Pursuit of Race and Gender Equity in American Academe.* New York: Praeger.

Witt, S. and N. Lovrich. 1988. The Sources of Stress Among Faculty and Gender Differences. *Review of Higher Education* 11(3): 269-284.

Wolfson, R. 1986. *Job Satisfaction of Industrial Arts/Technology Teacher Education Faculty in the U.S.* Unpublished dissertation, Ohio State University.

Woody, B. 1989. Black Women in the Emerging Services Economy. *Sex Roles* 21(1/2): 45-67.

Wyche, K., and S. Graves. 1992. Minority Women in Academia: Access and Barriers to Professional Participation. *Psychology of Women Quarterly* 16: 429-437.

Wylie, A. 1995. *The Contexts of Activism on Climate Issues.* In McMenemy, C. (ed.) Breaking the Anonymity: The Chilly Climate for Women Faculty, Waterloo, Ontario, CA: Wilfrid Laurier University Press.

Yogev, S. 1981. Do Professional Women Have Egalitarian Marital Relationships? *Journal of Marriage and Family* (Nov.): 865-871.

Young, C. 1986. Afro-American Family: Contemporary Issues and Implications for Social Policy. In D. Pilgrim, *On Being Black: An In-Group Analysis.* Bristol, IN.: Wyndham Hall.

____. 1989. Psychodynamics of Coping and Survival of the African-American Female in a Changing World. *Journal of Black Studies* 20 (Dec): 208-223.

Zaghal, A. 1984. Social Change in Jordan. *Middle Eastern Studies*, 20(4): 53-75.

Zimbler, L. 1990. Faculty in Higher Education Institutions, 1988. 1988 National Survey of Postsecondary Faculty (NSOPF-88). *National Center for Education Statistics.* Washington, D.C.: U.S. Department of Education.

Zuckerman, H. 1987. Citation Analysis and the Complex Problems of Intellectual Influence. *Scientometrics* 23: 329-338.

Zuckerman, H., J. Cole, and J. Bruer. 1991. *The Outer Circle: Women in the Scientific Community.* W. W. Norton and Company Publishing.

Zumeta, W. 1984. *Extending the Educational Ladder: The Changing Quality and Value of Post Doctoral Study.* Lexington, MA: D.C. Heath & Company.

*I*ndex

discretionary, 85

I
India faculty, 123
Israel faculty, 125

J
Japan faculty, 119
Jordan faculty, 127

K
Korea faculty, 121

N
National Association of Colored Women, 19-20
National Research Council, Survey of Doctorate Recipients, 17, 21, 26, 43, 69
National Science Foundation, 36
National Survey of Black Americans, 6, 61
Netherlands faculty, 130
New Zealand faculty, 135
Norway faculty, 128

P
Personal characteristics, 66, 84-86
Pilot study, 82
PWI, see Predominantly White institutions
Predominantly White institutions, 12, 15-16, 39, 41, 44, 60, 63
Puerto Rico faculty, 110

R
Recommendations
    to academic leaders, 98

*A*bout the Author

Sheila T. Gregory is a professor, researcher and educational consultant. She received her B.A. from Oakland University, M.P.A. in Health Care Administration from Wayne State University, and Ph.D. in Higher Education Administration from the University of Pennsylvania, where she graduated with highest distinction. She received a dissertation award from the American Association for Higher Education Black Caucus and has been the recipient of numerous grants. She is the author of three books, a dozen articles, and is editor of the National Congress of Black Faculty Newsletter. Recently, she has been a Visiting Research Scholar at the University of the West Indies, the American University of Cairo in Egypt, and the University of South Australia. Her research interests are in the areas of academic achievement, recruitment and retention, and leadership with special emphasis on minority and international women, faculty, and students.